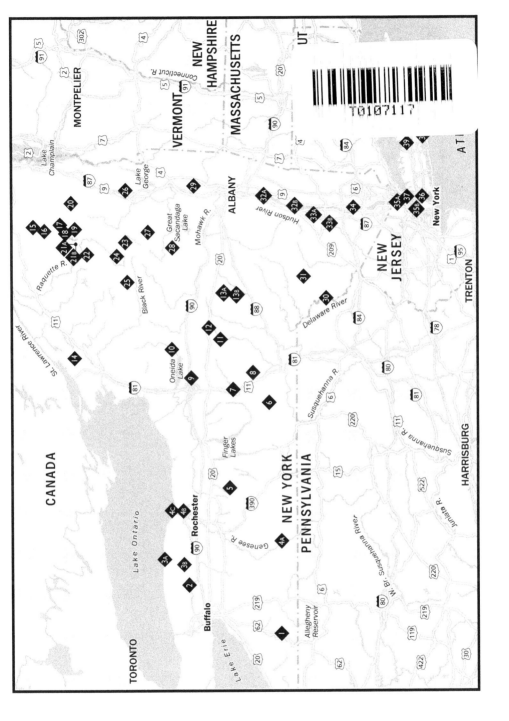

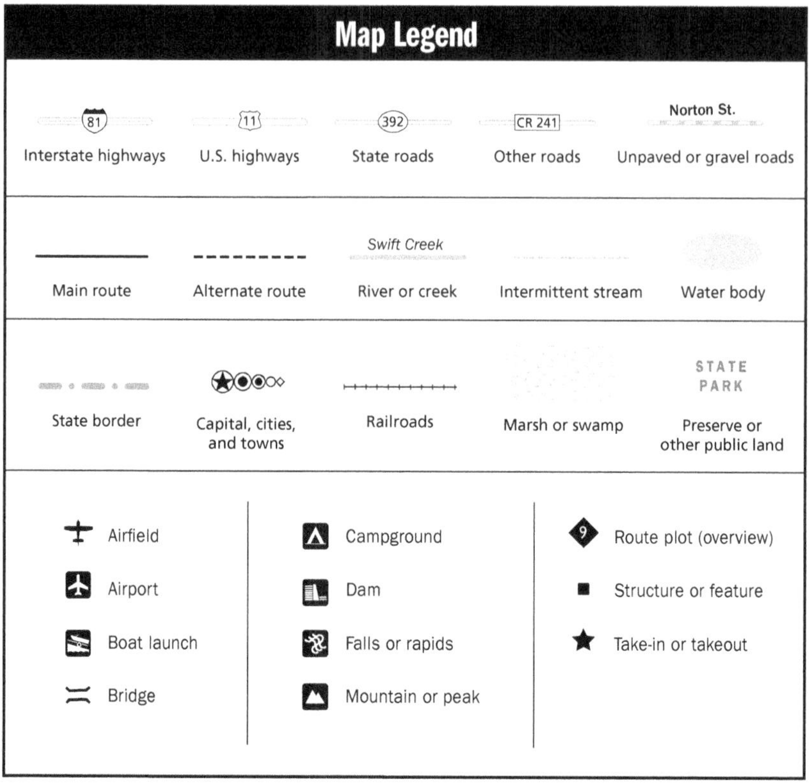
Map Legend
81
Interstate highways
11
U.S. highways
392
State roads
CR 241
Other roads
Norton St.
Unpaved or gravel roads
Main route
Alternate route
Swift Creek
River or creek
Intermittent stream
Water body
State border
Capital, cities, and towns
Railroads
Marsh or swamp
STATE PARK
Preserve or other public land
Airfield
Airport
Boat launch
Bridge
Campground
Dam
Falls or rapids
Mountain or peak
9
Route plot (overview)
Structure or feature
Take-in or takeout

OTHER MENASHA RIDGE PRESS PADDLING GUIDES

The Alaska River Guide
Canoeing & Kayaking Florida
Canoeing & Kayaking Georgia
A Canoeing & Kayaking Guide to the Ozarks
A Canoeing & Kayaking Guide to the Streams of Kentucky
Canoeing & Kayaking West Virginia
Carolina Whitewater

CANOEING & KAYAKING
NEW YORK

To Laura and AnnaGrace—I love you both more than words can say.

—K.S.

CANOEING &
KAYAKING
NEW YORK

Kevin Stiegelmaier

MENASHA RIDGE PRESS
www.menasharidge.com

Copyright © 2009 by Kevin Stiegelmaier

Published by Menasha Ridge Press
Distributed by Publishers Group West
Printed in the United States of America
First edition, first printing, 2009

Library of Congress Cataloging-in-Publication Data

Stiegelmaier, Kevin.
    Canoeing & kayaking New York/by Kevin Stiegelmaier.—1st ed.
        p. cm.—(Menasha Ridge paddling guides)
    Includes index.
    ISBN-13: 978-0-89732-668-1
    ISBN-10: 0-89732-668-7
    1. Canoes and canoeing—New York (State)—Guidebooks. 2. Kayaking—New York (State)—Guidebooks. 3. Rivers—New York (State)—Guidebooks. 4. New York (State)—Description and travel. I. Title. II. Title: Canoeing and kayaking New York.
    GV776.N7S75 2009
    797.12209747—dc22
                                    2009000153

Cover and interior photos by Kevin Stiegelmaier
Author photo by Laura Stiegelmaier
Maps by Scott McGrew and Kevin Stiegelmaier
Cover and text design by Alian Design
Typesetting and composition by Annie Long
Indexing by Rich Carlson

Menasha Ridge Press
P.O. Box 43673
Birmingham, Alabama 35243
www.menasharidge.com

CONTENTS

ACKNOWLEDGMENTS

Many people played a part in the writing of this book, and they have my utmost gratitude and appreciation. First, I would like to thank Russell Helms for giving me the opportunity to write the book and Bob Sehlinger and the editors at Menasha Ridge Press for all of your help and guidance throughout the process. I would also like to thank Molly Merkle for answering my never-ending questions and Ritchey Halphen for making everything come together.

Once I embarked on the immense task of writing this book, a few amazing friends jumped right in and offered me whatever assistance they could. Gretchen Schaentzler, Doug Elliot, Lori Dropp, and Ed Maloney all helped me in the early portion of this project with some organizing, planning, and equipment loans. I would not have known where to begin without them. Other friends—Dave Mutter, Ed Fontana-Daguerre, Jeff Schaentzler, and Edward Schaentzler—tagged along on some of my paddling trips and made the research of those rivers a bit easier and much more enjoyable. I thank you all for taking the time out of your own busy lives to join me.

Paddling unfamiliar rivers can sometimes be a daunting challenge. Luckily, I was able to call on the local knowledge of Michael Hunter from the Bronx River Alliance, Dick Williams from the Chenango River Landing, William Andrews from the Department of Environmental Conservation, and fellow paddler Phil Wirsing in helping me plan some of my trips.

Most importantly, I must thank my family for their help and support during the writing of this book. My in-laws, Sharon and Marc Hopfenspirger, provided me with many hot meals, a warm bed, and lots of early-morning coffee, while Mike Landor gave me tons of river, route, and road advice. I am extremely grateful that I was able to share some of my paddling adventures with my own father, Doug Stiegelmaier. I can never repay him or my mother, Susan, for all they did to help with this book and for fostering my love of the outdoors. I hope it was worth all of those sleepless nights worrying about my crazy adventures.

Finally, I must thank my incredible wife, Laura, for helping make this dream of mine come true. Only a truly amazing woman can take care of a child, run a house, and maintain a career on her own while her husband is off paddling some river in a far-off corner of the state. Laura did all of this, and then some, with ease. Her faith and support encouraged me to take on this project, her loving words got me through its tougher times, and only with her help did this book finally come to be.

Although I have always been a lover of the water, most of my early adventures were centered around rocks, dirt, and wooded trails. Weekends and vacations during high school and college were almost always spent riding a mountain bike or hiking a trail somewhere within the state. In fact, it wasn't until my senior year of college that I first went kayaking. And even then it took two more years, and the encouragement of a new coworker, before my interest in paddling began to grow.

Soon, however, kayaking became more of a passion than an occasional hobby, and I started to devote more and more time to its pursuits. Local paddles filled my weekday schedules. Longer trips took up most weekends. Overnighters and extended excursions were how I spent my vacations. I began venturing farther away from my local waters and was soon traveling up and down the entire East Coast looking for the perfect paddling destinations. Yet even among the rocks and lighthouses of Maine's coast, the sandy barrier beaches of Virginia and North Carolina, and the mangrove islands of southern Florida, New York's waters remained my favorites.

Eventually, for no reason other than my own enjoyment, I began keeping a journal of my kayak trips near my home on Long Island. With my wife's encouragement, this small hobby slowly evolved into a potential paddling guidebook about the island, which ultimately developed into plans for a guidebook for the entire state of New York. When Menasha Ridge Press offered me the chance to write *Canoeing & Kayaking New York*, I excitedly jumped into the process headfirst and never looked back.

As anyone who has ever paddled in New York will tell you, there are hundreds of lakes, rivers, streams, and ponds within the state's boundaries that are perfect for canoeing and kayaking. Ask any ten people to name their favorite stretches of water, and you'll surely get ten completely different answers. So how does one choose 50 rivers to include in a guidebook out of so many potential locations? I asked ten people their opinions. Then I asked ten more. And more after that, marking each location on a large map. I checked out Web sites, books, and paddling outfitters. With each step, my map became more marked up until a few patterns began to emerge and some locations seemed more popular than others. Using these patterns to help whittle down my possibilities, I ended up with a list of about 75 paddling destinations that seemed worthy of a visit.

Finally, I began traveling across New York with my Jeep, bicycle, and two kayaks in search of the best rivers to include in this book. This is when the true fun

My hope is that people use this information in finding their own paddling adventures and enjoy them as much as I do mine.

began. Along the way I stumbled upon a music festival in Cooperstown, paddled into the middle of a tugboat race off Manhattan, saw an osprey capture a pigeon in midair on the East River, surprised two river otters playing on the ice on the Sacandaga River, paddled through the middle of the world-famous Bronx Zoo, saw the most beautiful sunrise over the mountains from Canandaigua Lake, and met more friendly and kind people than I can remember. On the downside, I also crashed my bicycle during a shuttle, swamped my boat, lost a GPS unit, broke my rudder, lost a paddle, got poison ivy and sunburn, was rained on, developed blisters on my feet, was bitten by every type of insect in the state, received a speeding ticket, and got lost more times than I care to admit. I even had to portage around a herd of cattle blocking an entire river.

Ultimately, I was forced to remove some rivers from my list and found a few others to add to it, until I finally came up with 50 amazing river trips across the state. These selections are, in my opinion, among the best that New York has to offer. Did I miss one or two rivers that deserve to be included? Possibly. However, my goal in writing this book was not to give away all of New York's paddling secrets. Rather, it was meant to be a guide for paddlers to use as they explore the state's wonderful waters. I searched out the most convenient put-in and takeout locations, looked for the most scenic and popular stretches of water, and researched the best conditions to paddle all of these places. My hope is that people use this information in finding their own paddling adventures and enjoy them as much as I do mine.

STONE FOOTBRIDGE IN COOPERSTOWN

The runs I've chosen for this book are located on the most popular and most easily accessible sections of many New York rivers, including a wide variety of water: slow-moving streams, fast-moving whitewater, urban water trails, and Wild and Scenic Rivers. These waterways are scattered across the state as evenly as New York's geography allows. I've grouped them into "best of" categories in the following lists:

BEST SCENERY

Marion River (page 111)
Bog River Flow (page 105)
St. Regis Canoe Area (page 87)

BEST FOR WILDLIFE

Bog River Flow (page 105)
Oak Orchard Creek: Iroquois National
    Wildlife Refuge (page 29)
Sangerfield River (page 65)

BEST FOR SECLUSION

Sangerfield River (page 65)
Fish Creek Ponds (page 91)
Cedar River Flow (page 108)

BEST FOR KIDS

Peconic River (page 192)
Old Erie Canal (page 53)
Fish Creek Ponds (page 91)

BEST WATERFALLS

Genesee River: Turning Point Park to
    Lower Falls and Back (page 36)
Raquette River: Axton Landing to
    NY 3/30 (page 100)

BEST GEOLOGICAL SIGHTS

Genesee River: Turning Point Park to
    Lower Falls and Back (page 36)
Hudson River, Part Three: Yonkers to
    Tarrytown (page 163)
Hudson River: Part Two (page 157)

BEST FALL FOLIAGE

Hudson River: Cold Spring to
    Peekskill (page 157)
Sangerfield River (page 65)
Marion River (page 111)

BEST WATER TRAILS

Conewango Creek (page 19)
Old Erie Canal (page 53)
Hudson River (all runs)
East River (page 172)
Bronx River (page 176)

LOWER FALLS ON THE GENESEE RIVER

USING THIS GUIDE

A great deal of useful information is supplied for each river in this book. First, a brief description of each river identifies basic facts about its location, length, history, and wildlife. Then a map of the river, a run profile, and some At-a-Glance information is provided. This information includes GPS coordinates for put-ins and takeouts, U.S. Geological Survey (USGS) quadrangles, mean monthly water temperatures (where available), shuttle directions, and gauge information (again, where available).

THE MAPS

Detailed maps, which include put-ins and takeouts, are provided. These maps also identify points of interest such as bridges, parks, confluences with tributaries, rapids, and other structures on the river. Statewide and regional overview maps are provided as well. While all of these maps are extremely helpful in navigating the rivers, I recommend using them in tandem with more-detailed topographic maps, especially those in an atlas such as the *DeLorme Gazetteer* or printed by the USGS. Such maps are available online at the USGS Store (**store.usgs.gov**) and from Trails.com (**www.trails.com**).

RUN PROFILES EXPLAINED

DESCRIPTION

Every run is fully described in a run profile. This profile describes specific put-in and takeout spots, as well as other points of interest that may be found in between. In many cases, the history of the river and its surrounding areas is also given, along with information on what plants and animals can be observed while paddling. River features such as rapids, portages (or "carries," in local parlance), rest spots, and side trips are also mentioned in this section.

AT-A-GLANCE INFORMATION

A condensed list of useful information for each run is provided in an **At-a-Glance** box. Here, a river's **class, length, paddle time, runnable months, hazards, number of portages, rescue access, gauge, level, gradient,** and **scenery** rating are listed.

Rivers around the world are rated by **class** using a system developed by American Whitewater. This scale identifies the difficulty of these rivers as well as the skill level required to negotiate their dangers. It is divided into six classes, ranging from Class I to Class VI (see Appendix D for more-detailed information on these ratings). Trip **length** is listed, in miles, from the put-in to the takeout. The distances of side trips, optional paddles, and alternative put-ins or takeouts have been listed in the run descriptions. The average **time** for each trip is listed in hours. These times are only meant to be a guide, however, and can change depending on how many breaks, lunch stops, or photo opportunities are taken. The best, and sometimes only, **runnable months** for a river are then given. Rivers may be navigable at times other than those listed, though.

Hazards on the river may include rapids, boat traffic, strong currents, strainers, deadfall, waterfalls, and the like. The number of **portages** needed to complete a run is also given here, although the exact locations and descriptions of these portages are described in detail in the run profile. Ease of **rescue access** is listed according to the following scale: *Easy* (rescues can be accomplished throughout an entire run), *Limited* (rescues can be accomplished at some points along a run), *Difficult* (rescues can be accomplished only in a few areas during a run), and *Very difficult* (rescues are impossible in all but one or two isolated spots along a run).

The best method of obtaining **gauge information** (Web, phone, visual) is listed as well. **Web** indicates that paddlers can use the Internet to find water data. **Phone** means that local outfitters and organizations can be called for the latest conditions. **Visual** tells paddlers that water conditions should be checked in person before running a river. The optimum paddling **level** of a river is then listed, in feet or cubic feet per second (cfs). Some rivers in New York state are runnable year-round and will be indicated as such. Others may be tidal or have no level information available (indicated by *N/A*). **Gradient** refers to the slope of a river in feet per mile. Although the gradient can help indicate the difficulty of a river—for example, the steeper the gradient, the faster the water flows—it can be somewhat misleading. Many variables, such as the size and length of rapids and the number of strainers, or drops, for example, combine to influence the overall difficulty of a particular run. Finally, **scenery** is listed using a scale of A to D. An *A* rating indicates that a river flows through very beautiful, mostly pristine areas; a *B* means a river flows through areas that are more developed but still very scenic. A *C* describes an area with much more development. A river with a *D* rating flows through areas that are extremely overdeveloped, possibly polluted, and have been stripped of their natural beauty.

GPS COORDINATES

The coordinates of the put-in and takeout spots for each run are provided in two different formats, UTM (Universal Transverse Mercator) and longitude–latitude. The UTM system, developed by NATO during World War II, is based on a grid system somewhat like latitude and longitude. Listed first is the UTM longitude zone. The globe is divided into a total of 60 such zones; most of New York, for example, lies within zone 18. Each longitude zone is then divided into 20 latitude zones, labeled C through X, skipping the letters I and O (which look too similar to numbers). In this case, most of New York lies within zone T. Listed following the zone, the survey datum used to arrive at the coordinates in this book is WGS84 (versus NAD27 or WGS83), so make sure that your GPS unit is set to navigate accordingly. Finally, easting and northing numbers are given, representing east–west and north–south positions, respectively, within the zones. The USGS offers a good deal of information regarding UTM coordinates at its Web site, **www.usgs.gov.**

Most people are likely more familiar with the latitude–longitude grid system, listed immediately after the UTM coordinates. In this system, lines of latitude run horizontally across the globe, equally distant from each other. Each line of latitude, or degree, is roughly equal to 69 miles, although there is a slight variation because the earth is not a perfect circle but an oval. Nevertheless, the equator is considered 0°, while the North Pole is 90° north and the South Pole is 90° south. Lines of longitude run vertically on the globe, perpendicular to latitude lines. Instead of being equally distant, however, they converge at the poles. As a result, they are widest at the equator (about 69 miles apart) and become increasingly narrow as they move north or south. The Prime Meridian (located in Greenwich, England) is designated as 0° longitude. From this point, the degrees continue to the east and west, until they meet 180° later at the International Date Line in the Pacific Ocean. Each degree of latitude and longitude can also be divided into 60 minutes and 60 seconds. Seconds can be divided even further (tenths, hundredths, thousands) depending on how precise a measurement is needed. These divisions are then listed numerically, with latitude being listed first and longitude second. For example, the summit of Mount Marcy, New York's highest elevation, is found at N 44° 06' 46.24", W 73° 55' 24.08".

To learn more about how to enhance your outdoor experiences with GPS technology, refer to *GPS Outdoors: A Practical Guide for Outdoor Enthusiasts* (Menasha Ridge Press).

USGS QUADRANGLES

Probably the most popular and useful USGS maps are the 7.5-minute, or 1:24,000-scale, series known as quadrangles. These "quads" provide a good amount of detail and are quite useful for navigation. For this reason, the quads that include particular sections of rivers being described are listed before each run profile.

MEAN WATER TEMPERATURES BY MONTH

The USGS maintains hundreds of river-gauge stations that collect various data useful to paddlers. Some of these stations take frequent water-temperature readings that can be viewed online at **waterdata.usgs.gov/nwis/rt.** A number of private organizations, such as fishing clubs, hatcheries, and academic institutions, also measure water temperatures. Mean temperatures are listed by month whenever this data is available.

SHUTTLE DIRECTIONS

Specific shuttle directions to each put-in and takeout spot are given from a major road or highway. Other shuttling options, such as trains, buses, or subway systems, are also listed wherever possible.

GAUGE

Finally, river gauges most useful in obtaining information on river conditions are listed.

RIVER HAZARDS AND SAFETY

As with most outdoor sports, canoeing and kayaking are fairly safe activities, although they do pose their share of inherent risks. Paddlers can expect to encounter any number of the following hazards on a river.

Strainers are any kind of tree, branch, or other vegetation that is at least partially submerged in a river. The term *strainer* refers to the tendency of such obstacles to allow only water to flow through, trapping everything else in their clutches. **Deadfalls** are similar to strainers but usually block a stream completely and are difficult to get by. Rocks can sometimes get **undercut,** or eroded below the water's surface, creating holes or cavities that can trap things. Rivers also may contain turbulent, sometimes unpredictable sections of water, known as **rapids. Holes** are usually associated with rapids. Such features are created when water flows over an obstacle with enough velocity to form a wave that curves, sometimes violently, back upstream against itself. Wherever a river takes an appreciable drop, usually more than six feet, a **waterfall** is created. There may sometimes be **standing waves,** or waves that do not change position on a river as water flows past them. Depending on weather and prevailing conditions, a river may sometimes flow over its banks, creating **flooding** conditions. Rivers can also flow beneath **tunnels** and **bridges,** sometimes for long distances. They may be impounded by **dams** and require portages or flow into areas with increased **boat traffic.** In addition, paddlers may risk dangerously lowering body temperatures and **hypothermia,** or overexposure to the sun and **sunburns.**

RESCUE AND EVACUATION

As stated previously, kayaking and canoeing have certain inherent dangers that may not always be avoided. Although such dangers may be slight and may even lead to a more enjoyable experience, they can make paddling a very risky adventure. In fact, times may arise when a boater ends up in such a dire situation that rescue and evacuation are required. Regardless of experience and skill level, all canoeists and kayakers should be prepared for such circumstances and know how to react should the need arise.

Most paddlers will, at times, find themselves paddling in remote wilderness areas. In fact, many actively seek such locations. While these spots make for great paddling destinations, they can make rescues difficult to accomplish. There are usually few roads in such areas that come close enough to a river to make access possible. There may also be mountains, cliffs, or steep banks between roads and rivers that make rescues extremely difficult. Furthermore, certain areas may lack cellphone coverage, making calling for help impossible. A large portion of the Adirondack Park and much of western New York, for example, are without cellular service altogether.

Fortunately, paddlers have many options for minimizing risks and keeping their minds at ease. Perhaps the easiest precaution to take is simply to let someone know exactly where you will be and what your itinerary is. When cellular service is sketchy, paddlers should look to alternative means of communication. Satellite phones, for instance, work anywhere there is an unobstructed view of the sky and are very reliables piece of safety equipment. While they can be quite expensive to buy, they're usually available to rent. Some serious outdoorspeople may also choose to carry a personal locator beacon, or PLB. Although this device cannot be used like a satellite phone to call whomever you want, it can be activated to send a distress signal to search-and-rescue groups in the event that help is needed. Like satellite phones, PLBs can cost quite a bit of money. Luckily, they also are available for rent.

While all of these electronic devices may help save a person's life in an emer-

gency, they are no substitute for careful planning and preparation. Paddlers should always check topographic and highway maps before heading out on a trip and ensure that water conditions are optimal for a run. Always paddle within your skill level, and remember that there is safety in numbers. Finally, basic safety equipment, including a first-aid kit, extra food and water, and emergency camping gear (space blanket, matches, and such), should accompany you on every trip.

HELPFUL INFORMATION

RIVER GAUGES

The USGS measures water conditions on an incredibly large number of rivers in the United States. These river gauges usually measure water height and discharge, although water and air temperatures may also be measured at times.

Basically consisting of a float attached by wire to a recording device, these gauges measure water height, in feet, as it rises and lowers. In many cases this data is sent directly to the USGS via satellite. It is also converted into flow rates, in cubic feet per second (cfs), using rating curves created by the USGS.

Information on water levels and flow rates is invaluable to paddlers. It can often mean the difference between a trip spent grinding over every rock or sandbar in a river and rushing uncontrollably downstream through strainers and deadfalls. Knowing the best water levels for paddling a river can make for the most pleasurable trip possible. In some instances, the best water levels for paddling are not known. In others, such water data may not be collected on a river at all. In these cases, water conditions can be checked visually or by calling a local outfitter.

WATER LEVELS

Real-time water data is made available for all to see on the USGS Web site (**water data.usgs.gov/nwis/rt**). Here, paddlers can find information on gauge heights and discharge for rivers across the United States. This data is available in table and graph format, showing trends and averages as well as current conditions.

While the USGS site is probably the most convenient to use, groups such as American Whitewater (**www.awa.org**) and Waterline (**www.h2oline.com**) also list water data at their Web sites. Keep in mind, however, that these sites get their information from the USGS river gauges.

WEATHER BY SEASON

In general, New York state experiences a fairly moderate climate, with few instances of severe weather, other than snowstorms or nor'easters. Its weather can be greatly affected by geography, however, changing greatly due to elevation, topography, and proximity to large bodies of water. In fact, few, if any, states in the country experience such a wide variety of weather patterns.

ADIRONDACK HIGH PEAKS FROM THE
AUSABLE RIVER

❖ **WINTER** Most of New York experiences fairly mild winters compared with New England. Long Island, New York City, and most of the Lower Hudson River Valley, for example, see average winter temperatures around 31°F and may see temperatures fall below 0°F in only two or three winters per decade. Such conditions are due in part to these locations' proximity to water. The Atlantic Ocean and Long Island Sound retain their summer warmth for quite some time and warm the land near them as a result. They usually receive about 3.5 inches of rain each winter and average anywhere from 3 to 10 inches of snow per month.

New York's Finger Lakes region and Upper Hudson River Valley together experience slightly colder winters. Their average winter temperature is 26°F; they may see up to 15 days of below-zero temperatures and can receive more than 40 inches of snow in a season. The longest and coldest winters in the state are usually seen in the northern reaches. There, temperatures as low as 16°F are the average, with lows often reaching –25°F. Snow amounts can reach 90 inches by the end of the season and stay on the ground until early April.

Although the Great Lakes region of New York experiences winter temperatures similar to Long Island's, it sees much greater snowfall amounts due to the lake effect. This phenomenon occurs when cold-air masses flow over the warmer waters of Lake Erie and Ontario, making them evaporate. The water vapor then cools as it rises and condenses into clouds, eventually falling as snow. The lake effect is so pronounced that some snowstorms can last for days and drop up to eight feet of snow at a time. Approximately 60 percent of the region's winter snow falls as a result of this effect.

❖ **SUMMER** Summers in New York state are usually quite comfortable. Much of northern New York, including the Adirondacks, along with the Catskills and the Finger Lakes region, experiences cool summer temperatures averaging in the mid-60s Fahrenheit. Because of their topography, these areas may see nightly temperatures near freezing during early- and late-summer days. Higher temperatures are usually seen on Long Island, near New York City, and in the Lower Hudson River Valley. These areas are also considerably more humid during the summer months because of their proximity to large bodies of water. Pleasantly warm conditions prevail over much of the remainder of the state, with fairly low humidity and temperatures ranging from the upper 70s to the mid-80s.

❖ **SPRING AND FALL** The Great Lakes and Atlantic Ocean play a large part in moderating the spring and fall climates of New York. The waters warm slowly during the spring, cooling the air considerably. As a result, temperatures may remain in the 50s until mid-May throughout much of the state. Conversely, these bodies of water retain their summer heat and help warm the land near them. Many areas in the state see September and October temperatures hovering in the mid-60s and mid-70s as a result.

WILDLIFE

✧ **BUGS** While no dangerous species are native to New York state, there are three that cause an abundance of discomfort and annoyance: the blackfly, mosquito, and deer tick.

Blackflies and mosquitoes are, unfortunately, found throughout New York, although blackflies seem to predominate in the Adirondack region. Both pests are aggressive biters and cause welts that burn and itch. They often occur in swarms that have been known to follow a person for long distances. These insects are most active during the spring and early summer but can remain active well into the fall in some places. Dozens of repellents exist; everyone has a personal favorite. The most common include bug nets that can be worn over the head and bug spray. Most people agree that sprays containing DEET work the best, although there is some evidence that the chemical can lead to certain health problems. Organic sprays sometimes work just as well as the others. Keep in mind that different repellents may work for different people, so try a few and find the one that works best for you.

Deer ticks are tiny parasites that live by feeding on the blood of other animals. (In general, they are much smaller than wood, or dog, ticks—about the size of a freckle—and are uniformly dark in color, whereas wood ticks usually have white spots.) They can be found throughout New York state but are most prevalent in the southeastern parts, especially Long Island. In addition to being a nuisance, these ticks have been found to carry Lyme disease and can transmit it to their hosts.

You can use several strategies to reduce your chances of a tick bite while portaging or camping. Some people choose to wear light-colored clothing, so ticks can be spotted before they make it to the skin. Bug repellent also keeps them away. Most important, be sure to visually check your hair, the back of your neck, your armpits, and your socks while outdoors. Take a moment to do a more-complete body check while bathing or showering. For ticks that are already embedded, removal with sharp tweezers is best: place them as close to skin as possible and gently rotate out, taking care not to squeeze the tick. Use disinfectant solution on the wound. To be on the safe side, you may want to visit a physician as soon as possible and follow his or her advice on taking a course of antibiotics to ward off a possible case of Lyme disease. (It takes a few hours for an embedded carrier tick to infect the person it's bitten.)

✧ **MAMMALS** There are few, if any, mammals that might cause harm to paddlers on the water. Black bears are likely the only ones that may bother humans on land. Exercising common sense and following some preventative measures when camping and hiking will help prevent encounters, though. For example, all food should be cooked and stored far from any tents (100 yards is suggested). All surplus food supplies should be stored in bear-proof containers and hung from trees ten at least feet high and four feet from trunks. Finally, campers should never sleep in or keep clothes in their tents that were worn when cooking. Bears are attracted to the smell of food and may come to investigate.

✧ **REPTILES** New York state is home to relatively few dangerous species of reptiles. It is home to 13 different species of snakes, only 3 of which are poisonous: the timber rattlesnake, the eastern massasauga, and the copperhead. Of these three, the timber rattler is the most likely to be encountered, although even this snake is extremely rare—it is usually found in a small section of the eastern Adirondacks and in the southeastern part of the state, with the exceptions of New York City and Long Island. The rattler's most obvious feature is, of course, the rattle, found at the tip of its tail. This snake is most active during prime paddling season (April to October) and usually prefers wooded areas that have rugged terrain. As a result, paddlers should take care when portaging or camping in such areas.

The eastern massasauga is found only in two small parts of New York state, near the cities of Syracuse and Rochester. Like the timber rattler, the massasauga has a rattle on the end of its tail and is active during paddling season. It favors boggy, swampy areas such as marshes and floodplains but is extremely rare and almost never poses a threat to anyone or anything, except maybe mice and other small rodents.

The third venomous snake in New York, the copperhead, is relegated to a small area in the Hudson River Valley, south of Kingston. This snake eats small mammals and birds, though, and usually does not pose a problem to anyone.

The only other reptile that may be of concern is the snapping turtle. This fairly large turtle can be found throughout the state in both fresh and salt water. While it usually steers clear of humans, it will bite if disturbed. And with its sharp, hard, beaklike mouth, the snapping turtle can do a lot of harm. The best advice when dealing with any reptile, known or unknown, is to leave it be. Give it a wide berth and it should leave you alone.

CAMPING

Many paddlers often find camping an enjoyable alternative to staying at a hotel or inn. Luckily, New York state has a large variety of campgrounds and other places where paddlers can pitch their tents and throw down their sleeping bags. Many of these campgrounds are privately run and are usually fairly reasonable in price. Locations, availability, and rates can be found at Web sites such as **www .koa.com**, **www.nycampgrounds.com**, and **www.reserveamerica.com**. In addition, many New York State Parks allow camping on their property; visit **nysparks .state.ny.us/parks** for more information. The state Department of Environmental Conservation (DEC) also maintains 52 campgrounds in both the Catskill and Adirondack parks. The DEC Web site, **www.dec-campgrounds.com**, provides information about locations and schedules. Of all the sites above, however, ReserveAmerica is perhaps the most convenient place to find a campground. This site combines most of the information found in the other sites into one large database, with locations provided, maps shown, amenities described, and best of all, reservations taken.

While the campgrounds I've mentioned are convenient and fairly inexpensive, they are not usually among the quietest, nor do they provide a lot of privacy. Paddlers searching for a secluded, uncrowded campsite should look for one of the many DEC backcountry camping sites instead. These sites usually contain primitive lean-tos or tent platforms, or may simply consist of a flat, clear piece of land suitable for a tent. Nevertheless, they almost always provide a quiet, peaceful place to spend a night. In addition to such sites, New York state allows backcountry camping in any part of the Catskill and Adirondack parks as well as any state forest, as long as tents are set up at least 150 feet from any body of water, road, or trail. Go to **www.dec.ny.gov** for more rules and regulations regarding backcountry camping.

When camping, it is important to follow the "Leave No Trace" philosophy. Campers should always strive to make as little impact on an area as possible. Tents should be set up only in designated areas; campfires, when allowed, should be kept small and within a fire pit and fueled only with wood found near the campsite; garbage should be picked up and carried away; human waste should be buried eight inches deep in a small hole dug at least 200 feet from a camp, water, or trails; and cookware should be washed with water and biodegradable soap at least 200 feet from any water.

More information about camping in the Empire State can be found in *The Best in Tent Camping: New York State* (Menasha Ridge Press).

YOUR RIGHTS ON THE RIVER

Paddlers in New York state have a "public right of navigation," which allows them to navigate on freshwater rivers and streams, as well as lakes and ponds, for both commercial and recreational purposes. The state holds all waterways that are "navigable-in-fact" in a trust for its people, giving them the right to paddle on waterways within the state, regardless of whether they are bordered by public or private property. It also gives them the right to utilize riverbeds and banks, on both public and private lands, whenever necessary to portage around obstacles such as waterfalls and rapids.

As with most laws, however, there are gray areas within these access rights. In order to avoid confrontations with angry landowners and face possible legal trouble, paddlers should exercise common sense and do whatever possible to be respectful and courteous whenever dealing with others. While most fresh water in New York state is considered navigable, paddlers should not access such water via private property. Instead, public roads that run near a river or bridges that cross it usually make for much better put-in spots. When such spots are not available, asking permission from landowners before entering private property is strongly suggested. Likewise, paddlers should use private property such as riverbanks and beds when portaging only when absolutely necessary. The meaning of *necessary* may be open to interpretation. However, good judgment and common sense usually rule here. Incidentally, hiking downstream to scout the river ahead is included in this bit of law.

An important item to keep in mind when paddling is the importance of safety when dealing with others. Arguing with and/or physically confronting angry landowners, even those who are on the wrong side of the law, is never a wise thing to do. Access and navigability laws can be interpreted many different ways. Such ambiguities are best dealt with by politicians and lawyers, not canoeists and kayakers. Be courteous, respectful, and gracious toward everyone with whom you may deal in your paddles, and with any luck they will reciprocate. If they don't, choose an alternate spot for putting-in or portaging. Finally, be sure to report any violations of navigational rights to the DEC or local law enforcement to help ensure the public's rights to paddle New York's waterways.

PARKING AND SECURING VEHICLES

While researching and writing this book, I drove and parked all over New York state, learning a few tips and tricks along the way. State and county parks, fishing-access points, and campgrounds are often the best places to park. Some of these places do require a small fee, however, so check before leaving your car there. I also found that leaving my car on the sides of roads with wide shoulders, in private parking lots, at train stations, and in bus depots were also excellent options. I strongly advise asking permission first, though. I often found that most people were excited to talk about my paddling trips and

were more than happy to lend a hand. The best advice I can give, though, is to use common sense. If leaving a car just doesn't feel right, don't do it. I've had to alter my trips more than a few times because I didn't feel comfortable leaving my car in some places.

It is possible to use public transportation when shuttling between put-ins and takeouts in many parts of the state, especially near cities. For example, although I did receive some questioning looks riding the Manhattan subways with my paddling gear, my trips there were made much easier because of the subway system. I also made good use of the shuttle services provided by many of the outfitters across the state. Such businesses will often pick you up or drop you off for a small fee, or sometimes for no fee at all. Finally, when no other options existed, I used my bicycle to get from one end of a river to the other. While it is much easier to leave a bicycle in some places than it is a car, many of the same parking rules apply.

RIVER ETIQUETTE

There is no official agreed-upon standard of paddling protocol. Speaking to ten different people often results in ten different thoughts on the subject. Many commonalities do exist, though. For example, paddlers should never put themselves in a position in which they are paddling beyond their own skill level. Doing so not only puts the paddler at risk but also can endanger fellow paddlers. Furthermore, if a rescue is absolutely necessary, be as helpful and gracious as possible. Buying dinner or beverages for everyone who helped in your rescue is usually a very good idea.

Another rule of thumb is to give the right of way to paddlers heading downstream on a river. If you are downstream, waiting in an eddy, for instance, always look back upstream to make sure you do not get in another paddler's way when exiting. In the same vein, upstream paddlers should try to pick lines that do not interfere with paddlers downstream from them. While these rules sound good, there may be times when they do not apply. For example, in some situations it may be impractical to yield the right of way to an upstream boat. Instead, take precautions and make maneuvers so as to avoid each other. Common sense and good paddling skills should help prevent incidents.

Some river sections may become quite crowded during prime paddling conditions. When paddlers are faced with long lines of boats, it is important not to crowd one another. Be sure to pace yourself and not get too close to the boaters in front of you. If you must pass a downstream boater, do so on calmer sections of water, never in rapids. Also, do not hog holes or eddies. Either make room for other paddlers to share the space or move on as soon as possible.

Paddlers should also be as courteous as possible to other people on the river or nearby. Paddling groups should be limited to small numbers and remain fairly quiet and in control on rivers. Of course cheers, hoots, and hollers are OK. But too much yelling and carrying on can be disturbing to others. Similarly, small groups make it easier to pass anglers and other nature lovers

who may be on the river with you. Remember—they have as much right to use the river as you do.

Finally, it is important to respect both public and private property when on the river and on land. Ask permission before entering private property, keep a healthy space between your campsite and others, and practice minimal-impact camping (leave only footprints).

PADDLING SKILLS

New York state has many rivers that are perfect for paddlers of all skill levels. Expert whitewater paddlers can find what they want here, as can families looking to spend a quiet, serene day on the water. Not every river is suitable for everyone, however. Paddlers should always keep in mind their abilities when choosing rivers to run. The length of and time needed to complete trips should be considered when thinking about running a river just as much as its rating and hazards. Weather and tidal influences should also play an important part in the decision. A good rule of thumb to keep in mind when paddling is "When in doubt, don't go out."

Paddlers interested in increasing their knowledge and bettering their skills might consider taking a kayaking or canoeing class. Such classes are offered throughout the year by dozens of groups across the state and are usually sponsored by the American Canoe Association. Check its Web site, **www .americancanoe.org**, or contact a local outfitter for more information on the courses available.

NEW YORK STATE RIVERS

HISTORY AND GEOLOGY IN BRIEF

Within its 54,471 square miles, New York state contains a varied geology. Its landscape tells the lengthy, complex story of its geologic history, which includes everything from drifting continental plates, ice ages, and glaciers to erosion. Just as varied as the forces that shaped New York are the geologic features they created. The relatively young, 1.1-billion-year-old Adirondack Mountains, the glacially carved Finger Lakes, and the sandy outwash that formed Long Island, for example, are just some of the results of the amazing forces that have shaped New York. In fact, the state contains everything from mountainous highlands to marine and coastal lowlands. It is home to river valleys, glacial lakes and ponds, and tidal estuaries. It also boasts more than

50,000 miles of rivers and streams, spring-fed, tidal, and surface run-off included. Geologists divide the state and all of its features into eight major geologic regions. In order to more easily organize the rivers listed in this book, I have chosen to divide the state into five geographic regions instead: Western New York, Central New York, Northern New York–Adirondacks, the Hudson River Valley, and Southeastern New York–Long Island).

Both the **Western** and **Central New York** regions are part of the larger geologic area known as the Great Lakes Lowland. This section of fairly even topography is marked with rolling hills and fertile soil that extends roughly from Lake Erie to Syracuse, although the Western region identified in this book ranges from Lake Erie to Rochester. The Central Region then continues on to Oneonta. Rivers in these areas generally tend to run northward with slow flows and gentle gradients. Many, like the Chenango River, tend to

FISHING ON THE RAQUETTE RIVER

react greatly to rainfall, often swelling quickly and falling slowly. River gauges should be watched carefully when planning trips in this area.

Whereas the Western and Central portions of the state are relatively flat, **Northern New York** sees some higher altitudes. Consider that the highest point in New York, Mount Marcy, resides in the heart of this region in the geologic division known as the Adirondack Upland. Rivers in the Adirondack Park, as well as those in the areas west of the park, usually have fairly large gradients, often resulting in stretches of exciting whitewater. On the other hand, some of these same rivers are held back by dams or flow into ponds and lakes, in effect creating a network of interconnected flat-water routes. The key word in this area is *variety*.

The St. Lawrence Lowland, found northwest of the Adirondacks, sits in contrast to the high peaks of the Adirondacks. This area and its low-lying plains were formed from the silt and sediment left behind by glacial streams. The majority of rivers here run north toward the St. Lawrence River in gentle, braided flows.

To the south of the Adirondacks lies the **Hudson River Valley.** This area roughly extends from the Adirondack border to the north, Amsterdam to the west, Massachusetts to the east, and Westchester County to the south. It is characterized by the northeast trending, low mountains of the Catskills and Taconics and a deeply gouged river valley through which the Hudson flows. Parts of this river valley are reminiscent of Norwegian fjords, especially the area

STILL WATER ON THE SUSQUEHANNA RIVER

just north of Peekskill. Like the fjords of Norway, the Hudson in this area is influenced by marine waters and tides. Remarkably, these tides reach as far north as Troy.

The **Southeastern** corner of New York state is part of the low-lying geologic zone known as the Atlantic Coastal Plain. Although some of the topography here is a result of glacial carving, most of it was formed when the retreating glacier deposited sediments and debris known as till. Because of the incredibly flat nature of this outwash plain, the rivers in this area are sluggish and slow flowing, except for those acted on by ocean tides. The Nissequogue River on Long Island and the Hudson River off Manhattan, for example, are two rivers that are almost impossible to paddle against the tides.

WATERSHEDS

The state's rivers flow into 54 individual watersheds that are almost as diverse as the rivers that feed them. Of these 54 watersheds, 17 major drainage basins are usually identified.

The Niagara River and Lake Erie drain a good portion of western New York's waters, including Tonawanda Creek and the Buffalo River, and make up the second most populated watershed area in the state while also defining the westernmost part of the state line. Rivers to the south of this area flow into the Allegheny River instead, eventually making their way to the larger Ohio River Basin. The Genesee River collects the water from lands east of the Niagara Basin and carries them north to New York's other Great Lake, Lake Ontario.

Located in central New York, the seven Finger Lakes stretch from north to south, encompassing more than 208 square miles. All of this water, plus that from the area's rivers and streams, drains into the Oswego, Seneca, and Oneida rivers, eventually emptying into Lake Ontario. The Black River also empties into Lake Ontario, after it drains a relatively small area in the western Adirondacks and most of the Tug Hill area. Although the watershed area is smaller than many others in the state, it is more widely used by agriculture, tourism, and recreation. Many of the rivers with southern flows drain into the 444-mile-long Susquehanna River and follow its course through the largest watershed on the east coast (it ultimately empties into the Chesapeake Bay). The Chemung River also drains a portion of this area, itself being a major tributary of the Susquehanna.

In the northern tip of New York lies its largest watershed, the St. Lawrence River Basin. The basin drains a whopping 300,000 square miles in its entirety, 5,600 of which are within New York state. Most of the water in the northwestern reaches of the Adirondacks flows into the St. Lawrence River, as does the water in the lower river valleys on its eastern shore. The eastern Adirondack rivers flow into the similarly impressive Lake Champlain Basin, while the central and southern waters empty into the Upper Hudson River, which itself begins its flow in the Adirondack Park's High Peaks region on Mount Marcy. The portion of the river called the Upper Hudson reaches its southernmost point at the federal dam in Troy. Below this dam, the Hudson is known as the Lower Hudson River. Interestingly enough, this part of the Hudson is not really a river at all, but a tidal estuary. Nevertheless, it drains more than 5,000 square miles of land, which makes it one of the largest watersheds in the East Coast if considered along with the Upper Hudson and Mohawk River basins.

The Hackensack-Ramapo and Housatonic watersheds drain significant areas of southern New York, along with the larger Delaware River. The latter begins its flow in the Catskill Mountains, makes up a portion of the New York–Pennsylvania border, and eventually flows into Delaware Bay and the Atlantic Ocean. Separate from this flow is the Atlantic Ocean–Long Island Sound watershed, which collects all of the water from Long Island, New York City, and much of Westchester County, north of the city.

PADDLING SEASONS

As one would expect from such a varied topography, paddling seasons differ greatly across New York state. With its moderate climate, Long Island sees a paddling season that can last all year long. Rivers there do not tend to freeze over very often, although they do become quite cold. Likewise, the lower portions of the Hudson River Valley may be accessible to canoeists and kayakers throughout a good portion of the year. Paddling in the Adirondack region and other northern New York areas is severely limited by winter, however. In such environs, optimal paddling conditions may occur only between April and October. Low water levels and freeze-overs are the limiting factors there. Central and Western New York usually see paddling seasons that last from late March to October or early November. Many rivers in these areas run so low by the end of summer that they are unnavigable. In addition, they usually freeze over by midwinter and do not begin to thaw until March.

Forget-me-nots, Upper Carmans River

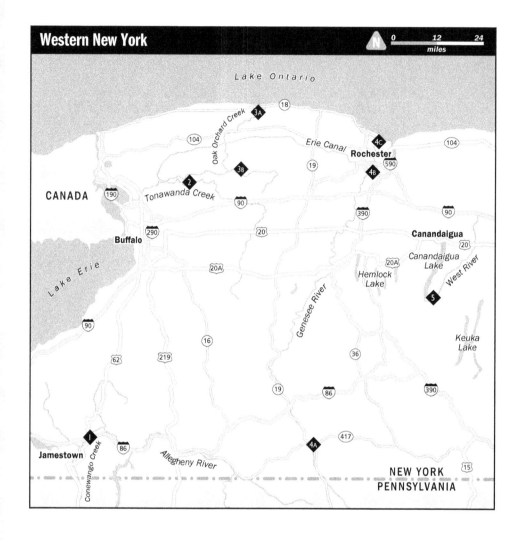

Western New York

1   CONEWANGO CREEK

Western New York's Conewango Creek has been described in a few different ways. Native Americans called it *Conewango,* or "walking slowly," an allusion to its casual, meandering flow. Today, the creek is known for being muddy, its chocolate-colored waters obvious to all who visit its banks. Even so, the Conewango is considered a paddler's paradise, perhaps the most fitting description of the three.

New York's Chautauqua County recently recognized the creek's appeal to paddlers and developed the Marden E. Cobb Waterway Trail along 25 miles of the Conewango's length. With the designation of this trail came the construction of four launch sites, improved parking, and even some lean-tos for camping. Maps are available online at **co.chautauqua.ny.us/parks/trailslist/cobb.htm** (click on "Get Map") and also at each launch site along the trail.

Though a popular destination, the Conewango is not without its problems. Because of its slow-moving water, the creek sees a great deal of change in water levels throughout the year. As a result, it may be running so low at times as to be unnavigable. The Conewango also sees many trees fall into its waters each spring, some of which can pose a danger to unwary paddlers. These issues can be alleviated by watching river gauges and planning trips accordingly.

USGS Quadrangles   KENNEDY (NY), IVORY (NY), JAMESTOWN (NY)

DESCRIPTION Once you are on the water at the Clarks Corners launch site, a few things about the Conewango become obvious. The first is the chocolate-milky color of its water. The second is its slow flow, which makes it possible to paddle in either direction. Finally, and most welcome, is the sense of peace and solitude one gets from the surrounding environment. Indeed, time seems

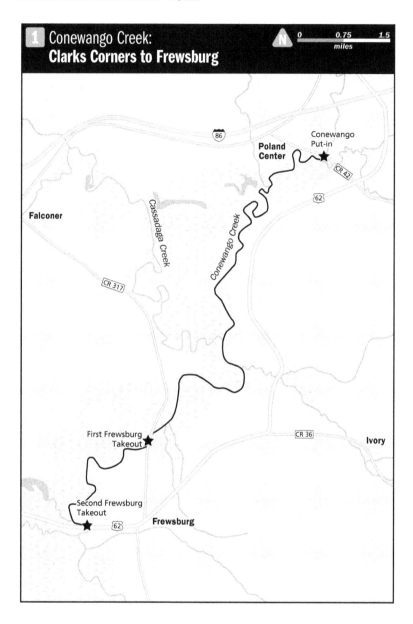

Conewango Creek:
Clarks Corners to Frewsburg

GPS Coordinates (UTM Zone 17T, WGS84)

Put-in:		Takeout:	
Easting	656482	Easting	650976
Northing	4665961	Northing	4657223
Latitude	N 42° 07' 48.54"	Latitude	N 42° 03' 09.24"
Longitude	W 79° 06' 24.12"	Longitude	W 79° 10' 31.92"

to slow as you get into your boat and push off the grassy riverbank into a lush, green woodscape.

Conewango Creek is only about 50 feet wide at this point, flowing with wide, graceful curves and turns between banks filled with silver maple and ash trees, the bases of which are completely covered by immense groups of ferns and wild grapevines. A solitary house sits along the creek's route and is visible 0.5 miles south of Clarks Corners. Otherwise, the only forms of life that occupy the creek are red-tailed hawks, kingfishers, wood ducks, Canada geese, and beavers, to name just a few species. I even spied a great horned owl the last time I paddled the Conewango, as well as a large herd of wading cattle.

After 1.5 miles of paddling, the creek's twists and turns tighten a bit, leading to an accumulation of broken

Clarks Corners to Frewsburg

Class	I
Length	10.8 miles
Time	3.5 hours
Runnable Months	EarlyA pril–late October
Hazards	Strainers
Portages	2
Rescue Access	Limited
Gauge	Visual, Web
Level	2.5 feet
Gradient	5.6
Scenery	A

tree limbs and fallen logs. As a result, quite a few strainers must be dodged, climbed over, or carried around between the first 1.5 to 2 miles. The creek does straighten out a bit after 2 miles, however, leaving only one or

WADING CATTLE ON CONEWANGO CREEK

two more large strainers to deal with before you reach mile 4.

Conewango Creek is joined by Cassadaga Creek about 5 miles south of Clarks Corners. The Conewango continues heading to the south (left) here, and so should boaters. The first landing site in Frewsburg can be found 2 miles later, just after the County Road 317 Bridge on creek-left. The second site in Frewsburg is just 2.5 miles farther. It can also be found on the left side of the creek, just before the Main Street Bridge in Frewsburg.

✧ **SHUTTLE DIRECTIONS** To get to the put-in at Clarks Corners, take Interstate 86/NY 17 to Exit 14 (US 62). Head

south on US 62 1.5 miles before taking the first right turn onto Mud Creek Road (CR 42). The put-in is 1.5 miles down the road on the right-hand side.

To get to the takeout in Frewsburg, head south on US 62 but do not turn right onto Mud Creek Road. Instead, head an additional 7 miles into the town of Frewsburg. Follow US 62 as it turns right, and head 1 more mile west to the bridge over the Conewango.

✧ **GAUGE** Water conditions on Conewango Creek can be checked visually at the Clarks Corners put-in or at the river gauge on the Conewango in Russell, Pennsylvania (visit **waterdata .usgs.gov/nwis/rt** to check online).

---

2 TONAWANDA CREEK

The Tonawanda is a small creek in Western New York that has a lot of big things going for it. Although it is only 90 miles long, the creek can boast about flowing through two fairly large towns and three cities, running over a 30-foot-high waterfall, passing through a Native American reservation and a wildlife-management area, and being part of the Erie Canal. Consider, too, the remarkable plant and animal life found along its banks, and it is easy to see why so many paddlers are drawn to the Tonawanda throughout the year.

Boaters on the Tonawanda can expect to see willow, eastern cottonwood, maple, and butternut trees growing out over the water's edge, while cattails, swamp milkweed, swamp rose,

yellow pond and fragrant water lilies, buttonbush, and purple loosestrife plants fill in every other inch of available space. Wood ducks, black ducks, great blue herons, red-winged blackbirds, goldfinches, and many other birds can be found floating, flitting, and flying overhead, just as beaver, muskrat, raccoon, and deer are all easily spotted from the seat of a boat.

Tonawanda Creek is navigable for much of its length, although the stretch from Wolcotsville to the Niagara River is the most popular. The creek does become more developed as it flows farther west, however, so those looking for peace and quiet are better off paddling east of NY 78 in Millersport.

USGS Quadrangles WOLCOTSVILLE (NY), CLARENCE CENTER (NY)

 DESCRIPTION Although paddling upstream on the Tonawanda Creek

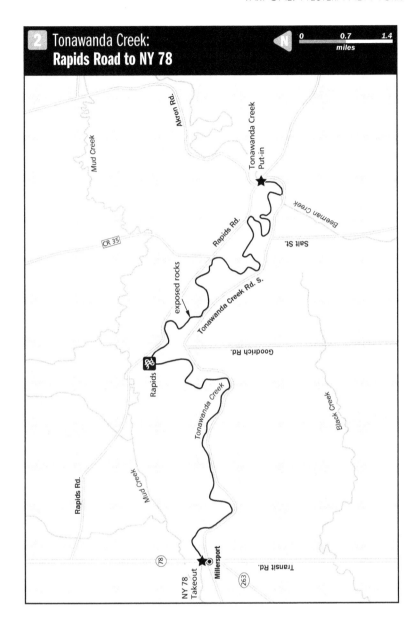

2 Tonawanda Creek: Rapids Road to NY 78

0   0.7   1.4
miles

GPS COORDINATES (UTM ZONE 17T, WGS84)

Put-in:		Takeout:	
Easting	696510	Easting	687438
Northing	4771749	Northing	4772985
Latitude	N 43° 04' 22.80"	Latitude	N 43° 05' 11.10"
Longitude	W 78° 35' 10.56"	Longitude	W 78° 41' 49.92"

Rapids Road to NY 78

Class	I
Length	11.1 miles
Time	4 hours
Runnable Months	May–October
Hazards	Strainers, submerged rocks
Portages	1
Rescue Access	Easy
Gauge	Visual, Web
Level	60 cfs
Gradient	0.2
Scenery	A

from the Rapids Road boat launch is not a possibility because it is blocked by a large pileup of downed trees and broken logs, the way downstream is free and clear of almost all snags and strainers and should make for a fairly smooth trip to the NY 78 takeout. Paddlers will find a creek that is about 50 feet wide, with a current so slow as to be almost imperceptible. On its way west, the Tonawanda winds through areas of forest that include maple, willow, butternut, ash, and eastern cottonwood trees. One of the best characteristics of a cottonwood tree is the way its leaves rustle when the wind blows through them. No other trees make quite as pleasing a sound as they do.

A few houses can be seen on the banks of the creek whenever the Tonawanda runs close to a road. These buildings disappear from view quite quickly and should not spoil the paddle for anyone. Some things that might ruin a trip, however, are the rocks that sit across the creek bed at mile 4.8. While neither large nor in swift water, these rocks could potentially cause damage to or capsize the boats of unwary paddlers. Luckily, there are huge gaps between them, allowing easy passage downstream. More of the same occurs 0.5 miles later, where more rocks appear near the Goodrich Road Bridge. One-quarter mile later you'll reach some small riffles, which I assume gave rise to the area name of Rapids. As with the rocks before them, common sense and a bit of attention should get you through unscathed.

The Tonawanda turns to the right and finally straightens out a bit 8 miles from the put-in. The takeout just after the NY 78 bridge is only about 2 miles west from there. Look for a steep, grassy trail on the north side of the creek that leads to the side of NY 78.

✧ **SHUTTLE DIRECTIONS** To get to the put-in on Rapids Road, take Interstate 90 to Exit 49 (NY 78). Head north on NY 78 9.5 miles into the town of Millersport. Look for the junction of NY 78 with NY 263 on the left. Turn right just after this junction onto Tonawanda Creek Road South. Take Tonawanda Creek Road South 6 miles east before turning right onto Rapids Road. Continue east on Rapids Road 3.3 miles until you reach a T. Turn left here and look for the boat launch on the right-hand side of the road.

To get to the takeout, head back to NY 78 and look for the wide shoulder on the west side of the highway just north of the bridge. Boats can be taken out here, but cars should be parked in the bank parking a bit farther north.

✧ **GAUGE** Water levels on Tonawanda Creek are best determined by checking the gauge on the creek in Rapids, New York (visit **waterdata.usgs.gov/nwis/rt** to check online). Conditions on the creek can also be checked visually from the NY 78 Bridge or the Rapids Road Bridge.

....

3   OAK ORCHARD CREEK

Oak Orchard Creek, which is actually a small river, is just west of the city of Rochester. It rises near the Oak Orchard Swamp north of Batavia, cruises west through the Oak Orchard Wildlife Management Area and the Iroquois National Wildlife Refuge, then heads north, passes through Medina, and empties into Lake Ontario. Although canoeing and kayaking opportunities along the creek are limited, two sections can be paddled: the Oak Orchard Swamp and the lower creek north of Lake Alice.

The Europeans were the first to call the area Oak Orchard after they settled here in the early 1800s. When they saw how the native Seneca Indians had drained parts of the swamp and cleared some of the land, it reminded them of an orchard of oak trees, thus providing the swamp's name. Although these settlers did not fare very well farming the area, waterfowl and other birds came to rely on it as a stopover point during their seasonal migrations. Nowadays, almost 100,000 Canada geese migrate through the swamp each spring, as do a few thousand ducks and other waterfowl. Come summer, shorebirds such as sandpipers, killdeer, and yellowlegs dominate the scene, although more than 250 other species of birds have been spotted in the swamp. Seeing how the area was a vital habitat for so many avian species, the federal government created the Iroquois National Wildlife Refuge in 1958, forever protecting the swamp and its waters.

Although paddling through the refuge is only permitted between Knowlesville Road and NY 63, there is much to see within this 6-mile stretch. Wooded riverbanks, freshwater marshes, and winding waters are all found here, inhabited by deer, muskrat, beaver, bass, carp, northern pike, and many other animal species. A pair of nesting bald eagles have also been spotted within the refuge's boundaries.

The stretch of Oak Orchard Creek north of the Lake Alice dam, though quite different from the Oak Orchard Swamp, is just as inviting. Because river ice is melted by warm water flowing from the power plant at the Lake Alice dam and the Orleans County Marine Park public boat launches in Point Breeze provide easy river access, canoeing and kayaking are possible almost all year long. Fishing is also extremely popular in this section, so paddlers may have to share the creek with anglers. Luckily, speed limits are kept low, and most fishermen are quite friendly and welcoming.

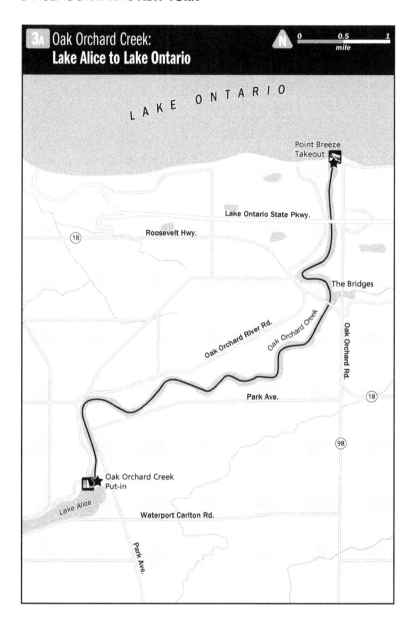

3A Oak Orchard Creek:
Lake Alice to Lake Ontario

L A K E   O N T A R I O

Point Breeze
Takeout

Lake Ontario State Pkwy.

Roosevelt Hwy.

(18)

The Bridges

Oak Orchard River Rd.

Oak Orchard Creek

Oak Orchard Rd.

Park Ave.

(18)

(98)

Oak Orchard Creek
Put-in

Lake Alice

Waterport Carlton Rd.

Park Ave.

N

0   0.5   1
mile

GPS Coordinates (UTM Zone 17T, WGS84)

Put-in:		**Takeout:**	
Easting	723871	Easting	727533
Northing	4800856	Northing	4805872
Latitude	N 43° 19' 37.98"	Latitude	N 43° 22' 16.44"
Longitude	W 78° 14' 19.56"	Longitude	W 78° 11' 29.64"

USGS Quadrangles Run 3A:
Kent (NY); Run 3B: Oakfield (NY),
Knowlesville (NY)

**Lake Alice to
Lake Ontario**

Class	I
Length	5.5 miles
Time	2 hours
Runnable Months	Year-round, weather permitting
Hazards	Boat traffic
Portages	None
Rescue Access	Easy
Gauge	Visual, phone
Level	N/A
Gradient	3.8
Scenery	A

DESCRIPTION Although Oak Orchard Creek flows for quite some time before emptying into Lake Ontario, it is held back by a dam that forms Lake Alice just south of Point Breeze. As a result, anyone wanting to paddle the creek to Lake Ontario must use the Department of Environmental Conservation fishing access spot downstream of the dam on the east side of the creek. Although its location is perfect, there is a steep, rocky trail down to the creek's edge, making launching somewhat of a chore. Two sets of steady hands and sure feet should be able to accomplish the task without much trouble.

Oak Orchard Creek flows quite swiftly north of the dam. It is lined with low-lying, dense trees whose branches lean way out over the creek, though there is more than enough room to paddle down the middle of the creek and stay out of trouble. The creek begins flowing through a series of gentle, sweeping curves after 1 mile, and slows down quite a bit as a result. Yellow pond lilies and fragrant water lilies are able to take advantage of the slower-moving water and begin to colonize a good portion of the creek here. Likewise, cattail marshes pop up 1.5 miles downstream of the dam, wherever the maple, ash, sycamore, and oak trees have not taken hold.

A series of bridges are reached after about 4 miles of paddling, in an area aptly named The Bridges. Paddling into the cove and its small feeder stream on the right is possible, and can provide a welcome diversion from the powerboats on the creek. It is the bridge on the left that marks the way to Lake Ontario, though. The creek makes one more sweeping turn once it passes through The Bridges, then runs almost due north toward the lake. It passes under the Lake Ontario State Parkway Bridge at mile 5 and comes to the Orleans County Marine Park and its boat ramp 0.5 miles later on the right.

✧ **SHUTTLE DIRECTIONS** To get to the put-in downstream of the Lake Alice dam, take NY 98 north and turn left onto Park Avenue, 3.6 miles north of NY 104. Head west on Park Avenue 3 miles, looking for the brown Department of Environmental Conservation fishing access sign on the right side of the road. The trail to the creek is in the far right corner of the parking lot.

To get to the takeout on Lake Ontario, head north on NY 98 from Park Avenue. After 2 miles, follow the sign for the town boat launch on Oak Orchard Creek.

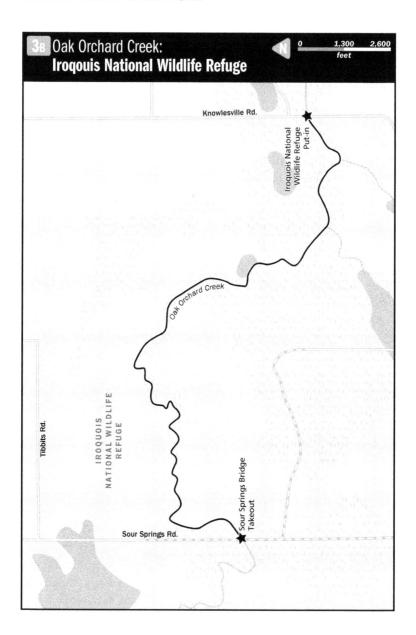

3B Oak Orchard Creek:
Iroqouis National Wildlife Refuge

GPS COORDINATES (UTM ZONE 17T, WGS84)

Put-in:		**Takeout:**	
Easting	717615	Easting	717615
Northing	4777675	Northing	4777675
Latitude	N 43° 07' 13.98"	Latitude	N 43° 07' 13.98"
Longitude	W 78° 19' 29.94"	Longitude	W 78° 19' 29.94"

✧ **GAUGE** The best spot to visually check on water conditions is at the fishing access just downstream of the Lake Alice dam. Oak Orchard Canoe and Kayak also can give updated water conditions. Call them at (585) 682-4849.

3B **DESCRIPTION** The put-in on Knowlesville Road provides the easternmost access point on Oak Orchard Creek for anyone wanting to paddle through the Iroquois National Wildlife Refuge. From there, the creek begins its circuitous flow through this amazing place. It starts by passing through a densely wooded area of silver maple, cottonwood, and willow trees, flowing along with a barely perceptible current. A few of these trees have fallen into the creek along the way, sometimes leaving only the narrowest of passages open. On other occasions, beaver dams have been built that, likewise, can impede progress downstream. After 0.4 miles, however, the tree-lined banks give way to groves of cattails, swamp milkweed, lizards' tail, and buttonbush, all characteristic of wetland environments. Indeed, this marshy area extends along the creek for quite some time, until a more forested scene reemerges 1.5 miles later.

Whether paddling beneath a forested canopy or through cattails gently waving in the breeze, paddlers should keep an eye out for one of the bald eagles that have nested within the refuge. I was lucky enough to encounter one of them sitting quite low on a branch in a dead tree within the first mile of paddling the creek. Usually a bit easier to spot are the feisty carp that swim just beneath the water's surface.

Look for their dorsal fins above the surface as they cruise the shallows hunting for a meal.

There are only a few options when paddling Oak Orchard Creek within the Wildlife Refuge from Knowlesville Road. Paddlers may take out at the bridge on Sour Springs Road, 4 miles west of their put-in. They may also continue 2 miles farther and take out on NY 63. Or they may simply turn around and return to the Knowlesville Road put-in. No matter which version of the trip you choose, your experience on Oak Orchard Creek will surely be a memorable one.

✧ **SHUTTLE DIRECTIONS** To get to the put-in on Knowlesville Road, take Interstate 90 to Exit 48A (NY 77). Head north on NY 77 6.5 miles and turn right onto Lewiston Road. Turn left after 2.5 miles onto Knowlesville Road and follow the signs into the Iroquois National Wildlife Refuge. Look for the put-in on the south side of the bridge

Iroquois National Wildlife Refuge	**B**
Class	I
Length	8 miles (round-trip)
Time	2–3 hours
Runnable Months	March–November
Hazards	Strainers
Portages	None
Rescue Access	Difficult
Gauge	Phone, visual
Level	N/A
Gradient	0.7
Scenery	A+

crossing Oak Orchard Creek 2 miles after turning onto Knowlesville Road. There is ample parking in the lot just 0.25 miles farther north.

To get to the Iroquois National Wildlife Refuge Visitor Center, take NY 77 north but do not turn right onto Lewiston Road. Instead, head 1 mile farther north, to Casey Road. Turn left onto Casey Road and follow the signs to the center.

✧ **GAUGE** Water levels on Oak Orchard Creek can best be determined by calling the Iroquois National Wildlife Refuge at (716) 948-5445 or by checking them directly from the bridge on Knowlesville Road.

4   GENESEE RIVER

The Genesee, one of New York's most well-known rivers, actually has its source in Pennsylvania, just south of the town of Genesee. It heads north from there, entering New York state near the town of Wellsville, and flows a total of 157 miles until it empties into Lake Ontario in the city of Rochester. In doing so, the Genesee effectively cuts the state in two (no other river in the state can claim such a feat).

The Genesee passes through some varied topography on its way north, running between rolling hills, through wooded forests, between sprawling fields, over more than a few waterfalls, and down the middle of a river gorge. These features all add their own touch of beauty to the river. In fact, the Native American name for the Genesee means "Pleasant Valley," the perfect description for such a place.

Nowhere is the stunning scenery of the Genesee more obvious than in Letchworth State Park. Located about halfway along the river's run through New York, this park is situated where the Genesee began carving out its famous gorge. In doing so, it left cliffs almost 600 feet high, hence the nickname "Grand Canyon of the East." The river also cascades over three spectacular waterfalls within this park's boundaries, making it an immensely popular travel destination.

With three waterfalls and a 600-foot-deep gorge, kayaking within Letchworth State Park is not for everyone, although whitewater enthusiasts can register to paddle the Class II and III waters within some portions of the park. The 50 miles of river above Letchworth, especially from Wellsville to Belmont, are much more suitable for flat-water paddlers. The river is also a paddler's delight north of the park, as it flows for almost 60 miles toward the city of Rochester. It is at the northern end of this stretch that the Genesee Waterways Center makes its home, providing boat rentals, canoeing and kayaking instruction, and group paddles on the river. Once north of the Waterways Center and in the heart of Rochester, the Genesee plunges down three final waterfalls, then runs uninterrupted to Lake Ontario. The picturesque Turning Point Park is located along the banks on this final section of river and makes it easy for paddlers of all abilities to experience its beauty.

USGS Quadrangles RUN 4A:
WELLSVILLE SOUTH (NY), WELLSVILLE NORTH (NY); **RUN 4B:** WEST HENRIETTA (NY); **RUN 4C:** ROCHESTER EAST (NY), ROCHESTER WEST (NY)

Wellsville to Scio A

Class	I
Length	6.4 miles
Time	2–3 hours
Runnable Months	April–June (or longer depending on rain)
Hazards	Dams
Portages	2
Rescue Access	Easy
Gauge	Web, visual
Level	5 feet
Gradient	6.5
Scenery	B–

DESCRIPTION While the boat launch at Wellsville's Island Park is very convenient, it puts boaters on the water near a highly developed section of the Genesee. Paddling along the grass fields of the park is pretty enough but only lasts for about 0.2 miles, at which point a small dam must be carried around via a small landing area on the left. The river then passes under a highway bridge 0.1 mile later and becomes contained within a concrete flood control channel.

Some paddlers might feel despair at this point and wonder why they chose to paddle this particular stretch of river. Not to worry, though. The Genesee enters a more natural area just a short distance north of Wellsville, but not before it flows over one more small dam a mile after the put-in and past a small shopping mall 0.25 miles after that. The lush, green landscape that begins to emerge after 1.5 miles of paddling dominates the scenery from then on. As if there were any doubt when this transformation was complete, an impressive, stately silver maple tree grows out over the river at mile 2 in such a way that seems to welcome boaters downstream.

The Genesee turns almost due north after 2.5 miles, flowing parallel to a low mountain just west of it. From here on it runs almost directly toward

Scio, turning slightly east, then west, and back east again. It does this all the while flowing past large sycamore and willow trees; between banks lined with beautiful crown vetch, monkey flower, and bird's-foot trefoil flowers; and underneath dozens of bank swallows, cedar waxwings, kingfishers, and red-winged blackbirds cruising the skies above. A few houses pop up around mile 3 and some road noise becomes obvious when the river nears NY 19 after 5.5 miles. Thankfully, little else exists to distract from the natural beauty of the river through the takeout in Scio. Paddlers who are enjoying the river may choose to head even farther north to the town of Belmont, adding an additional 5 miles to their paddle. The takeout in Belmont is right before the town dam. There is also a good takeout spot in Scio just beyond the County Road 9 bridge on the left riverbank.

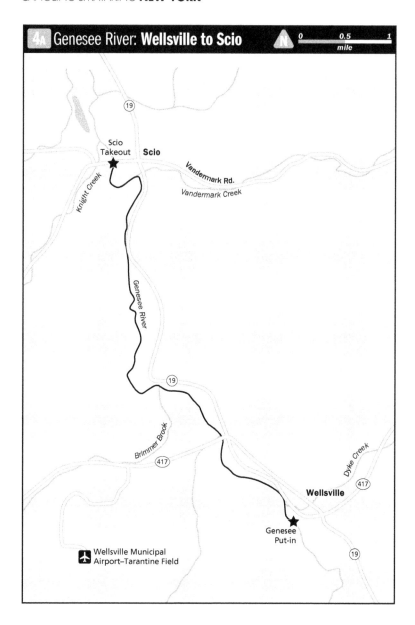

Genesee River: **Wellsville to Scio**

GPS Coordinates (UTM Zone 18T, WGS84)

Put-in:		**Takeout:**	
Easting	256562	Easting	256385
Northing	4666773	Northing	4667009
Latitude	N 42° 06' 55.02"	Latitude	N 42° 07' 02.46"
Longitude	W 72° 56' 40.68"	Longitude	W 77° 56' 48.72"

WILDFLOWERS ON A GENESEE RIVERBANK

⟐ SHUTTLE DIRECTIONS To get to the put-in at Wellsville, take NY 17/Interstate 86 to NY 19 (Exit 30). Take NY 19 south 13 miles, through the towns of Belmont, Scio, and finally Wellsville. Once in Wellsville, turn right onto West Dyke Street and enter Island Park. Boats can easily be launched next to the large wooden bridge over the creek.

To get to the takeout in Scio, take NY 19 back north into the town of Scio and turn left onto River Street. The takeout can be found on the right in 0.3 miles, just after crossing the bridge.

⟐ GAUGE The gauge most useful in determining water levels is on the Genesee in Wellsville (visit **waterdata .usgs.gov/nwis/rt** to check online). Water levels can also be checked visually at a number of spots along its length from NY 19.

DESCRIPTION The Genesee River flows south for 55 miles from the Genesee Waterways Center before it reaches the impassable falls in Letchworth State Park. There are quite a few paddling options within these 55 miles, many of which make use of eight different access sites between the Waterways Center and the state park. For example, the town of Avon is a respectable 25-mile paddle, while Industry is 13 miles and Scottsville is 11 miles, each one being perfect for a full day's outing. The Ballantyne Bridge, however, is only about 3.5 miles from the Waterways Center, making it the perfect destination for a half-day paddle on the Genesee.

When heading south from the center, the Genesee passes under a small footbridge and crosses the Erie Canal 0.3 miles later. There can be

B Genesee Waterways Center to Ballantyne Bridge and Back

Class	I
Length	6.6 miles (round-trip)
Time	2–3 hours
Runnable Months	March–Oct.
Hazards	Boat traffic
Portages	None
Rescue Access	Easy
Gauge	Web
Level	900 cfs
Gradient	2.4
Scenery	A

some heavy boat traffic here, so it is very important to look both ways when crossing its width. Once across the boat channel, paddlers can head down either riverbank while heading south where the abundant plant life can be more easily appreciated. Black locust, basswood, cottonwood, red oak, and willow trees make up most of the foliage here, although purple loosestrife and wild grapevines seem to be everywhere as well. Unfortunately, there is quite a bit of noise from roads and a nearby airport. There are also a few houses situated right on the eastern riverbank about 2.5 miles south of the center. Nevertheless, the Genesee River remains an enjoyable, scenic body of water throughout its run.

A good takeout can be found a very short distance up Black Creek, which empties into the Genesee 3.2 miles south of the Waterways Center. Paddlers may also make their trip round and head back downstream to their starting point.

✧ **SHUTTLE DIRECTIONS** To get to the put-in at the Genesee Waterways

ROUTE 104 BRIDGE CROSSING
THE GENESEE RIVER GORGE
(SEE RUN 4C, PAGE 36)

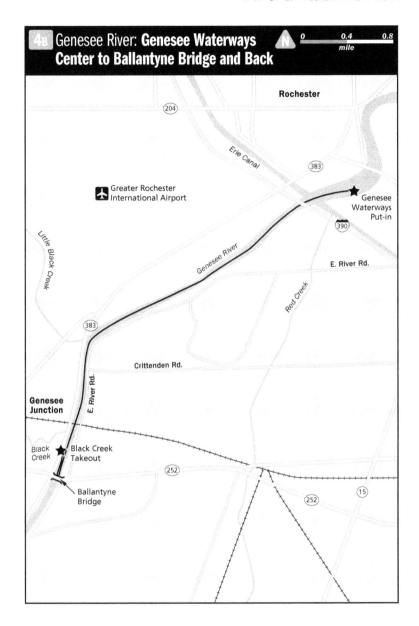

4B Genesee River: **Genesee Waterways Center to Ballantyne Bridge and Back**

Rochester

Greater Rochester International Airport

Genesee Waterways Put-in

Genesee River

Erie Canal

Little Black Creek

Red Creek

E. River Rd.

Crittenden Rd.

Genesee Junction

E. River Rd.

Black Creek Takeout

Black Creek

Ballantyne Bridge

GPS Coordinates (UTM Zone 18T, WGS84)

Put-in:		**Takeout:**	
Easting	285540	Easting	285540
Northing	4777785	Northing	4777785
Latitude	N 43° 07' 20.76"	Latitude	N 43° 07' 20.76"
Longitude	W 77° 38' 10.74"	Longitude	W 77° 38' 10.74"

Mean Water Temperatures by Month (Degrees Fahrenheit)					
	Jan	Feb	Mar	Apr	May	Jun
Mean	N/A	N/A	N/A	49	55	72
	Jul	Aug	Sep	Oct	Nov	Dec
Mean	77	76	69	55	N/A	N/A

Center, take Interstate 390 to Exit 17 (NY 383/Scottsville Road). Head north on Scottsville Road for 0.5 miles and turn right onto Elmwood Road. Turn right into Genesee Valley Park after 0.25 miles. The Waterways Center is just beyond the public pool.

To get to the Black Creek takeout, head south on Scottsville Road instead of north. Turn right onto Black Creek Road just before the Ballantyne Bridge, almost 3 miles south of Interstate 390. The boat ramp will be on the right-hand side of the road.

✧ **GAUGE** The gauge most useful in determining water levels on the Genesee is on the river in Avon (visit **water data.usgs.gov/nwis/rt** to check online).

4c DESCRIPTION The lower Genesee River, flowing through Rochester to Lake Ontario, is quite an interesting stretch of water to paddle. Unfortunately, river access is limited. The boat launches shown on the New York state atlas near the mouth of the river are all either within private boat marinas or not easily accessible. Luckily, though, there is a free and convenient boat launch in nearby Turning Point Park that serves as the perfect spot to begin a trip up- or downstream on the lower Genesee. A small cart or a partner to help shoulder the weight of a boat is highly recommended as the trail to the river's edge from the parking lot is long (0.25 miles) and quite steep. Once on the river, the hard work is over and the fun begins. The Genesee empties into Lake Ontario just 2.5 marina-lined miles to the north, making it an easy and attractive paddling destination for some. The impressive Lower Falls lie just 4 miles to the south, themselves a worthy destination.

The first 0.5 miles of river south of the boat launch bring paddlers past a large wooden bulkhead used by tankers and other large ships to unload cargo. Once past the tankers and tugboats, paddlers can revel in the nature that abounds. Huge cattail marshes line the riverbanks with stands of oak, maple, willow, and cottonwood trees colonizing the steep canyon walls above.

C Turning Point Park to Lower Falls and Back

Class	I
Length	7.5m iles (round-trip)
Time	2–3 hours
Runnable Months	April–June (or longer depending on rain)
Hazards	None
Portages	None
Rescue Access	Difficult
Gauge	Visual, Web
Level	900 cfs
Gradient	4.4
Scenery	A+

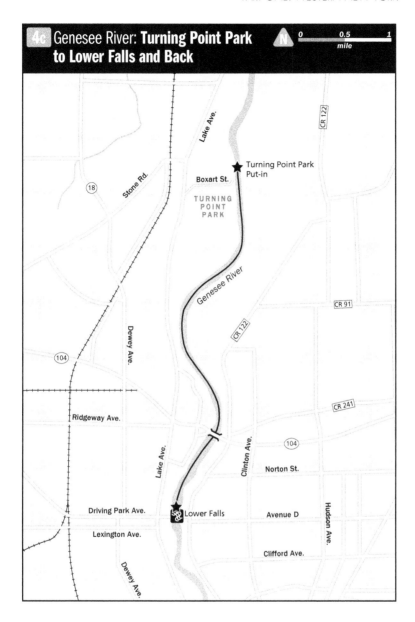

4c Genesee River: **Turning Point Park to Lower Falls and Back**

GPS Coordinates (UTM Zone 18T, WGS84)

Put-in:		**Takeout:**	
Easting	287523	Easting	287523
Northing	4789688	Northing	4789688
Latitude	N 43° 13' 48.24"	Latitude	N 43° 13' 48.24"
Longitude	W 77° 36' 59.52"	Longitude	W 77° 36' 59.52"

MEAN WATER TEMPERATURES BY MONTH (Degrees Fahrenheit)					
JAN	FEB	MAR	APR	MAY	JUN
MEAN N/A	N/A	N/A	49	55	72
JUL	AUG	SEP	OCT	NOV	DEC
MEAN 77	76	69	55	N/A	N/A

Incredibly, the large trees and high walls block out almost all the sights and sounds of Rochester, even though the river flows through the heart of the city. As a result, paddlers may hear only the screeches of red-tailed hawks circling overhead, the cascading of water as it falls down the canyon walls in small waterfalls, and the chattering of kingfishers and red-winged blackbirds that search for prey in the marsh grasses.

The pristine river setting is broken up by the appearance of an industrial plant 2.25 miles south of Turning Point Park and a footbridge 0.25 miles after that. For the most part, however, the river remains a thing of beauty. Even the NY 104 Bridge at mile 3 is a stunning sight, with its graceful arches and stone supports.

The low rumble of the falls can be heard about 0.5 miles south of the NY 104 bridge, around the same time a small island is reached. This island is navigable on both sides, although the water on the east side can be quite shallow. The lower falls lie just south of this island and can be reached by paddling through the rocks that dot the water there. Boats also may be landed onshore near the island, where foot trails lead to the falls as well. Once paddlers have had their fill, all that is left to do is turn around and head back to Turning Point Park.

✧ **SHUTTLE DIRECTIONS** To get to the put-in at Turning Point Park, take Interstate 90 to Exit 46 (Interstate 390). Head north on I-390 for 14 miles before turning right onto NY 104. Stay on NY 104 for two and a half miles, and then turn left onto Lake Avenue before crossing the Genesee River. Stay on Lake Avenue for 2.2 miles and turn right onto Boxart Street. Turning Point Park is at the end of Boxart Street, about 0.5 miles later.

✧ **GAUGE** Water levels within the Genesee River Gorge can best be determined by checking the gauge on the Genesee at the Ford Street Bridge in Rochester (visit **waterdata.usgs.gov/ nwis/rt** to check online).

5   WEST RIVER

In an area of New York state that is relatively flat with few paddling opportunities, the West River is a blessing. Found south of Canandaigua Lake in the beautiful High Tor Wildlife Management Area, the West gives canoers and kayakers a river to explore, abundant wildlife to observe, and scenic mountains at which to gaze. In fact, the word *tor* means "a high, rocky hill or peak," used here in reference to the area's topography.

The New York Department of Environmental Conservation protects High Tor and the portion of the West

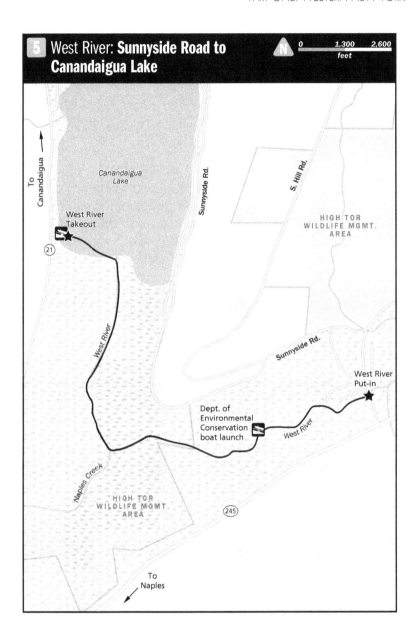

5 West River: **Sunnyside Road to Canandaigua Lake**

GPS Coordinates (UTM Zone 18T, WGS84)

Put-in:		Takeout:	
Easting	308917	Easting	306297
Northing	4725287	Northing	4726723
Latitude	N 42° 39' 22.80"	Latitude	N 42° 40' 06.96"
Longitude	W 77° 19' 52.80"	Longitude	W 77° 21' 49.56"

Sunnyside Road to Canandaigua Lake

Class	I
Length	3 miles
Time	2 hours
Runnable Months	April–November
Hazards	None
Portages	None
Rescue Access	Limited
Gauge	Visual
Level	N/A
Gradient	2.0
Scenery	A+

River that flows through it, maintaining its natural beauty and charm. They also have constructed two launches on the river specifically for canoes and kayaks and maintain a third near the river's mouth for powerboats as well as paddlecraft. These powerboats are encountered more frequently the closer the river gets to Canandaigua Lake, but their presence benefits paddlers in a way. If left unchecked, water plants such as lilies, duckweed, and arrow arum can clog the narrow channel leading to the lake, making navigation impossible. The fishermen and their boats maintain an open waterway, however, by frequently traveling this stretch of river and keeping those plants from taking root. As a result, paddling from the Sunnyside Road or NY 245 launches to Canandaigua Lake is quite easy and enjoyable.

The West River is also navigable to the east of Sunnyside Road, although the way upstream is usually blocked by beaver dams and plant growth after a few miles. This short side trip is a good alternative for those not wishing to deal with powerboats, as long as an out-and-back paddle is OK (there are no good takeouts east of Sunnyside Road).

USGS Quadrangles MIDDLESEX (NY)

DESCRIPTION The West River seems like just another average river when you're setting out from the Department of Environmental Conservation fishing access spot on Sunnyside Road. Paddlers first encounter a few floating mats of duckweed and yellow pond lilies as they head west on the river. Maple trees, one of the usual inhabitants of wetlands, line the riverbanks in between clusters of cattails and arrow arum plants. Some bullfrogs croak, a couple of geese swim by, and a few carp splash at the surface. But the river curves to the right after little more than 1,000 feet, opening up to gorgeous views of a small mountain in the High Tor Wildlife Management Area called Sunnyside Point. And it only gets better from here.

The pond lilies and duckweed seem to take their cue and begin to carpet almost the entire river surface from bank to bank, leaving only a small but obvious channel to paddle through. Likewise, the cattails increase in number, creating a huge marsh that begins 0.5 miles after the put-in and extends out of sight. Numerous side creeks and channels can be found in this marsh, all of which beg to be explored.

I witnessed red-winged blackbirds, Canada geese, great blue herons, kingfishers, and swallows inhabiting the marsh when I paddled the West River, and could also identify northern flickers, goldfinches, eastern kingbirds, and warblers in the trees beyond. Beautiful swamp rose flowers added a splash of pink color to the verdant green surroundings, dozens of carp swam beneath my boat, and even a beaver was kind enough to make its appearance, swimming across from bank to bank.

The river comes to a T 1.5 miles west of the put-in, where Naples Creek joins it in flowing north to Canandaigua Lake. As before, the duckweed and yellow pond lilies begin to grow so densely that they almost block any clear path down the river. A section suitable enough for paddling usually stays open on the far left side of the river, however, and leads to the lake 1 mile distant. Once on the lake,

paddlers can explore the area, return to the Sunnyside Road put-in, or simply head west to another DEC fishing access and take out there. That boat ramp is located just left of the very first house on the lake's shore.

✧ **SHUTTLE DIRECTIONS** To get to the put-in on Sunnyside Road, pick up NY 245 north of the town of Naples and head north 4 miles. Turn left onto Sunnyside Road and look for the parking lot just before the bridge over the West River on the left.

To get to the takeout on Canandaigua Lake, head back to Naples along NY 245 and turn right onto NY 21. Take NY 21 north 3.5 miles to the fishing access point on the right.

✧ **GAUGE** The best spot to check water conditions is at the bridge over the West River on Sunnyside Road.

MORNING MIST ON THE WEST RIVER

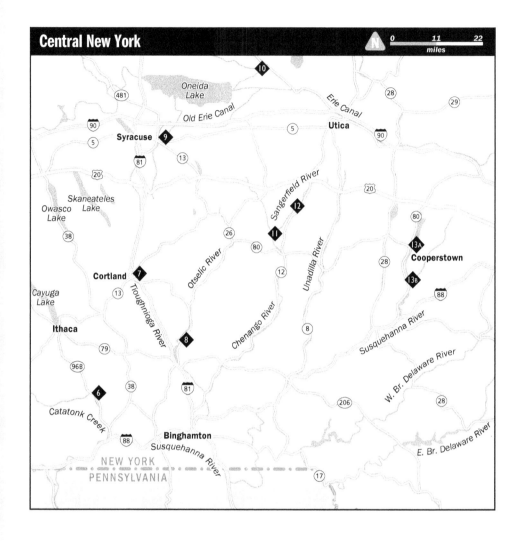

Oneida Lake

481

Old Erie Canal

Erie Canal

28

29

90

5

Syracuse   9

Utica

5

90

81

13

20

Skaneateles
Owasco   Lake
Lake

Sangerfield River

20

38

26

80

12

11

Cooperstown

13A

80

Cortland   7

Otselic River

12

Unadilla River

28

13B

88

Cayuga
Lake

13

Tioughnioga River

Ithaca

Chenango River

8

79

8

Susquehanna River

96B

W. Br. Delaware River

6

38

81

Catatonk Creek

206

28

88

Binghamton

Susquehanna River

NEW YORK

E. Br. Delaware River

PENNSYLVANIA

17

6   CATATONK CREEK

In his book *No Two Rivers Alike,* Alec Proskine describes Catatonk Creek as an "intimate small creek [good] for beginning paddlers." In truth, though, it is perfect for anyone with a boat and a paddle.

Although the Catatonk is paddleable from its beginnings in Spencer, the best spot to begin a trip is in the town of Candor, below the lower dam. From there, heading downstream to Owego is a pleasant and easy paddle that contains a bit of light whitewater, some developed areas, lots of natural beauty, and tons of fun. Towering oak, willow, and hemlock trees abound along the forested banks with sprawling farmland interspersed in between. Kingfishers, nuthatches, wood ducks, red-winged blackbirds, swans, and geese all call the creek home. Signs of beavers are everywhere. Muskrats swim from bank to bank. Largemouth and smallmouth bass swim just under the surface. With all of these attractions, it's easy to see why Proskine recommends the Catatonk as a place to get beginners hooked.

USGS Quadrangles CANDOR (NY), OWEGO (NY)

DESCRIPTION In the first 0.3 miles below Candor, the Catatonk is quite narrow (about 20 feet wide) and swift. From Candor, it twists and turns its way south through a marshy area filled with large oak, beech, and willow trees on both riverbanks. These trees and the land beyond create a pleasing area to paddle through, despite the buildings and farms that are visible just beyond the creek's banks.

The Catatonk passes under the Kelsey Road Bridge and makes a sharp right turn 1.5 miles downstream of Candor as it begins to run parallel to NY 96. As expected, some noise can be heard from the road, although NY 96 remains far

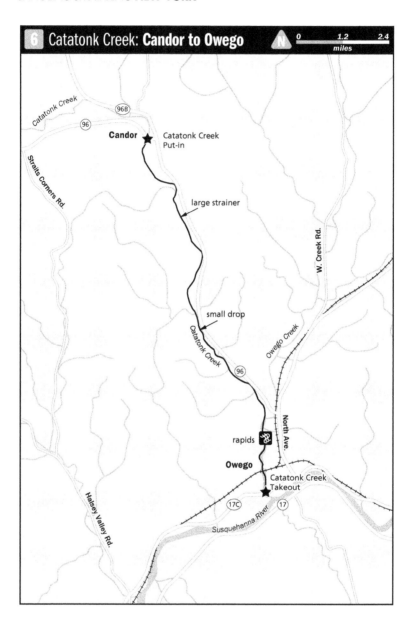

6 Catatonk Creek: Candor to Owego

GPS Coordinates (UTM Zone 18T, WGS84)

Put-in:		**Takeout:**	
Easting	389774	Easting	394405
Northing	4675948	Northing	4661472
Latitude	N 42° 13' 40.56"	Latitude	N 42° 05' 53.64"
Longitude	W 76° 20' 08.58"	Longitude	W 76° 16' 37.14"

enough from the creek that the din of traffic is never too distracting. The Catatonk is then divided by a small island 1 mile after the bridge. Both sides of the island are navigable, though both entrances are guarded by fairly large strainers. I once swamped my boat navigating the left passage and lost an expensive GPS unit on the bottom of the creek. Anyone not wishing to attempt the challenges of either side may simply pull his or her boat across the small sandbar in the middle of the creek, bypassing the strainers altogether—something I wish I had done that fateful, wet day.

Catatonk Creek slows down and straightens out a bit after flowing past the small island at mile 2.5 and continues heading south toward Owego. Unfortunately, the creek also comes very close to NY 96 around mile 5.5 and gets quite noisy with the sounds of traffic from the road above. A small drop (two feet) 0.5 miles later creates a slightly faster flow on the water, and it also marks the point where more houses than trees line the creek's banks. The Catatonk meets Owego Creek 3 miles after this small drop and speeds up once again with the increased volume of water. As the pace of the creek quickens, so do paddlers' pulses as the rumble of whitewater grows from a dull echo to a loud groan. The rapids here are not very long or difficult to navigate, especially during low-water conditions. No large rocks or holes exist, leaving an easy, straight path. As always, care should be taken when running rapids, especially when water levels are higher and currents faster. One mile later,

Candor to Owego

Class	I–II
Length	10.8 miles
Time	3.5 hours
Runnable Months	April–June
Hazards	Strainers
Portages	None
Rescue Access	Easy
Gauge	Visual, Web
Level	2 feet
Gradient	8.5
Scenery	A

the Catatonk passes under a railroad trestle and reaches the takeout in Owego 0.5 miles after that.

✧ **SHUTTLE DIRECTIONS** To get to the put-in at Candor, take Interstate 86/NY 17 to Exit 64 (Owego/Ithaca). Get off NY 17 and head north on NY 17C, cross the Susquehanna River, and enter the town of Owego. Once across the river, continue north on NY 17C until it joins NY 96 (0.2 miles). Turn left onto NY 96 and head north 10 miles until you reach Main Street in Candor. Turn left onto Main Street and head west 0.25 miles. Turn right onto Academy Street and park in the Moyer Park lot.

To get to the takeout in Owego, get back on NY 96 and head south 10 miles until you reach NY 17C (Main Street) in Owego. Turn right onto NY 17C and head west 0.8 miles. Look for a large park with a couple of baseball fields on the right side of the road just before the bridge over the Catatonk. Turn right into this park and look for

SPRING ON THE CATATONK

the dirt parking area near the northwest corner.

An alternative to shuttling by car is to use the Tioga County Public Transit system. Paddlers can make good use of the bus stops in both Candor and Owego to get from one end of the creek to the other while only paying $2 for the ride.

✧ **GAUGE** Water levels on Catatonk Creek in Owego are a good indication of conditions upstream. Paddlers may check these levels visually in Moyer Park or look up the Owego Creek gauge in Owego at **waterdata.usgs.gov/nwis/rt.**

7 TIOUGHNIOGA RIVER

The Tioughnioga is a 70-mile-long river that flows through Central New York, east of the Finger Lakes region. It begins its long run in two separate branches, the West Branch arising in Tully and the East Branch flowing out of Cuyler. These two branches join in Cortland and flow south to their confluence with the Chenango River in Binghamton. Amazingly, this large flow then makes its way almost 400 miles to the south before it empties into the Chesapeake Bay in Maryland.

Although it has seen many changes since its banks were first settled more

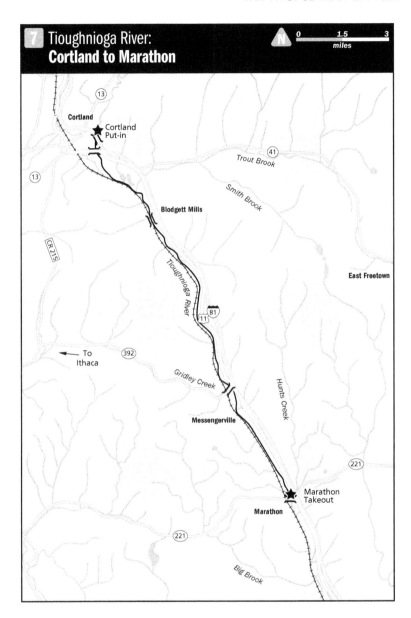

7 Tioughnioga River: Cortland to Marathon

0   1.5   3
miles

Cortland

Cortland Put-in

13

13

Trout Brook   41

Smith Brook

Blodgett Mills

CR 215

Tioughnioga River

East Freetown

81
11

To Ithaca   392

Gridley Creek

Hunts Creek

Messengerville

221

Marathon Takeout

Marathon

221

Big Brook

GPS Coordinates (UTM Zone 18T, WGS84)

Put-in:		**Takeout:**	
Easting	405041	Easting	414855
Northing	4717975	Northing	4699110
Latitude	N 42° 36′ 30.1″	Latitude	N 42° 26′ 22.7″
Longitude	W 76° 09′ 27.7″	Longitude	W 76° 02′ 06.9″

Cortland to Marathon

Class	I–II
Length	14.3 miles
Time	4 hours
Runnable Months	April–October
Hazards	Strainers
Portages	None
Rescue Access	Easy
Gauge	Web
Level	3.2 feet
Gradient	4.9
Scenery	A+

than 200 years ago, the Tioughnioga remains an important river in New York state. Its narrower sections provide perfect habitats for brook and brown trout, while its wider sections are inhabited by great quantities of both large and smallmouth bass, all of which are widely fished for. In addition, the river, with its ease of access, gentle flow, and beautiful views, is a favorite among canoeists and kayakers. Thus, it comes as no surprise that both the Cortland Line Company, a fishing-line manufacturer, and the Grumman Canoe Company started their businesses along the Tioughnioga.

Although much of the Tioughnioga is navigable, its most popular stretch runs between Cortland and Marathon. Cortland's Yaman Park and Marathon's Lovell Field are the perfect spots for putting boats on the water and taking them out. Likewise, the scenery found on the river between these two places can be breathtaking at times. Paddlers can usually understand, after just one

trip down the Tioughnioga, why the Native Americans named the river "waters with flowers hanging over their banks."

USGS Quadrangles
McGraw (NY), Marathon (NY)

7 **DESCRIPTION** Although the Cortland put-in is a convenient place to start a trip on the Tioughnioga, it puts paddlers on the water in an overdeveloped area bustling with houses, office buildings, roads, and a sewage-treatment plant. With a bit of faith and a lot of patience, however, paddlers will soon be treated to a more natural, scenic river that passes through some extremely picturesque areas. In fact, this is one of the prettiest rivers I have ever paddled.

Views of distant mountains abound once paddlers head under a railroad overpass 1 mile from the put-in. From this point on, the Tioughnioga passes through mostly undeveloped areas lined with low-growing shrubs and taller maple, beech, and willow trees. Caution should be exercised in this upper section, though. Numerous fallen trees and strainers also line the riverbanks, threatening to snag or overturn unsuspecting boaters. Such strainers can be especially troublesome when water levels are higher than normal. Luckily, the river is about 20 feet wide here, making it easy to avoid getting caught up in any branches along the shore.

The Tioughnioga comes fairly close to Interstate 81 about 3 miles south of the put-in and runs roughly parallel to it until the takeout in Marathon. Plenty of distance exists between the two, however, making it all but impossible to hear any road noise. One mile later, the river is crossed by the Blodgett

AUTUMN ON THE TIOUGHNIOGA

Mills Bridge. There is access to the river on the southwest side of this bridge, making it a good alternative to putting in near Cortland.

The river quickens a bit and enters a more wooded area 2 miles after it flows beneath the Blodgett Mills Bridge. In fact, it flows just beneath Snyder Hill, a small mountain 7.5 miles south of the put-in whose hemlock-lined eastern slope seems to drop right down into the river. The Tioughnioga then continues flowing through a shallow gorge of sorts, heads under the NY 392 Bridge in Messengerville, and encounters an exciting patch of swift-moving water 1 mile south of the bridge. There, the river enters a figure-eight-shaped section of water that draws boats in, speeds them up, sends them through a few S-turns, and shoots them out the other side. While it does not require expert paddling skills, this pulse-quickening experience does require boaters to pay close attention to their surroundings. Just as before, the riverbanks are lined with strainers ready to grab hold of gear or clothing and swamp boats. Once through, however, most people yearn for a chance to paddle this section of river again.

The landscape surrounding the river seems to flatten after Messengerville, and the Tioughnioga begins to pass farmland and come closer to the interstate once again. The river then enters the town of Marathon after 13 miles, passes under the NY 221 Bridge, and reaches the takeout by Lovell Field in Marathon at mile 14.3.

✧ **SHUTTLE DIRECTIONS** To get to the put-in at Cortland's Yaman Park, take I-81 to Exit 11 (NY 13). Head north on NY 13 for 0.1 mile and take the first right onto Kennedy Parkway. Continue east on Kennedy Parkway for 0.5 miles and enter Yaman Park. The put-in is located in the far-right corner of the park.

To get to the takeout in Marathon, pick up US 11 in Cortland and head south for 13 miles to NY 221. Turn right onto NY 221 and head west for 0.2 miles, taking the second left onto Peck Street. The takeout is located at the far end of the southernmost parking lot.

✧ **GAUGE** The gauge most useful in determining water levels on the Tioughnioga River is the Tioughnioga at Cortland (visit **waterdata.usgs.gov/ nwis/rt** to check online).

---

8   OTSELIC RIVER

The Otselic River is a slow-moving, peaceful waterway just east of the Finger Lakes region. It begins flowing in the town of Georgetown and heads south for 45 miles, passing through woodlands and farmlands until it is impounded to form Whitney Point Lake in Whitney Point.

Willet to Upper Lisle

Class	I
Length	8.8 miles
Time	2.5 hours
Runnable Months	April–October
Hazards	None
Portages	None
Rescue Access	Limited
Gauge	Web
Level	1.4–2
Gradient	3.6
Scenery	A+

Although the Otselic parallels NY 26 for most of its length, the road stays almost completely hidden from sight and sound. Instead, paddlers are treated to a quiet, almost pristine setting. The river contains long, straight runs broken up by tight S-curves that flow through low-lying areas of shrubs, wildflowers, and dense sections of deciduous and evergreen forests. It also acts as a home to a wide variety of wildlife, including great blue herons, wood ducks, kingfishers, and muskrats. With such natural beauty, easy access in the towns of Lower Cincinnatus and Willet, and a convenient takeout in Upper Lisle, the Otselic has long been a favorite among paddlers.

USGS Quadrangles WILLET (NY)

DESCRIPTION Although many people begin their trips on the Otselic River just south of NY 26 in Lower Cincinnatus, another put-in exists in the town of Willet, just north of the NY 26/41 Bridge. Its ample parking and easy river access make this a

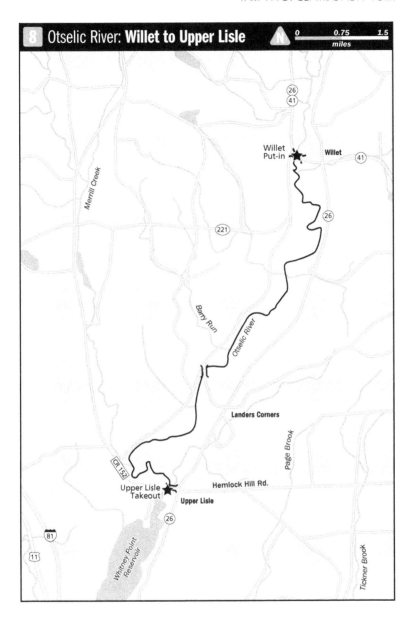

GPS Coordinates (UTM Zone 18T, WGS84)

Put-in:		Takeout:	
Easting	424389	Easting	420950
Northing	4702541	Northing	4694294
Latitude	N 42° 28' 17.5"	Latitude	N 42° 23' 48.9"
Longitude	W 75° 55' 11.3"	Longitude	W 75° 57' 37.8"

popular spot for paddlers looking to explore the lower portion of the Otselic.

After entering the water and passing under the bridge immediately south of the put-in, boaters will notice the low-lying, marshy setting through which the Otselic flows. Many freshwater-loving plants grow in this area, including arrow arum and the ever-abundant Japanese knotweed. Red oak trees also inhabit the flatlands there but are replaced by huge stands of white pines and hemlocks after 1.5 miles of paddling.

Paddlers reveling in the quiet and solitude of the river should not despair when a large house comes into view at mile 1.7. This house is one of the few signs of civilization on the river and will be left behind rather quickly. In fact, one of the Otselic's most beautiful stretches lies just 2 miles after the house. Amazing quantities of eastern hemlock trees can be seen on both sides of the river in this section. American beech trees also populate this area in incredible numbers. Their silvery bark and autumnal colors have always captivated me. Always among the last of the trees to lose their leaves, beeches allow forests to retain some sense of color before succumbing to winter's grasp.

The Otselic flows under a second bridge after 5 miles of paddling. There is access to the river just south of this bridge for those looking for an alternative to putting in near Lower Cincinnatus or Willet. Three miles later, the Otselic flows into a vast floodplain with steep, sandy banks and numerous turns. The takeout can be found just after these turns, immediately south of the NY 152 Bridge in the Whitney Point Multiple-Use Area. South of this takeout lies Whitney Point Reservoir, a large lake created by damming the Otselic in Whitney Point for flood control.

✧ **SHUTTLE DIRECTIONS** To get to the Willet put-in, take Interstate 81 to Exit 9 in the town of Marathon. Follow the exit ramp to County Road 221 and head east 7 miles. CR 221 will end at an intersection with NY 26/41. Turn right onto SR 26/41 and head east 600 feet. Look for a brown Department of Environmental Conservation sign marking the parking area on the left side of the road.

To get to the takeout in Upper Lisle, continue east on NY 26/41 for 0.5 miles and turn right onto NY 26 once it separates from NY 41. Head south on NY 26 for 6 miles and turn right onto CR 152. Head west on CR 152, cross over the bridge, and park in the dirt lot of the multiuse area immediately after the bridge on the left side of the road.

✧ **GAUGE** The gauge most useful in determining water levels on the Otselic River is the Otselic at Cincinnatus (visit **waterdata.usgs.gov/nwis/rt** to check online).

9   OLD ERIE CANAL

"Low bridge, ev'rybody down!
Low bridge, for we're comin' to a town!
And you'll always know your neighbor,
You'll always know your pal,
If you've ever navigated on the
    Erie Canal."

Although Thomas S. Allen wrote these words in 1905, they could very well be describing the Erie Canal today. There are still many low bridges to pass under. There is access in a good number of towns along the route. And the people on and about the canal are always very friendly. The only major difference between the canal in 1905 and the canal today is its function. Originally serving as a major thoroughfare between Albany and Buffalo, what is known today as the Old Erie Canal is closed off, with little more than 36 miles preserved for human-powered boats.

Many people foresaw the need for a canal across New York state years before it was actually constructed. In fact, the building of such a canal through Central New York was first proposed in 1699. However, construction did not start until 1817, when Governor DeWitt Clinton finally OK'd the project. The 363-mile-long Erie Canal was opened 8 years later. It was improved 9 years later and was used for 84 additional years before it was replaced by the New York State Barge Canal. The Old Erie Canal fell into disrepair and was filled in at many spots along its length. This important piece of New York state history seemed destined to be lost forever, and it might very well have been if state and town governments had not stepped in to preserve segments of it. One such stretch now makes up the Old Erie Canal State Historic Park. Running 36 miles from DeWitt to Rome, this park is used by an incredible number of people each day who are looking for a peaceful place to jog, ride a bike, observe nature, or paddle.

Even though the historical significance of the canal is hard to ignore, many paddlers are more interested in observing nature in the area. And there is plenty to keep them just as busy as the history buffs. Immense snapping turtles lurk just under the murky green water. Red-winged blackbirds, black-capped chickadees, song sparrows, woodpeckers, swallows, red-tailed hawks, and many other bird species flit about or soar overhead. Muskrats and beavers can often be seen swimming across the canal or

DeWitt to Canastota

Class	I
Length	14.5 miles
Time	6 hours
Runnable Months	April–November
Hazards	Low bridges
Portages	1
Rescue Access	Easy
Gauge	Visual
Level	N/A
Gradient	0.1
Scenery	A+

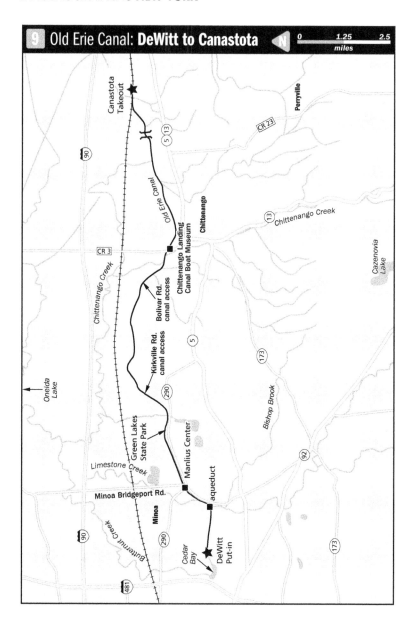

9 Old Erie Canal: **DeWitt to Canastota**

GPS COORDINATES (UTM ZONE 18T, WGS84)

Put-in:		**Takeout:**	
Easting	415685	Easting	436092
Northing	4766175	Northing	4769495
Latitude	N 43° 02' 36.90"	Latitude	N 43° 04' 31.69"
Longitude	W 76° 02' 06.60"	Longitude	W 75° 47' 06.10"

nibbling away on something onshore. I even encountered a fairly large water snake swimming past my kayak the last time I paddled here. Consider too the plant life along the canal, and it is easy to see its appeal to nature lovers. Thank goodness 19th-century engineers had the capability to build such a canal and 21st-century politicians and civic leaders have the desire to preserve it.

USGS Quadrangles
SYRACUSE (NY), MANLIUS (NY), AND CANASTOTA (NY)

DESCRIPTION Paddlers only have one option when using the boat launch in beautiful Cedar Bay Park, and that is to head east. The only question is how far to go. After all, this segment of the Old Erie Canal runs all the way to Rome, New York, with access at almost every road crossing.

The canal is about 50 feet wide for most of its length, with trees lining the southern bank and a walking path alongside the northern bank. Although this path was originally designed to allow horses and mules to tow barges up and down the canal, it sees more use today from joggers and bicyclists. Paddlers will find that the path is heavily used, especially during warm spring and summer days. Be ready for arms that hurt just as much from waving at passersby as from actually paddling.

You'll reach the boat access point at Burdick Street just 0.75 miles after Cedar Bay. This spot is a suitable parking alternative whenever the Cedar Bay lot is full. Just 0.5 miles beyond that is a beautiful aqueduct built in 1856. This structure gives paddlers a small taste of

what the Erie Canal might have looked like in its prime. Although long abandoned, the aqueduct still makes for an excellent photo opportunity. The canal then passes the Manlius Center 2 miles later, where boaters can easily enter or exit the water depending on how far they plan on paddling.

The canal turns slightly to the right after Manlius Center and enters a more wooded area that is home to the beautiful Green Lakes State Park. In fact, the wooden bridge that is visible just after this turn marks the perfect spot to access the park from the canal. It is hard to resist the shaded picnic areas, wooded walking paths, and stunning green-water lakes found in the park. There are also bathroom facilities, a top-notch golf course, and campsites rounding out the amenities. As if these weren't enough, Green Lakes State Park is also home to what is considered the largest stand of old-growth forest in Central New York.

The canal passes the boat access on Kirkville Road 1 mile past Green Lakes State Park. As before, paddlers can exit the water here, although many choose to simply turn around and head back to Cedar Bay. Those who continue heading east will reach yet another access point at Bolivar Road in 3.5 more miles and will come to the Chittenango Landing Canal Boat Museum in another mile. This museum is an excellent place to stop and look back into the past, when canal boats continuously traveled the Erie Canal. It is also a good place to turn around and head back west to the Bolivar or Kirkville Road takeout. If not, paddlers

GREEN LAKES STATE PARK

will be faced with a somewhat difficult portage around a bridge near mile 13 that has been blocked by beaver dams. Apparently two very industrious beavers chose the only two open passageways under the bridge as the best places to build their elaborate dams. Paddlers wishing to continue to Canastota and beyond must portage their boats up and over this bridge through some thick undergrowth. Once back in the water, though, the takeout on Beebe Bridge Road is only a short paddle away.

✧ **SHUTTLE DIRECTIONS** To get to the put-in at Cedar Bay Park, take Interstate 481 to Exit 3 East toward Fayetteville. Head east on NY 5 after leaving the interstate and turn left

onto Lyndon Road after 0.7 miles. Lyndon Road will turn into Cedar Bay Road after 0.75 miles. Look for the entrance to Cedar Bay Park on the left after 0.5 miles.

To get to the takeout in Canastota, continue heading east on Cedar Bay Road until it turns into Burdick Street. Stay on Burdick Street 1 mile, until it meets NY 5. Turn left onto NY 5 and head east 12.8 miles. Turn left onto Beebe Bridge Road and head north 0.5 miles. The parking lot for the Old Erie Canal multiuse path will be on the left, just before the train tracks.

✧ **GAUGE** Due to the absence of any flow, the Old Erie Canal is paddleable year-round, weather and ice permitting, of course.

---

10 FISH CREEK (ONEIDA LAKE)

Fish Creek presents multiple personalities. It contains sections in its upper reaches that many whitewater paddlers consider to be some of the best kayaking spots in New York, if not in the entire Northeast. But it also has a more mellow personality, especially in its last few miles when it lazily passes through areas of natural beauty and twists and turns its way between farms and fields. Bank swallows, wood ducks, red-winged blackbirds, beavers, muskrats, deer, pike, and bass are just some of the wildlife that call Fish Creek home. Willow, aspen, birch, and maple trees line the riverbanks, with sumac, water

willow, and other understory species taking up the spaces in between.

Fish Creek joins the New York Barge Canal just before it empties into Oneida Lake in the town of Sylvan Beach. The town was founded in 1840 as an important shipping port for Lake Oneida and its lakeshore towns. Sylvan Beach became an even bigger and more important transport hub when the Barge Canal was constructed to run through it. Sylvan Beach remains a bustling, busy place today, although in a slightly different manner. Its residents and visitors now enjoy the town's popularity as a resort community with beautiful beaches, an amusement park, great restaurants, shops, and cozy rental cottages.

Whether the hustle and bustle of the town is a distraction or a draw for

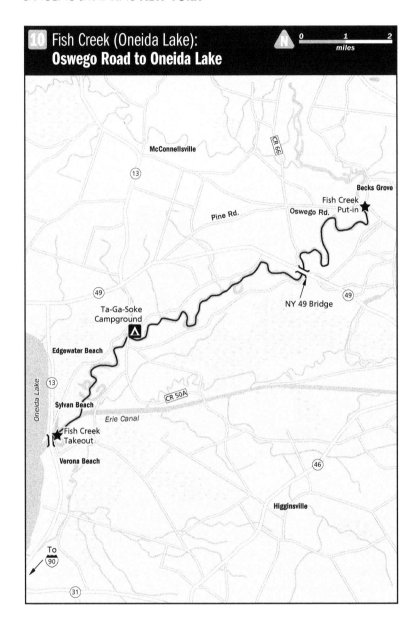

Fish Creek (Oneida Lake):
Oswego Road to Oneida Lake

McConnellsville

Becks Grove

Fish Creek
Put-in

Oswego Rd.

Pine Rd.

NY 49 Bridge

Ta-Ga-Soke
Campground

Edgewater Beach

Sylvan Beach

Erie Canal

Fish Creek
Takeout

Verona Beach

Higginsville

To 90

Oneida Lake

CR 66

CR 50A

GPS Coordinates (UTM Zone 18T, WGS84)			
Put-in:		**Takeout:**	
Easting	450554	Easting	440659
Northing	4789613	Northing	4782674
Latitude	N 43° 15' 27.72"	Latitude	N 43° 11' 40.25"
Longitude	W 75° 36' 33.07"	Longitude	W 75° 43' 49.25"

boaters on Fish Creek is truly up to the individual. Many paddlers do not mind the crowds and actually enjoy the social interactions both on the creek and off. For those paddlers, the portions of the creek nearest the lake are best. Many others go out of their way to avoid such crowds, seeking the privacy and solitude of the more natural sections of the creek. For them, staying between Oswego Road and the NY 13 Bridge is advisable. Still, others may seek out the more exciting, adventurous rapids on Fish Creek. These thrill-seekers will appreciate the run from Taberg south to NY 49. In short, Fish Creek truly has something for everyone.

USGS Quadrangles

LEE CENTER (NY), VERONA (NY), AND SYLVAN BEACH (NY)

DESCRIPTION Although the upper sections of Fish Creek contain some pretty big Class III and IV rapids, the water tends to flatten a bit as it heads southwest toward Taberg. There are still some Class II rapids south of Taberg, though, that should only be run by boaters who are confident in their whitewater skills. The creek becomes much more subdued after about 0.5 miles of paddling from Taberg and finally enters an area where wildlife is more plentiful than rapids.

Boaters may notice very highly eroded banks on both sides of the creek as they head south past Oswego Road. While such erosion makes for an unsightly scene, the sandy cliffs are perfect nesting spots for bank swallows. These amazing birds live in colonies along the riverbanks that

Oswego Road to Oneida Lake

Class	I (Class II if using Taberg put-in)
Length	11.5 miles
Time	3.5 hours
Runnable Months	April–November
Hazards	None
Portages	None
Rescue Access	Easy
Gauge	Visual, phone
Level	2 feet
Gradient	3.2
Scenery	B

can sometimes include thousands of individuals, all of which dip, dive, and flit about after flying insects. Paddlers not sure if the bird they are watching is a bank swallow need only look for a white-colored chest with a dark band encircling just under the neck.

Fish Creek continues to twist and wind its way southwest from sometimes towering cliffs and eventually passes under NY 49 3.5 miles south of Oswego Road. Those looking for a shorter trip to Oneida Lake can put in here instead of off Oswego Road. There is more than enough room to park a car or two on the side of NY 49 just before and after the bridge. Another stop is found 5 miles later at the Ta-Ga-Soke Campground and Country Store. Weary paddlers can take a break, pick up some snacks and supplies in the store, and use the restrooms if necessary.

Boaters not interested in dealing with the crowds of Sylvan Beach or paddling along shores lined with houses,

EROSION ON FISH CREEK

private docks, and RV parks may choose to turn around after the campground and head back to their starting point. For those who choose to head farther downstream, Fish Creek will reach the Erie Canal 2 miles farther and Oneida Lake 1 mile after that. It is possible to paddle onto the lake and head beyond the breakwater. Strong winds can kick up quickly, though, so paddlers should only venture out into open water when the weather is calm.

If a foray onto Oneida Lake is out of the question and heading back upstream is not favorable, paddlers may end their trip anywhere along the long concrete canal wall, although the spots nearest ladders are the most suitable. If powerboats have taken up all of the available spaces, canoes and kayaks can be landed quite easily on the southern side of the canal directly under the NY 13 Bridge.

✧ **SHUTTLE DIRECTIONS** To get to the put-in off Oswego Road, take Interstate 90 to Exit 34N toward Oneida. Take a right on NY 13 after the exit ramp and head north 11 miles until NY 13 meets NY 49. Turn right onto NY 49 and head east 2.3 miles, looking for Pine Road on your left. Turn left onto Pine Road and stay on it for 2.7 miles until it ends. Pick up Oswego Road just across the intersection at this point, and continue heading east. You will cross Fish Creek 1.2 miles later. Once over the creek, look for a dead-end road on your right. Park there and follow the short path down to the water.

If using the Taberg put-in, turn left at the intersection of Pine Road and Oswego Road instead of heading east on Oswego Road. Head north on CR 66 for 3 miles, looking for a large shoulder on the right-hand side of the road. Fish Creek comes fairly close to the road here, making put-ins easy.

To get to the takeout in Sylvan Beach, return to Pine Road and retrace your route back to NY 49 and NY 13. Take NY 13 south into the town of Sylvan Beach. Turn left onto Fourth Avenue just before crossing the Erie Canal at the southern end of town, and follow it under the bridge to a large pier and parking lot.

✧ **GAUGE** It is best to determine water conditions on Fish Creek in person. An unofficial gauge painted on the NY 69 Bridge in Taberg should read 2.5 to 3 feet for the best water conditions. Another painted gauge can be found on the County Road 50A Bridge in Sylvan Beach; it should read 1 foot or more for the best conditions. Paddlers can also call Northern Outfitters, (315) 449-1208, for information on water levels.

....

11 CHENANGO RIVER

Ask paddlers to name some of their favorite rivers in the Central New York area, and they will all likely mention the Chenango. This river begins its slow flow in the Morrisville Swamp, near the town of Morrisville, and heads south through the beautiful Chenango Valley. It eventually joins the Susquehanna River in Binghamton, but only after covering 119 miles, with an average gradient of only four feet per mile. In fact, the Chenango is among the most gently sloping rivers in the state.

Due to its slow movement and gentle gradient, the Chenango is greatly affected by rain. It is subject to flooding throughout the spring and often takes two or more days to return to its normal water levels after periods of heavy rain. As a result, the river gauge in Sherburne has become the best friend of many a Chenango paddler.

Finicky water levels aside, the river is navigable for more than 70 miles of its length, with no dams, rapids, or other portages to contend with. Furthermore, access is easily available

Earlville to North Norwich	
Class	I–I+
Length	12.9 miles
Time	4 hours
Runnable Months	April–September
Hazards	Strainers nd deadfall
Portages	None
Rescue Access	Easy
Gauge	Web
Level	450 cfs
Gradient	4
Scenery	B+

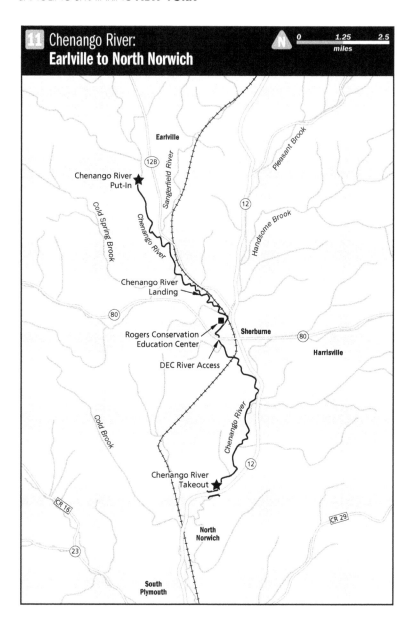

GPS Coordinates (UTM Zone 18T, WGS84)

Put-in:		Takeout:	
Easting	454612	Easting	457901
Northing	4732029	Northing	4718554
Latitude	N 42° 44' 21.96"	Latitude	N 42° 37' 05.79"
Longitude	W 75° 33' 16.26"	Longitude	W 75° 30' 48.01"

along the river in the towns of Earlville, Sherburne, North Norwich, Norwich, Oxford, Greene, and Chenango Forks. Factor in these qualities with the river's slow flow, beautiful scenery, and campgrounds in Sherburne and Chenango Forks, and it is easy to see why so many people love to paddle here.

MEAN WATER TEMPERATURES BY MONTH (Degrees Fahrenheit)						
	JAN	FEB	MAR	APR	MAY	JUN
MEAN	N/A	N/A	N/A	50	60	69
	JUL	AUG	SEP	OCT	NOV	DEC
MEAN	74	72	62	49	N/A	N/A

USGS Quadrangles
EARLVILLE (NY), NORWICH (NY)

DESCRIPTION As the Chenango flows through Earlville, both riverbanks are lined with houses and private property. The river takes on a wilder feel after only 0.2 miles, though, bringing paddlers through sections of woodland and open farmland. In fact, most of the land between Earlville and North Norwich is taken up by farms. While this makes for some stunning scenery, there are some dangers associated with it, namely strainers. These numerous fallen trees can trap paddlers and swamp or flip boats. Most of the Chenango is wide enough to allow easy passage between these hazards. Nevertheless, care should be taken when paddling.

The Chenango nears NY 12B 2 miles south of Earlville and parallels the road for most of the way to North Norwich. This, of course, raises the noise level of the road to a maximum. Don't despair, though. Traffic is usually light and is blocked from view by the many trees that line the riverbanks. A small stream joins the Chenango after 3 miles, increasing the river's volume and speeding its flow. With this new speed come some fun riffles and eddies to play in. Paddlers are sure

to find themselves enjoying certain sections so much that they will want to head back upstream and run them again. Such portages are easy to do and can be fun for those willing to expend a bit more energy.

The Chenango flows past the grounds of the Chenango River Landing after 4.5 miles, making it the approximate halfway point of the trip. With picnic tables and shade trees, it truly is the perfect spot for a rest stop and lunch. Just 1.5 miles downstream of the landing is Rogers Conservation Education Center. The farm boasts beautiful walking trails, wildlife viewing platforms, and a visitor center filled with educational exhibits. Boats can be tied up near any of the benches on the western riverbank, so paddlers can walk around enjoying the lovely scenery of this magnificent park.

The river passes under NY 80 in the town of Sherburne, just 0.5 miles past the game farm. The Department of Environmental Conservation maintains a river-access point on the west side of the river where paddlers may choose to take out. If not, they will find that the river flows quite near a beautiful high point known as Steam Sawmill Hill 4 miles south of the NY 80 takeout. It then passes under NY 12 in the town of North Norwich, where another DEC access spot exists. Paddlers taking out

SWIFT WATER ON THE CHENANGO

here should look for the boat launch just 150 feet south of the bridge.

✧ **SHUTTLE DIRECTIONS** To get to the put-in at Earlville, take the New York State Thruway (Interstate 90) to Exit 33 (NY 365). Head south on NY 365 3.6 miles, turning right onto NY 5 (Seneca Avenue) when NY 365 ends. Turn left onto NY 46 (Glenwood Avenue) after 0.3 miles and continue heading south on NY 46 an additional 15.6 miles. At this point, NY 46 will join NY 12B. Stay on NY 12B 9.5 miles, which will take you into the town of Earlville. Once in Earlville, turn right onto County Road 14 and look for the

bridge crossing the Chenango after 0.5 miles. Park on the side of the road and look for the put-in on the southeastern side of the river.

To get to the takeout in North Norwich, pick up NY 12B in Earlville and head south 5 miles, until it joins NY 12. Stay on NY 12 another 5.7 miles and park in the DEC boat access just south of the bridge crossing the Chenango.

✧ **GAUGE** The gauge most useful in determining water levels on the Chenango River is the Chenango at Sherburne (visit **waterdata.usgs.gov/ nwis/rt** to check online).

12 SANGERFIELD RIVER

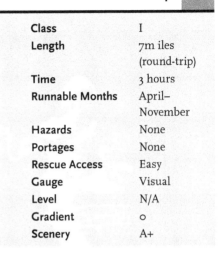

Ninemile Swamp

Class	I
Length	7m iles (round-trip)
Time	3 hours
Runnable Months	April–November
Hazards	None
Portages	None
Rescue Access	Easy
Gauge	Visual
Level	N/A
Gradient	0
Scenery	A+

The Sangerfield is a scenic, slow-flowing river near the towns of Hubbardsville and Sangerfield. While it is named after an early settler of the area, Jedediah Sanger, the river is most famous, or perhaps infamous, as a sanctuary for the notorious Loomis Gang. The patriarch of the Loomis family, George Washington Loomis, came to the area in 1802 and settled a 9-mile stretch of land along the Sangerfield. This property eventually became known as the Ninemile Swamp and served as a hideout for the Loomis family throughout their lives of crime.

While the Sangerfield runs roughly from NY 12 to the Chenango River, the most popular paddling portion is between Wickwire and Swamp roads. This section includes a good part of the Ninemile Swamp and is home to a large variety of plant- and wildlife. Beautiful wildflowers abound in the spring and summer here, while the striking red and orange colors of the swamp's maple trees burn strongly in the fall. Likewise, white-tailed deer, beaver, waterfowl, and hawks cruise the Sangerfield throughout the year. Some people have also claimed another more unusual sighting: that of George Loomis's ghost. Apparently, he can be seen near Swamp Road on October nights, especially as the anniversary of his death looms near. There have also been reports of ghostly horseback riders, possibly from the original Loomis Gang, galloping through the swamp. Whether these claims are fact or fiction, they only serve to add to the Sangerfield's appeal. After all, who wouldn't want to paddle a haunted river?

USGS Quadrangles

HUBBARDSVILLE (NY)

DESCRIPTION Although it is sometimes possible to launch on the Sangerfield from the Green Road Bridge in Hubbardsville, the best and most reliable put-in is on the north side of the bridge on Wickwire Road. This spot has ample room for three or four cars to park and features a sloped boat launch perfect for sliding a canoe or kayak into the river.

While the river south of Wickwire Road is often unnavigable, it can be a paddler's paradise to the north. As it flows through the Ninemile Swamp, the Sangerfield is about 20 feet wide,

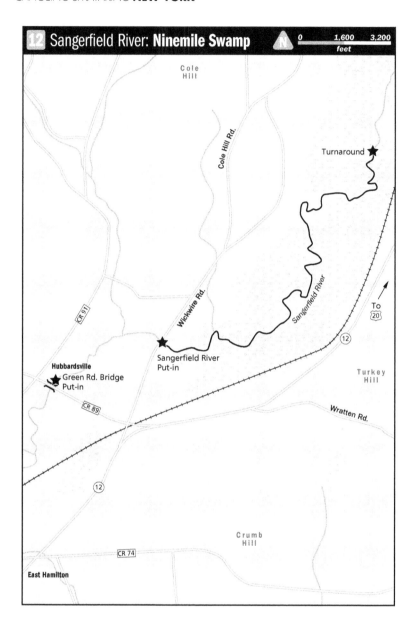

12 Sangerfield River: Ninemile Swamp

GPS COORDINATES (UTM ZONE 18T, WGS84)

Put-in:		**Takeout:**	
Easting	463481	Easting	463481
Northing	4741027	Northing	4741027
Latitude	N 42° 49' 15.36"	Latitude	N 42° 49' 15.36"
Longitude	W 75° 26' 48.30"	Longitude	W 75° 26' 48.30"

BEAVER DAM ON THE SANGERFIELD

with a current slow enough to make heading upstream incredibly easy. The best feature of the river, though, is its abundant natural beauty. Indeed, the only signs of civilization are a few houses sitting up on Cole Hill Road.

I last paddled here in early spring and, within five minutes of entering the water, had seen numerous deer feeding along the water's edge, had flushed four or five colorful wood ducks swimming along the riverbanks, and saw signs of beaver activity everywhere. After paddling for another hour or so, I was able to add great blue herons, kingfishers, Canada geese, mergansers, and muskrats to the list of species I had seen.

Although the amazing quantity and variety of animals alone made

this a worthwhile paddle, the plants of the swamp made it truly memorable. The true definition of a swamp is a "low-lying wetland with slow-flowing water that is dominated by large trees." Such a description fits the Ninemile Swamp perfectly. While the main course of the river is obvious and easy to follow, it is also possible to paddle among the many trees of the swamp, especially as the river twists and turns its way upstream. In fact, the presence of these large maple and willow trees, along with the other plants of the swamp, make for one of the most stunning places I have ever paddled.

Unfortunately, this same abundance of plant life may at times prevent clear passage to Swamp Road.

I was forced to turn around after 3.5 miles of paddling, 1 mile south of Swamp Road, when the plants closed in and blocked my progress. The water level was quite high at this time, which leads me to believe that continuing any farther would be all but impossible at lower levels. Nevertheless, my paddle downstream to Wickwire Road was just as enjoyable as my paddle upstream had been.

✧ **SHUTTLE DIRECTIONS** To get to the put-in on Wickwire Road, take Interstate 81 to Exit 6 North (Chenango Bridge). Continue north on NY 12 for 58 miles and turn left onto Wickwire Road. After about 700 feet you will cross a railroad track. Continue down Wickwire Road for 0.6 miles, where you will reach a bridge crossing the Sangerfield. Park at the boat access spot on the right side of the road before the bridge.

To get to Swamp Road from the put-in, head back north on NY 12 4 miles. Turn left onto Swamp Road and continue 0.5 miles until you reach the bridge over the Sangerfield.

✧ **GAUGE** The best way to determine water conditions on the Sangerfield is visually. The river may be unrunnable at times due to low water levels or during periods of dry weather.

13 SUSQUEHANNA RIVER

Most people would think a paddler crazy, hearing him or her talk of paddling from New York to Maryland. However, these disbelievers would change their minds if they knew of the Susquehanna River. At 444 miles long, it is the longest river on the East Coast of the United States, flowing from Otsego Lake in Cooperstown, New York, to the Chesapeake Bay in Maryland. In doing so, the Susquehanna passes through much of New York, Pennsylvania, and northeastern Maryland, draining an area of more than 27,000 square miles. Local folklore says that the name *Susquehanna* means "mile wide and foot deep." Whether or not this legend is true, the name fits.

As expected from a river of such length, there are dozens of paddling options between Cooperstown and Waverly (where the Susquehanna crosses into Pennsylvania for good). Beginning a trip on beautiful Otsego Lake is an extremely popular option because of both the popularity of the village of Cooperstown and the sheer beauty of the lake. James Fenimore Cooper recognized this beauty early on and referred to the lake in some of his stories as "The Glimmerglass." Paddlers on these early sections will find a narrow river that winds its way south through pastoral farmland, wooded riverbanks, fields of wildflowers, and lily-covered ponds.

Another common trip brings boaters to Goodyear Lake and (possibly) beyond. There is an excellent takeout spot on the lake's shore, but there is also a portage around the dam that enables paddlers

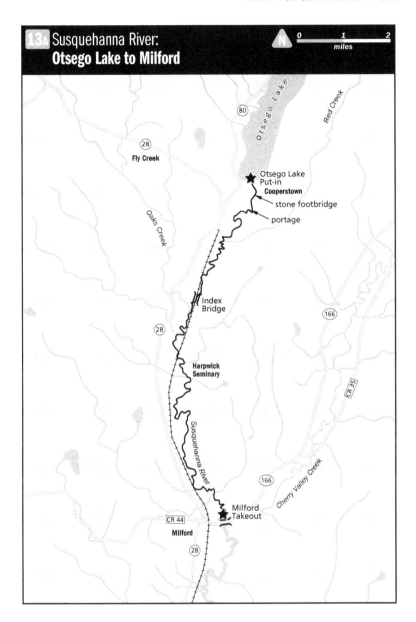

13A Susquehanna River: Otsego Lake to Milford

GPS Coordinates (UTM Zone 18T, WGS84)

Put-in:		Takeout:	
Easting	506376	Easting	505550
Northing	4727815	Northing	4715409
Latitude	N 42° 42' 10.08"	Latitude	N 42° 35' 27.90"
Longitude	W 74° 55' 19.74"	Longitude	W 74° 55' 56.46"

A   Otsego Lake to Milford

Class	I
Length	13.8 miles
Time	4 hours
Runnable Months	April–October
Hazards	Strainers
Portages	1
Rescue Access	Easy
Gauge	Visual, Web
Level	1,500 cfs
Gradient	3.1
Scenery	A

to travel farther downstream to Colliersville. The Susquehanna's annual canoe race makes use of this portage, running a total of 70 miles from Cooperstown to Bainbridge. The General Clinton Canoe Regatta, as it is called, is held every Memorial Day weekend to commemorate the 1779 voyage of General James Clinton and his forces from Otsego Lake to Tioga Point, Pennsylvania. In addition to the namesake race, there is a monument at the beginning of the Susquehanna, marking the spot where Clinton and his men built a dam to block the flow from the lake. Once the backup was large enough, the General had his men breach the dam so they could float down the surge of river water to Pennsylvania and join the fight against a group of Iroquois warriors loyal to Great Britain.

Those who paddle the Susquehanna, whether they are beginner boaters, nature lovers, canoe racers, or soldiers on their way to do battle, will surely fall under its spell. I have long considered it one of my favorite rivers to paddle and am sure all who experience it will find the same.

USGS Quadrangles
COOPERSTOWN (NY), MILFORD (NY)

13A **DESCRIPTION** The Susquehanna begins flowing out of the southern end of Otsego Lake just 0.3 miles east of the public boat launch in Cooperstown. It is hard to imagine the size of the river's immense watershed when paddling these early stages—the Susquehanna is only about 30 or 40 feet wide at this point and only a few feet deep. However, its beauty becomes apparent immediately upon heading south.

The Susquehanna passes under quite a few bridges as it heads south toward Milford. None are quite as stunning as the stone footbridge found just 0.25 miles south of Otsego Lake. Most people cannot resist its charm and beauty and must stop to take a few photos before continuing. Paddlers should not get too comfortable in their boats after passing this bridge, though, because a portage lies just 0.2 miles later. The small dam at Mill Street must be carried around using the short path on the left riverbank. Unfortunately, this trail is lined with poison ivy, so take great care when walking its length.

MEAN WATER TEMPERATURES BY MONTH (Degrees Fahrenheit)					
	JAN	FEB	MAR	APR	MAY	JUN
MEAN	N/A	N/A	N/A	51	61	69
	JUL	AUG	SEP	OCT	NOV	DEC
MEAN	75	73	66	50	46	N/A

The Susquehanna narrows a bit after the Mill Street portage and begins to twist and turn through sections of swift water lined with strainers and deadfall. Scrapes, scratches, and overturned boats can easily result from not paying close attention to the river and its surroundings. After zigging and zagging for 4 more miles, the river passes under the County Road 11C Bridge in Index and begins to straighten a bit and slow down. From there the river continues its course south, turning this way and that, until it enters an area with a slightly different feel 7 miles later. Gone is the closed-in, wooded landscape, which is replaced by a more open, scenic countryside. It is not at all uncommon to find deer bounding across the open fields and see cattle grazing at the fences. The NY 166 Bridge in Milford is just 1 mile later. The best takeout spot is on the muddy bank just under the bridge on the left-hand side.

✧ **SHUTTLE DIRECTIONS** To get to the put-in on Otsego Lake in Cooperstown, take Interstate 88 to Exit 17 (NY 28/7). Head north on Gersoni Road and NY 7 for 1.25 miles toward Cooperstown, until NY 7 joins NY 28. Continue north on NY 28 16 additional miles into the village of Cooperstown. NY 28 will continue to the left at this point. Head right on NY 80 instead, and it will come to Lake Street after 0.4 miles. Turn right onto Lake Street, head east 0.2 miles, and look for the Department of Environmental Conservation fishing access point on the lake side of the road. The public boat launch is found at the northernmost end of the parking lot.

To get to the takeout in Milford, return to NY 28 and head south 8.3 miles. Turn left onto NY 166 and head east 0.7 miles. Cross over the Susquehanna and look for a dirt turnoff and parking area on the left side of the road immediately after the bridge. A short trail at the end of this dirt road leads to the river's edge.

✧ **GAUGE** The gauge most useful in determining conditions on the Susquehanna is on the river in Unadilla (visit **waterdata.usgs.gov/nwis/rt** to check online). Water levels can also be checked visually at the NY 166 bridge in Milford and the Main Street Bridge in Cooperstown.

DESCRIPTION From Milford, the Susquehanna continues its slow flow south, once again twisting and turning through a beautiful countryside complete with silos, barns, cows, and all things normally associated with farms. Paddlers should keep to the

Milford to Goodyear Lake **B**	
Class	I+
Length	10.5 miles
Time	3 hours
Runnable Months	April–October
Hazards	None
Portages	1(if continuing past Goodyear Lake)
Rescue Access	Easy
Gauge	Web, visual
Level	1000 cfs
Gradient	0.4
Scenery	A+

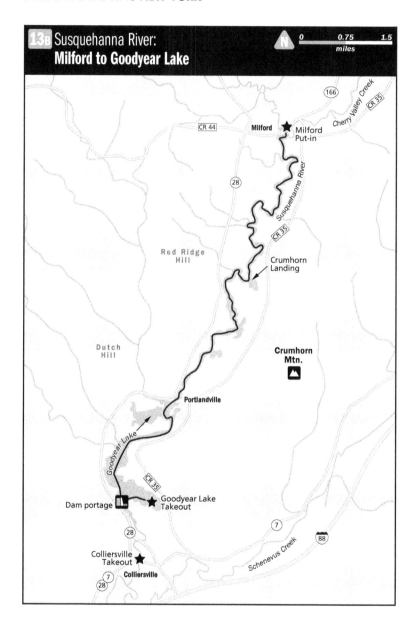

13B Susquehanna River:
Milford to Goodyear Lake

GPS Coordinates (UTM Zone 18T, WGS84)

Put-in:		Takeout:	
Easting	505550	Easting	501972
Northing	4715409	Northing	4705855
Latitude	N 42° 35' 27.90"	Latitude	N 42° 30' 18.20"
Longitude	W 74° 55' 56.46"	Longitude	W 74° 58' 33.60"

MEAN WATER TEMPERATURES BY MONTH (Degrees Fahrenheit)					
	JAN	FEB	MAR	APR	MAY	JUN
MEAN	N/A	N/A	N/A	51	61	69
	JUL	AUG	SEP	OCT	NOV	DEC
MEAN	75	73	66	50	46	N/A

right when the river forks just 130 feet south of the NY 166 Bridge and follow the main river flow. Anyone paddling this section of river, especially in the spring, will be truly amazed at the sheer numbers and varieties of birds that flit and fly above the water. Spotted sandpipers, orioles, kingfishers, northern cardinals, wood ducks, red-winged blackbirds, eastern kingbirds, and wood warblers are just a few examples of birds often seen on this part of the Susquehanna. Similarly, plant lovers will have no trouble finding a great many kinds of wildflowers growing along the riverbanks. Bright blue forget-me-nots, lady's-smock flowers, and wild geraniums are among those that add their beautiful and vivid colors to the river's scenery.

The river begins to flow through a more wooded section 3 miles south of Milford and provides gorgeous views of Crumhorn Mountain to the east. A few houses pop up around mile 3.7 but disappear 0.25 miles later, leaving paddlers undisturbed for the next 3 miles. The Susquehanna then makes a sharp right turn after 4.5 miles, immediately after an entrance to a shallow pond on the left. If time allows and water levels are high enough, this pond should definitely be explored. Small in area but big in beauty, it rivals other stunning lakes and ponds in such places as

the Adirondacks or Catskill Mountains. Looking past the hundreds of yellow pond lilies on the left side, paddlers will see a Department of Environmental Conservation boat launch and a picnic area named Crumhorn Landing. The landing is a perfect spot to break for lunch or to take out if one is not headed all the way to Goodyear Lake. Two equally scenic, albeit smaller, ponds lie on the right side of the river after Crumhorn Landing 1 mile later, with another larger pond on the left 0.5 miles after that. The river then passes under a railroad trestle in another 0.5 miles, turns left, and heads almost directly toward Goodyear Lake. Unfortunately, the Susquehanna's banks are mostly developed from this point on.

The Portlandville Bridge (1 mile after the railroad trestle) marks the beginning of Goodyear Lake. Even though the lake stretches out to the right (south) of this bridge, left is the way to go. Once through the large S-turn and the 1-mile-long, 300-foot-wide channel, boaters will enter the lower portion of the lake. There are two options from there: head due south to the portage around the Goodyear Lake Dam, or head southeast to another DEC fishing-access spot. Those choosing to portage should look for a steep but short path on the shore just to the left of the buoys warning of the dam. Paddlers can then continue 1.3 miles south and take out at the Colliersville fishing access point on the west side of the river. Those heading for the takeout on Goodyear Lake should look for a small set of concrete steps on the southern shore of the lake, 0.5 miles east of the dam. These steps lead to a short trail and a large parking area.

✧ **SHUTTLE DIRECTIONS** To get to the put-in at Milford, take Interstate 88 to Exit 17 (NY 28/7). Head north on Gersoni Road and NY 7 1.25 miles toward Cooperstown, until NY 7 joins NY 28. Continue north on NY 28 7.8 additional miles, until NY 28 enters the town of Milford. Turn right onto NY 166 at this point and head east 0.6 miles. Cross over the Susquehanna and look for a dirt turnoff and parking area on the left side of the road immediately after the bridge. A short trail at the end of this dirt road leads to the river's edge.

To get to the takeout on Goodyear Lake, take Gersoni Road north from Interstate 88 and turn right when it meets NY 7. Travel east on NY 7 for 0.6 miles, turning left when it meets CR 35. Stay on CR 35 for just under 1 mile, looking for Sillman Cove Road. Turn left onto Sillman Cove Road and head 0.4 miles toward the lake. Cross the railroad tracks and follow the sign for the Department of Environmental Conservation fishing access point. A short trail at the far end of the parking lot leads to Goodyear Lake.

✧ **GAUGE** The gauge most useful in determining conditions on the Susquehanna is on the river in Unadilla (visit **waterdata.usgs.gov/nwis/ rt** to check online). Water levels can also be checked visually at the NY 166 Bridge in Milford and the Main Street Bridge in Cooperstown.

RAILROAD TRESTLE CROSSING
THE SUSQUEHANNA

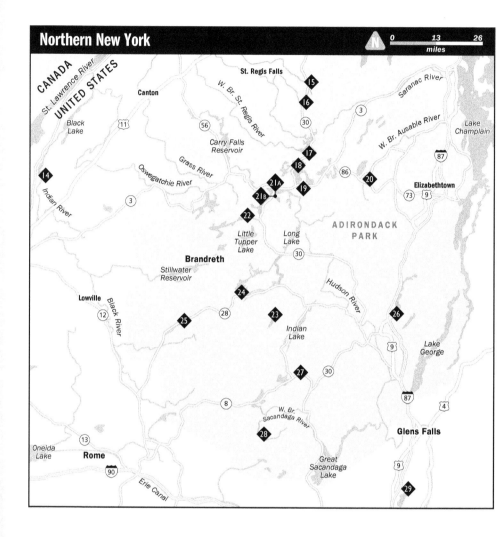

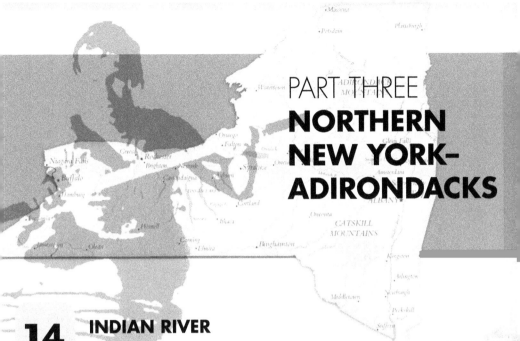

14 INDIAN RIVER

The Indian River lies to the west of the Adirondack Park in an area abundant with lakes, streams, and rivers to paddle. In fact, a 35-mile path, aptly named the Indian River Canoe Route, was designed to take advantage of these excellent paddling conditions. The route begins in Antwerp and heads southwest toward Evans Mills before turning north and running to Rossie. Paddlers on the route can expect a slow, steady current that will take them through the flat, scenic geography of northwestern New York.

USGS Quadrangles REDWOOD (NY), MUSKELLUNGE LAKE (NY)

DESCRIPTION From the state boat launch on Red Lake Road, it's possible to paddle upstream on the Indian River for 4 flat, easy miles to the dam in Theresa, or to follow the river downstream to Red Lake, Muskellunge Lake, and beyond. Out of these options, taking out on Red Lake is usually the most common choice. It lies just 2.5 miles away, but exploring its shores provides almost 360 acres of additional paddling to this trip.

Paddlers may doubt the logic of choosing a put-in immediately upstream of a housing development. After

Red Lake Road to Red Lake

Class	I
Length	2.5 miles
Time	1–2 hours
Runnable Months	May–October
Hazards	None
Portages	None
Rescue Access	Easy
Gauge	Visual
Level	N/A
Gradient	2.0
Scenery	B+

INDIAN RIVER

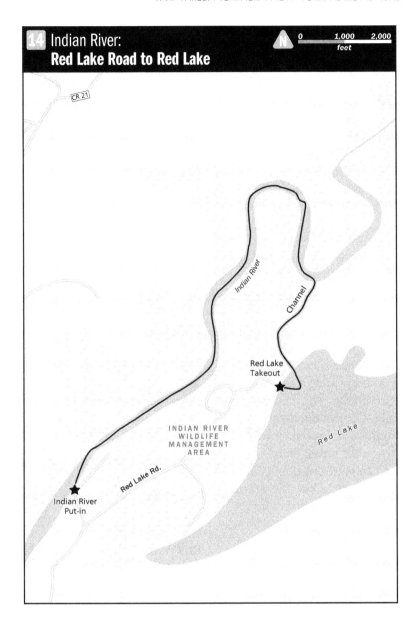

14 Indian River: Red Lake Road to Red Lake

0   1,000   2,000 feet

CR 21

Indian River

Channel

Red Lake Takeout

INDIAN RIVER WILDLIFE MANAGEMENT AREA

Red Lake Rd.

Red Lake

Indian River Put-in

GPS Coordinates (UTM Zone 18T, WGS84)

Put-in:		**Takeout:**	
Easting	439271	Easting	440426
Northing	4901567	Northing	4902182
Latitude	N 44° 15' 53.32"	Latitude	N 44° 16' 13.59"
Longitude	W 75° 45' 39.07"	Longitude	W 75° 44' 47.25"

all, how scenic can such a location be? Those with perseverance will very soon be treated with peace and solitude, as the trailers quickly disappear. Instead, natural riverbanks are filled with red and silver maple, black willow, hickory, and white ash trees, together with green grasses and pickerelweed plants. Unfortunately, Eurasian watermilfoil, a particularly aggressive and ruthless invasive plant, can be found in huge numbers just beneath the surface along this stretch of river as well.

Watermilfoil has become quite a nuisance throughout many of New York's waters, where it has spread almost uncontrollably and is crowding out native species. It has also become an impediment to many different forms of water recreation, as swimming and boating areas become inundated with the plant's feathery green stalks. Controlling the growth of watermilfoil has proved quite difficult, as even the tiniest bit of a stalk broken off can take root after drifting off and form a new colony. As a result, mechanical harvesting or cutting is ineffective. Blocking the plant's growth with large mats has worked in some locations, and some chemical and biological controls are being tested as well. Paddlers can do little to battle established watermilfoil colonies but can play an important role in preventing their further spread. All boats should be cleaned off and checked thoroughly after every paddle in order to stop hitchhiking plants from inadvertently being carried to other bodies of water.

The Indian River continues flowing northeast in much the same way for 2 miles until the small, narrow channel leading to Red Lake is reached. Although it is not technically located within the Adirondack Park, Red Lake appears much the same as many of the park's bodies of water. It is ringed with lush banks of white pine, spruce, and hemlock trees, which themselves are separated by high, exposed outcroppings of rock. A few houses dot the shores where the cliffs have flattened enough to allow them. However, much of the lake's shore is wild.

The takeout on Red Lake is just southwest of the channel that leads onto the lake from the Indian River. Note, however, that this particular boat launch seems to be a haven for mosquitoes. I was so ferociously attacked by these insects the last time I paddled here that I was forced to haphazardly throw my gear into my Jeep and loosely strap my boat to the roof before speeding away to a safer place where I could get out and re-sort everything.

✧ **SHUTTLE DIRECTIONS** To get to the put-in on Red Lake Road, take Interstate 81 to Exit 49 and follow NY 411 4.8 miles into Theresa. Turn left onto Commercial Street and again onto Bridge Street. Look for Red Lake Road just 0.2 miles later and turn left once more. The state boat launch will be reached 4 miles later on Red Lake Road

To get to the takeout on Red Lake, turn left after leaving the boat launch parking area and continue east on Red lake Road for 1 more mile. The takeout is at the end of Red Lake Road.

✧ **GAUGE** Water levels on this stretch of the Indian River are best checked visually from the boat launch on Red Lake Road.

15 DEER RIVER FLOW

The Deer River is a 70-mile-long waterway in the northern Adirondacks that stretches from humble beginnings a bit north of Paul Smiths to its confluence with the St. Regis River near Helena. The Deer River has something for every type of paddler along this run. Paul Jamieson describes the river perfectly in his book *Adirondack Canoe Waters: North Flow* as being "nearly everything a river can be except big." It boasts miles of scenic flat water, long stretches of spirited whitewater, and sections that run through some of the most remote parts of the Adirondack Park. Among all of this variety, one of the most popular portions remains the Deer River Flow.

Although it is only 3 miles long, the Deer River Flow has established itself as a favorite of Adirondack paddlers. With no campsites along its edges and only one location to launch a boat onto its waters, the Deer nonetheless has something special that brings people to it, and that is its scenic beauty. Picture a wide expanse of cold water dotted with floating mats of fragrant white water lilies and cattail groves; lined with balsam fir, red maple, spruce, tamarack, white cedar, and white pine trees; bustling with the activity of beavers, Canada geese, largemouth and smallmouth bass, deer, and the occasional bald eagle; and surrounded by majestic mountain views. Then you'll have some idea why the Deer River Flow is such a coveted place.

USGS Quadrangles
LAKE TITUS (NY)

DESCRIPTION The only access to the waters of the Deer River Flow is just off NY 30 on Cold Spring Road. This boat launch puts you on the flow at the tip of its southernmost arm, which leads north to a wider expanse of water. This arm passes one house on the left 0.25 miles downstream but flows beneath hundreds of fragrant water lilies floating in wide mats along its edges. Behind these mats, where the banks begin to rise out of the river, cattails have taken hold, with the balsam fir and tamarack trees standing proud watch over it all.

A few beavers have built their trademark dams along the southern arm of the flow, as some of the aquatic vegetation has begun to grow almost entirely across its width. Neither of these is enough to block the way north, however. In fact, the wider part of the Deer River Flow will be

NY 30 to Deer River Campsite and Back

Class	I
Length	4.8m iles (round-trip)
Time	3 hours
Runnable Months	May–October
Hazards	None
Portages	None
Rescue Access	Easy
Gauge	Visual
Level	N/A
Gradient	N/A
Scenery	A+

reached after only a little more than a mile.

Once you're out on the wider portion of the Deer River Flow, you have a few options. To the right stretches out another arm of the flow that leads to Horseshoe Pond. Just under 1.5 miles to the northeast, this pond is a popular destination for many day-trippers on the Deer River. Many others choose to head west on the flow and follow the left shoreline in search of the river's outflow and the small dam that holds its waters back. Still others simply head directly across the flow, toward the north shoreline and the various camps that can be found there. Much

of this shoreline is private, however, so landing is prohibited. Nevertheless, the scenery on the flow, especially the mountain views to the south, is spectacular and should not be missed.

✧ **SHUTTLE DIRECTIONS** To get to the put-in on Cold Spring Road, pick up NY 30 at Paul Smith's College and head north 15.3 miles. A large grass parking lot can be found on the corner of NY 30 and Cold Spring Road, and the boat launch is a bit farther west.

✧ **GAUGE** Water conditions on the Deer River Flow can be checked visually from the put-in on Cold Spring Road.

MOUNTAIN VIEWS ON THE DEER RIVER FLOW

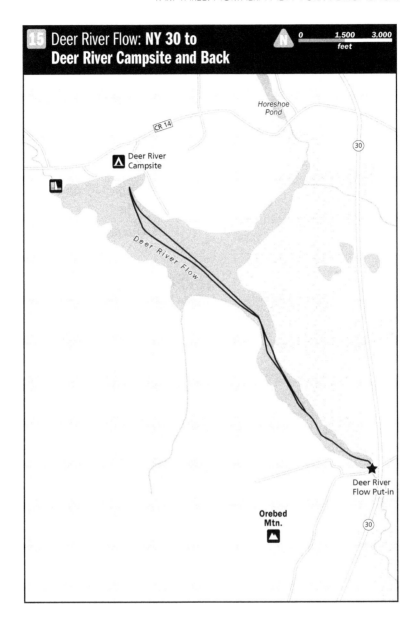

15 Deer River Flow: **NY 30 to Deer River Campsite and Back**

N   0   1,500   3,000 feet

Horeshoe Pond

CR 14

30

Deer River Campsite

Deer River Flow

Deer River Flow Put-in

Orebed Mtn.

30

GPS Coordinates (UTM Zone 18T, WGS84)

Put-in:		Takeout:	
Easting	557133	Easting	557133
Northing	4942456	Northing	4942456
Latitude	N 44° 37' 59.49"	Latitude	N 44° 37' 59.49"
Longitude	W 74° 16' 46.84"	Longitude	W 74° 16' 46.84"

16 OSGOOD RIVER

Though less than 15 miles long, the Osgood River is one of the true treasures of the Adirondack Park. From its start in Osgood Pond to its confluence with Meacham Lake, the Osgood flows through land that has remained almost completely untouched by development. As a result, stunning tamarack and spruce groves, sprawling marshes of alder bushes and grasses, and floating mats of pond lilies are encountered instead of camps, cars, and powerboats. With such pristine conditions comes a great variety of wildlife, such as beavers, muskrats, bass, pike, herons, kingfishers, and any number of other bird species common to evergreen forests.

While most of the Osgood's length is navigable, paddling upstream on the river from Meacham Lake and returning the same way is a much better alternative to trying to travel the entire length from Osgood Pond to Meacham Lake. This lower section, strung with scenic ponds and pine-filled eskers, provides some of the best cruising waters around, whereas the upper section disappears underground 2.5 miles north of Osgood Pond and becomes completely unnavigable for quite some distance.

USGS Quadrangles
MEACHAM LAKE (NY)

DESCRIPTION While the public boat launch at the northern end of Meacham Lake offers convenient water access, it forces paddlers to travel almost 2 miles south on the lake before reaching the outflow of the Osgood River. Putting in near the southern end of the lake is a much better option and is possible where the East Branch of the St. Regis River flows under NY 30. From there, a short upstream paddle on the St. Regis is necessary to reach Meacham Lake. This is more of a gift than an ordeal, though, as the outflow is exquisitely beautiful. The spires of many balsam fir trees proudly point skyward along this little stretch of water, with smaller, straggly tamarack trees growing in the more moist areas. When I last paddled here, just after a summer sunrise, every needle on every tree was covered with a fine layer of dew, glistening in the early-morning light and creating a scene I will never forget.

Once you are onto Meacham Lake, the Osgood River's outflow, where

Meacham Lake to Osgood River and Back

Class	I
Length	5.8m iles (round-trip)
Time	3 hours
Runnable Months	May–October
Hazards	None
Portages	None
Rescue Access	Difficult
Gauge	Visual
Level	N/A
Gradient	2.8
Scenery	A+

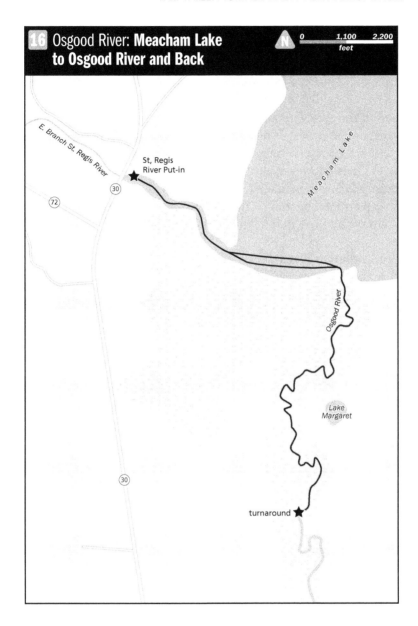

16 Osgood River: **Meacham Lake to Osgood River and Back**

0   1,100   2,200
feet

GPS COORDINATES (UTM ZONE 18T, WGS84)

Put-in:		**Takeout:**	
Easting	554973	Easting	554973
Northing	4933624	Northing	4933624
Latitude	N 44° 33' 13.88"	Latitude	N 44° 33' 13.88"
Longitude	W 74° 18' 28.31"	Longitude	W 74° 18' 28.31"

the true fun begins, can be found 0.3 miles farther along the southern shore. The twisting and turning starts almost immediately as you head upstream. In fact, I calculated that in my first 3 miles of travel on the Osgood, I barely covered 1 mile of true distance. This circuitous route can be quite confusing at times. However, a common trick is to follow the direction in which water plants are bending. This will most always lead you in the right direction.

The river continues this dizzying route south, through areas rife with large tamarack trees, thick alder bushes, and clumps of swamp milkweed. Anytime the Osgood flows near dry land, white pine and spruce trees begin to replace the plants better adapted for wetter areas. Beavers are quite active along the river and have created more than a few dams along its run. Thankfully, none are big enough to cause any major interruptions or wet feet. The Osgood runs in this way for quite a few more miles before it becomes impassable, making any trip from Meacham Lake an out-and-back paddle. Simply turn around whenever you've had enough, and allow the slow current to help you downstream.

✧ **SHUTTLE DIRECTIONS** To get to the put-in on Meacham Lake, head north on NY 30 from Paul Smith's College and look for a small turnoff on the right side of the road after 9.3 miles.

✧ **GAUGE** Water conditions on the Osgood River can be checked visually from the put-in on Meacham Lake or along Route 30.

MEACHAM LAKE SHORELINE

17 ST. REGIS CANOE AREA

Look at any map of the Adirondack Park, and the cluster of blue in its northern region will be hard to miss. A good portion of that blue is the St. Regis Canoe Area, the only true designated canoe area in the state. Amazingly, there are 18,000 acres in this canoe area, containing 58 bodies of water, all of which are closed to motorboats and seaplanes. Because of this, these lakes, ponds, and streams have remained wild in nature and striking in beauty.

The waters of the St. Regis area have long been a favorite destination for vacationers looking for a delightful way to spend a day or two communing with nature. Many guests of the old Paul Smith's Hotel or Saranac Inn would set out in canoes and spend most of the day paddling between the lakes and ponds of the area, making good use of the short and easy carries that connect the bodies of water to each other.

To this day, one of the most beloved of trips in the St. Regis Canoe Area is the route known as the Seven Carries. Seven portages may seem like a lot for a day trip. However, considering where they take you, there really is no reason to complain. As Paul Jamieson says in *Adirondack Canoe Waters: North Flow,* "Ten lakes and ponds for seven short carries seems a bargain. And you can cheat a little by omitting the first pond and carry." In fact, many paddlers do just that, launching directly on Little Clear Pond instead of tiny Little Green Pond right next door. Either way, the route takes you through some of the

most tranquil, pristine areas in the entire Adirondack Park, ultimately finishing at the canoe launch at Paul Smith's College.

Although the Seven Carries route has always been an all-time favorite among canoeists, a wealth of other routes through the canoe area exists. Everything from loops, half-day end-to-end trips, and overnighters is possible and easy to complete. In fact, with the dozens of backcountry campsites found throughout the area, the well-marked carries, and the solitude that is possible to achieve, it is easy to see why the St. Regis Canoe Area is often considered the ultimate Adirondack paddling destination.

USGS Quadrangles
UPPER SARANAC LAKE (NY),
ST. REGIS MOUNTAIN LAKE (NY)

DESCRIPTION From the access road off Fish Hatchery Road, it's possible to launch on either Little Green Pond or Little Clear Pond. Little Green

Little Clear Pond to Paul Smith's College

Class	I
Length	8 miles
Time	4–5 hours
Runnable Months	May–October
Hazards	None
Portages	6
Rescue Access	Limited
Gauge	Visual, phone
Level	N/A
Gradient	N/A
Scenery	A++

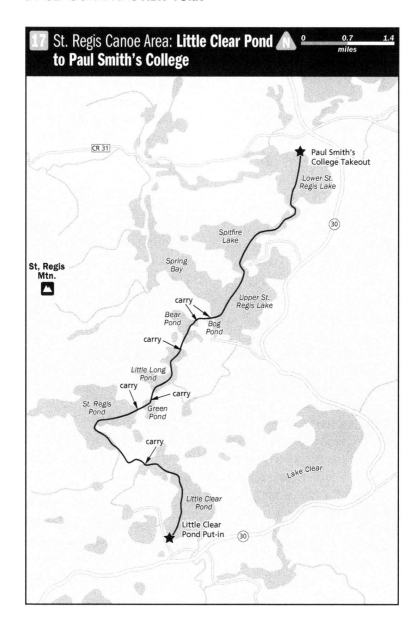

17 St. Regis Canoe Area: **Little Clear Pond** to Paul Smith's College

Paul Smith's College Takeout

Lower St. Regis Lake

CR 31

Spitfire Lake

St, Regis Mtn.

Spring Bay

Upper St. Regis Lake

carry

Bear Pond

Bog Pond

carry

Little Long Pond

carry

St. Regis Pond

carry

Green Pond

carry

Lake Clear

Little Clear Pond

Little Clear Pond Put-in

GPS Coordinates (UTM Zone 18T, WGS84)

Put-in:		Takeout:	
Easting	556429	Easting	559365
Northing	4911655	Northing	4920389
Latitude	N 44° 21' 21.50"	Latitude	N 44° 26' 03.70"
Longitude	W 74° 17' 30.90"	Longitude	W 74° 15' 14.70"

Pond, the traditional start of the Seven Carries route, is quite beautiful, though tiny, which is why many canoeists begin their trip on its southwestern shore. You can eliminate one carry, however, by launching directly onto Little Clear Pond from its southwestern shore instead. A short walk and an extra 15 or 20 minutes are all that differentiate between these options.

The scenic beauty that is synonymous with the St. Regis ponds becomes quite obvious once you have paddled a few feet away from shore. Little Clear Pond is surrounded by incredibly lush evergreen woodland that effectively blocks all signs of civilization. Heading north will bring you past a few small islands and through a narrowing stretch of water before the pond becomes marshier at its northwestern tip. After 1.5 miles, look for a white rectangular sign on this shore that points the way to the carry to St. Regis Pond.

The carry between Little Clear and St. Regis Pond is the longest, and perhaps roughest, of the route, although even this portage is not very difficult. Mostly carpeted with fallen pine needles, the trail has some rocky and muddy sections and finishes with a narrow wooden walkway over a shallow marsh. At its end lies a small creek that leads directly to St. Regis Pond. This pond is roughly the same size as Little Clear, although it stretches from west to east instead of north to south. Heading to its western shore will bring you to two carries, one of which leads to Grass Pond and the other to Ochre Pond. Grass Pond is basically a dead end as far as paddling routes go, but Ochre Pond leads farther to Fish Pond and the more remote western portion of the St. Regis Canoe Area.

At the eastern end of St. Regis Pond is a carry that leads to Green Pond, which seems very small compared

CARRY BETWEEN LITTLE CLEAR
AND ST. REGIS PONDS

with the previous two ponds; indeed, just a few dozen paddles stroke are all it takes to cross to its northern shore, where the carry to Little Long Pond can be found. In addition to the balsam fir, hemlock, and pine trees that dominate the foliage on the first three ponds, Little Long contains quite a few tamarack trees as well. Heading up its long and narrow length brings you through these beautiful tamarack trees and to the pond's northern tip, where yet another white sign indicates a carry. This next one is fairly short again and leads to C-shaped Bear Pond.

Surprisingly, Bear Pond's shores contain more deciduous trees than the previous ponds, with maple and birch becoming more prevalent than tamarack and hemlock. At the tip of the C's upper arm is the fifth carry of the six in the route, heading to the aptly named Bog Pond. Carnivorous sundew and pitcher plants can be found here in abundance, as can pond lilies, cranberry, and bog rosemary. Although Bog is the smallest pond along the route, it is easy to lose track of time here admiring the abundance of marsh plants. The last carry of the route can be found directly across the pond's width and leads to Upper St. Regis Lake.

Civilization reappears on Upper St. Regis Lake in a graceful, idyllic manner rather than the usual abrupt, intrusive way. Scores of beautiful, sprawling camps line the lake's shores as far as the eye can see, complete with docks and boathouses almost as big as the camps themselves. The lake is a true boat-lover's dream in

that inside almost every boathouse floats a classic canoe, motorboat, or sailboat. Many of these sailboats are members of the stunning Idem class, first commissioned by the St. Regis Yacht Club for its local races. Heading almost due north from the large island in the center of Upper St. Regis will bring you to a narrow channel marked with green and red buoys, at the end of which is Spitfire Lake. Skirt along its eastern shore and you will come to the 0.5-mile-long channel that braids through a marsh of pickerelweed and pond lilies to Lower St. Regis Lake. Paul Smith's College and its boat ramp are easy to find amid the scattered camps of Lower St. Regis Lake. Its brown and green buildings stand tall directly across the lake, just less than 1 mile to the north.

✧ **SHUTTLE DIRECTIONS** To get to the put-in on Little Clear Pond, pick up NY 30 at Paul Smith's College and head south 9.4 miles. Look for a sign for the fish hatchery and follow it to the right onto Fish Hatchery Road. Signs on the right side of the road will point to the parking area and boat launch on Little Clear Pond.

To get to the takeout at Paul Smith's College, head north on NY 30 and turn into the college's main entrance. Follow the campus signs to the parking lot and canoe launch.

✧ **GAUGE** Conditions in the St. Regis Canoe Area can be checked visually from the put-in on Little Clear Pond or Little Green Pond or by calling St. Regis Outfitters at (518) 891-8040.

18 FISH CREEK PONDS

Like the St. Regis Canoe Area to the north, the Fish Creek Ponds are a paddler's dream come true. The area contains a dozen separate ponds, each connected to the other by the area's namesake creek or by a short carry, which makes completing loops of varying lengths possible. It also plays host to two large public campgrounds and many backcountry campsites, all of which add to the area's popularity. Good or bad, this also mean large numbers of paddlers on the water. Amazingly, however, the ponds around Fish Creek never seem to be crowded, even during the busiest summer months.

A look at any good map of the Fish Creek area shows the endless opportunities it presents paddlers. Through-trips are possible, as are out-and-backs, circumnavigations, and loops. Of these alternatives, one loop stands out as the most popular. This particular trip begins at the Fish Creek Pond Campground boat launch, heads up Fish Creek, then passes through Copperas Pond, Whey Pond, Rollins Pond, Floodwood Pond, Little Square Pond, and back down Fish Creek to the boat launch. Completing this loop guarantees paddlers will encounter loons, beavers, and a large variety of waterfowl, so be sure to bring a camera. The loop also guarantees at least two portages (depending on water levels), so bring a good set of wheels as well.

USGS Quadrangles
UPPER SARANAC LAKE (NY)

DESCRIPTION One can launch a canoe from numerous spots in the Fish Creek area, although none seem as popular as the one in Fish Creek Campground. This ramp is open to all boaters, regardless of whether they are resident campers or (the latter need only pay a small fee), and it can get quite crowded, especially during summer months. Thankfully, most of the crowds and motorcraft stick to Square Pond and do not travel upstream on Fish Creek. Amazingly, quiet and solitude are often just a few paddle strokes away.

Once you're on Fish Creek, American black ducks, great blue herons, and beavers are more common than people. Pickerelweed and water lilies mark the boundary between the water and land, while alder bushes grow wide and tamarack trees point skyward as the land gets a bit drier. Balsam fir, white pine, and birch trees fill in the higher ground beyond. These

Fish Creek Loop

Class	I
Length	8.8 miles
Time	4–5 hours
Runnable Months	May–October
Hazards	None
Portages	2
Rescue Access	Limited
Gauge	Visual
Level	N/A
Gradient	N/A
Scenery	A++

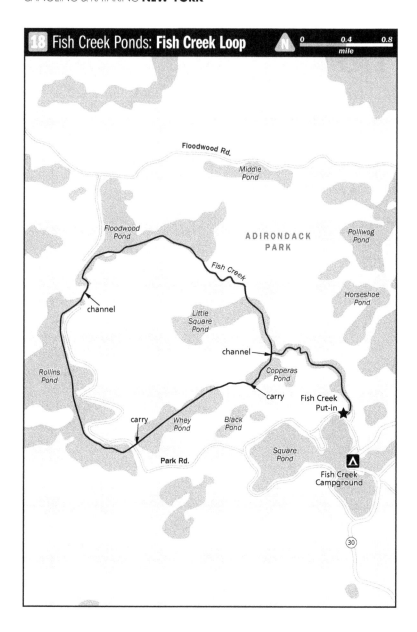

18 Fish Creek Ponds: **Fish Creek Loop**

Floodwood Rd.

Middle
Pond

Floodwood
Pond

ADIRONDACK
PARK

Polliwog
Pond

Fish Creek

channel

Horseshoe
Pond

Little
Square
Pond

channel

Rollins
Pond

Copperas
Pond

carry

Fish Creek
Put-in

carry   Whey   Black
Pond   Pond

Square
Pond

Park Rd.

Fish Creek
Campground

30

GPS Coordinates (UTM Zone 18T, WGS84)

	Put-in:		**Takeout:**	
Easting	550894		Easting	550894
Northing	4906328		Northing	4906328
Latitude	N 44° 18' 30.33"		Latitude	N 44° 18' 30.33"
Longitude	W 74° 21' 42.83"		Longitude	W 74° 21' 42.83"

plants part just 1.3 miles on the left to make way for the narrow channel that leads to Copperas Pond.

It only takes a few paddle strokes to cross tiny Copperas Pond, where a white sign marks the start of an easy carry to Whey Pond. Only slightly bigger than Copperas Pond, Whey Pond stretches 1 mile to the southwest, where the next carry is found. This carry leads to the southern tip of Rollins Pond and is quite easy as well. Heading north on Rollins Pond provides plentiful shoreline to explore, although most of the land on the right is taken up by waterfront campsites. At Rollins's northeastern tip is a narrow, rocky channel that leads to Floodwood Pond. It is possible to float through this passageway when water levels are high enough. However, drier times may force a short carry, which is possible on the left.

Floodwood Pond marks both the northernmost part of the Fish Creek Loop and its halfway point. The pond is shaped like a bow tie, with the channel from Rollins Pond emptying into it on the left and Fish Creek flowing out of it on the right. Once you're on Fish Creek, the last pond in the loop, Little Square Pond, lies just 0.5 miles downstream. From the point the creek enters the pond, much of its acreage stretches to the west. Paddlers can take the time to explore its shores or simply keep heading south on Fish Creek. The Fish Creek Campground boat launch is 1.2 miles downstream.

✧ **SHUTTLE DIRECTIONS** To get to the put-in at the Fish Creek Campground, pick up NY 30 at Paul Smith's College and head south 15.4 miles. Follow the signs on the right for the Fish Creek Campground and its boat launch.

✧ **GAUGE** Water conditions in the Fish Creek area are best checked visually from the Fish Creek Campground.

....

19 SARANAC RIVER

Although the name *Saranac* is thought to originate from the Native American word meaning "We rise here," the actual point of origin of the Saranac River is debatable. Its headwaters are so intertwined with the St. Regis and Raquette rivers that most people have no idea where the river begins. Some consider nearby Mountain Pond as the river's true source, while others argue for Grass Pond or Heller Pond.

Still others simply note Upper Saranac Lake as the river's starting point.

Regardless of where its true beginning is, the Saranac is a river of many faces. Outdoors writer Paul Jamieson describes it as "a stream both of upland marsh and lake and of rugged mountain pass. It is for novice and expert and gradations in between." Indeed, the river's lower sections are full of whitewater thrills and excitement, while the upper river is better known for its flat-water cruising.

One of the classic Adirondack canoe trips can be found in the Saranac's upper reaches. Known as

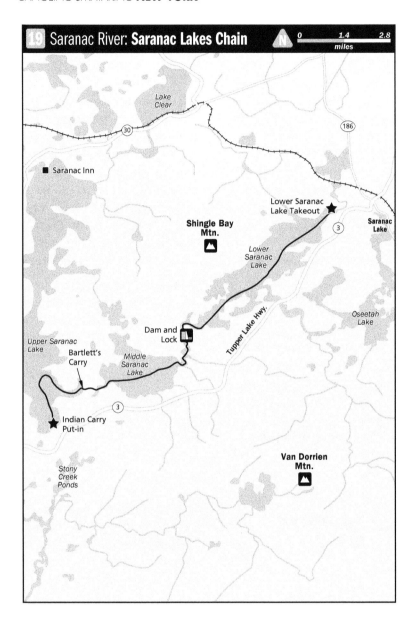

GPS Coordinates (UTM Zone 18T, WGS84)

Put-in:		Takeout:	
Easting	554715	Easting	567378
Northing	4898640	Northing	4908405
Latitude	N 44° 14' 20.18"	Latitude	N 44° 39' 32.82"
Longitude	W 74° 18' 53.25"	Longitude	W 74° 09' 17.90"

the Saranac Lakes Chain, the route stretches 18 miles from the northern end of Upper Saranac Lake to the eastern shore of Lower Saranac Lake. Along the way it includes a carry and a trip through a lock, and it provides an interesting contrast between development and nature: beautiful lakeshores lined with lush evergreen trees and exposed granite outcroppings that are also dotted with summer cottages, camps, and boat docks.

USGS Quadrangles
Tupper Lake (NY), Upper Saranac Lake (NY), Saranac Lake (NY)

DESCRIPTION For those wanting to paddle the classic Saranac Lakes Chain, two convenient put-ins can be found on Upper Saranac Lake: Saranac Inn and Indian Carry. Launching at Saranac Inn obliges paddlers to travel the entire 6-mile length of Upper Saranac Lake before reaching the channel to Middle Saranac Lake, whereas the Indian Carry put-in, at the southern tip, reduces the trip by about 5 miles. Upper Saranac is the most developed of the three lakes in the chain, making this shortcut a popular option for seekers of peace and solitude.

A few rocky, evergreen-topped islands sit off the boat launch at Indian Carry, blocking the rest of the lake from view. Like the lake's small islands, its shores are lined with pines, firs, and spruces, with the lighter bark of birch trees dotted throughout. Just 1 mile north on the right lies Chapel Island and its namesake church. This rustic church offers services Sunday mornings during the summer for all who wish to attend.

A deep, narrow cove sits to the east behind Chapel Island, where the carry to Middle Saranac Lake, Bartlett's Carry, can be found. It lies just out of view behind a small island, but a large white sign labeled CANOE CARRY points the way. Once out of the water, you must follow a dirt road up and down a small hill to a wooded trail that will ultimately lead you to Middle Saranac Lake. Altogether, this carry is 0.5 miles long and steep enough to get all but the strongest hearts thumping. A good set of wheels or a strong paddling partner can help make it much easier.

Middle Saranac Lake, the smallest of the chain, opens up at the end of a short, marshy channel, marked by a large boulder named Plymouth Rock. Beyond this rock lie a half-dozen or so islands, beyond which is the long, winding channel to Lower Saranac Lake. The last three of these islands, Norway Island, Second Island, and First Island, form a line that points almost directly to the channel's entrance, which may

Saranac Lakes Chain	
Class	I
Length	13.3 miles
Time	5 hours
Runnable Months	May–October
Hazards	None
Portages	1
Rescue Access	Limited
Gauge	Visual, phone
Level	N/A
Gradient	2.5
Scenery	A+

be difficult to spot. The channel is also marked with red and green buoys that are hard to miss. These buoys not only help paddlers find their way in the Saranac Lakes but also mark the limits of the safe-boating channel, so powerboats will not run aground or foul their propellers. Speeds on the channel between the lakes are limited, making conditions much safer for us all.

About 1 mile down the channel you will reach a unique and interesting structure of the Adirondack waters. A hand-operated lock is situated here, bypassing rapids leading to Lower Lake. If a lock tender is not on duty when you arrive, directions for operating the lock are printed on a large wooden sign next to the doors. Once you go through, the channel opens up to Lower Saranac just 1 mile later.

This last lake of the chain stretches 5 miles to the northeast, roughly paralleling NY 3 toward Saranac Lake Village. Few houses occupy the lake's shores, though quite a few campsites from the Saranac Lake Islands Campground can be found along its length. Ampersand Bay lies just 0.5 miles past the lake's most northern island, at the far end of the lake, where the state boat landing can be found next to the green-roofed Ampersand Hotel.

✧ **SHUTTLE DIRECTIONS** To get to the Indian Carry put-in on Upper Saranac Lake, take NY 3 12.5 miles south from Saranac Lake Village or 8 miles north from Tupper Lake, turning off at the sign indicating the parking area for Indian Carry.

To get to the takeout in Saranac Lake Village, head north on NY 3 toward Saranac Lake Village. Turn left onto Edgewood Road after 11.6 miles and follow it 0.25 miles before turning left onto Ampersand Bay Road. The takeout can be found 0.2 miles farther on Ampersand Bay Road.

✧ **GAUGE** Conditions on the Saranac Lakes can be checked visually from the Indian Carry put-in or from NY 30. You can also check by calling St. Regis Canoe Outfitters at (518) 891-1838.

PLYMOUTH ROCK ON
MIDDLE SARANAC LAKE

20 AUSABLE RIVER, WEST BRANCH

NY 73 to Conservation Monument	
Class	I
Length	5.3 miles
Time	2 hours
Runnable Months	May–August (or later after heavy rains)
Hazards	Dam and rapids
Portages	1
Rescue Access	Easy
Gauge	Visual
Level	3 feet
Gradient	4.2
Scenery	A+

The West Branch of the Ausable River has the worthy distinction of starting its flow from Mount Marcy, the highest peak in New York state. From this lofty beginning, the river runs northeast for 36 miles before it joins the East and Main branches of the Ausable River at Ausable Forks. The West Branch takes on many forms along the way, giving paddlers everything from beautiful and exciting whitewater runs to miles of swift-but-flat cruising water and rapids that many consider to be some of the most challenging in the area. For those seeking an enjoyable, relatively easy half-day paddle, there is no better section than the portion of river between NY 73 in Lake Placid and the Conservation Monument on NY 86.

Four access points exist along this stretch of the West Branch, making trips of varying lengths possible. Keeping in mind that the first location has some very shallow, rocky water after it and the second is very near private property, the third location (by the small iron bridge on Riverside Drive) is usually the best put-in to use. From this point, a consistent current flows downstream, carrying boats among banks lined with alder, swamp milkweed, balsam fir, gray birch, and spruce trees, and through spots with stunning mountain vistas. Lawrence Grinnell states in *Canoeable Waterways of New York State* that this particular portion of the West Branch is "the most charming small stream tour in the state." I don't think I would give it top billing in the state, but top five? Definitely.

USGS Quadrangles
LAKE PLACID (NY)

DESCRIPTION Unlike the shallow and rocky stretches of water above NY 73, the West Branch of the Ausable below the road is better suited for paddling. The first available launching site in this section of river is just downstream of the small bridge off County Road 21, 1 mile east of NY 73. The Ausable has quite a swift current here, pushing paddlers and their boats downstream with ease. On the downside, the rapid current also speeds paddlers past much of the scenic beauty that abounds on the river.

Worth eyeing closely are the large stands of swamp milkweed, the dense rows of alder bushes, the spirelike balsam fir trees, and rustic birch trees

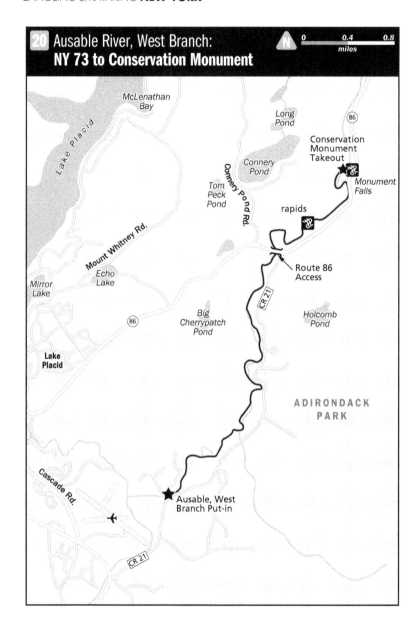

20 Ausable River, West Branch:
NY 73 to Conservation Monument

GPS Coordinates (UTM Zone 18T, WGS84)

Put-in:		Takeout:	
Easting	583755	Easting	586469
Northing	4902095	Northing	4906994
Latitude	N 44° 16' 02.20"	Latitude	N 44° 18' 39.80"
Longitude	W 73° 57' 02.20"	Longitude	W 73° 54' 56.90"

that call the riverbanks home. Time should also be spent watching the circuitous flight paths of cedar waxwings hunting for insects, the drifting and swimming of mergansers along the water's edge, the industrious workings of beavers, and the swimming of trout below the river's surface. Be sure to look forward once in a while, though—numerous fly-fishermen ply the Ausable for a chance at landing one of these desired fish and would not appreciate being knocked over by an errant canoe or kayak.

As the Ausable's West Branch continues to flow to the north, it remains beautifully scenic and quiet despite its proximity to CR 21. In fact, there is little to distract paddlers from the river's beauty but a few submerged rocks 0.8 miles north of the put-in and a couple of houses 1 mile later. One and a half miles later, the river passes under the NY 86 Bridge, leaving only 2 more miles before the takeout at the Conservation Monument.

There is access to the river from the west side of the NY 86 Bridge, just downstream of its span. Anyone not interested in portaging around a breached dam and some rapids would be well served taking out here instead of farther downstream. However, those who continue on can expect to reach the portage 1 mile after the bridge. Because this is not an easy carry, it's best to use the trail on the eastern riverbank to bypass the hazards on the river. Boats can be relaunched a few hundred feet later and paddled 1 mile farther downstream to the takeout in the small park containing the Conservation Monument. Another set of intimidating rapids lies just downstream of the monument, proving the necessity of landing here instead of traveling farther.

✧ **SHUTTLE DIRECTIONS** To get to the put-in off CR 21, pick up NY 86 in Lake Placid and head east 0.5 miles before turning right onto NY 73. Head south on NY 73 2 miles, then turn left on CR 21. Look for a small iron bridge on the left side of the road after 1 mile.

To get to the takeout at the Conservation Monument, continue heading north on CR 21 3 miles, turn right onto NY 86, and travel 1 additional mile. Look for the monument on the left side of the road.

✧ **GAUGE** Conditions on the West Branch of the Ausable River can be checked visually from the NY 86 Bridge or wherever CR 21 nears its flow.

----

21 RAQUETTE RIVER

The Raquette River, the second longest river in the state, begins its flow in the lake of the same name, nestled deep within the Adirondack Park. From there it flows north for more than 150 miles before joining the St. Lawrence River in the Mohawk Nation of Akwesasne. The Raquette's flow is anything but ordinary, though, taking on many different forms along its length. Author Lawrence Grinnell describes this variety best when he writes, "From that lake it undergoes seven metamorphoses: lake, river, lake, river, lake, river, to acquire its final fluvial form." Indeed, if you trace the river's path on a map, your finger will touch Raquette Lake, Forked Lake, Long Lake, and Tupper Lake.

Amazingly enough, almost every inch of the Raquette's long and varied route is paddleable, with trip options just as diverse as the river itself. The river is fairly flat in its upper stretches but does flow over Buttermilk Falls just before it enters Long Lake. A short carry around these falls is necessary, as is another longer carry around Raquette Falls after Long Lake. There is nothing but calm, albeit winding, water for the next 24 miles or so, until whitewater (up to Class V in some sections) arises in Piercefield. The Raquette enters a reservoir about 18 miles later and ends its northward run as a flat, peaceable river.

Although canoeists seem to love each and every part of the Raquette, the stretch between Axton Landing and Tupper Lake is arguably the most popular. It is not uncommon, especially during the summer months, to see dozens upon dozens of paddlers putting in at Axton Landing or on NY 30. Unfortunately, powerboats are also allowed on this stretch of river, which can make for quite a racket (no pun intended). Luckily, there always seems to be enough room for everyone on the river, even the wildlife that call it home.

As for the origin of the name Raquette, some believe it comes from the French word for "snowshoe." Specifically, some think it has to do with a pile of wooden snowshoes supposedly found on the shore of what is now Raquette Lake, while others are of the opinion that the mouth of the river resembles a snowshoe. Still others believe the name is an adaptation of the word *racket*, meaning "noisy" (the Native American name for the river was *Ta-na-wa-deh*, meaning "swift or noisy water"). Or perhaps it has something to do with large numbers of canoes floating down its course. We may never know for sure.

A Axton Landing to NY 3/30

Class	I
Length	7 miles
Time	3–4 hours
Runnable Months	May–October
Hazards	None
Portages	None
Rescue Access	Easy
Gauge	Visual, phone
Level	N/A
Gradient	4.5
Scenery	A+

USGS Quadrangles
TUPPER LAKE (NY)

DESCRIPTION The Axton Landing boat launch is found in an oxbow on the Raquette River, a bit downstream of Raquette Falls. When setting out from here, paddlers should head left to join the main body of the river, where the fun begins. Almost immediately, the Raquette begins twisting and turning, heading north, then south, then back north, then east, then, well, you get the picture. In fact, in the first 2 miles of flow below Axton Landing,

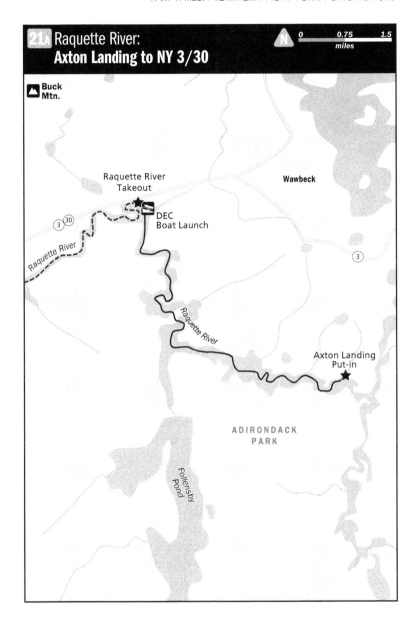

21A Raquette River:
Axton Landing to NY 3/30

0   0.75   1.5
miles

Buck
Mtn.

Raquette River
Takeout

Wawbeck

3 30

DEC
Boat Launch

Raquette River

3

Raquette River

Axton Landing
Put-in

ADIRONDACK
PARK

Follensby
Pond

GPS Coordinates (UTM Zone 18T, WGS84)

Put-in:		Takeout:	
Easting	553808	Easting	548936
Northing	4894692	Northing	4898622
Latitude	N 44° 12' 12.48"	Latitude	N 44° 14' 21.07"
Longitude	W 74° 19' 35.58"	Longitude	W 74° 23' 13.79"

GROUP PADDLE ON THE RAQUETTE RIVER

the river barely covers 1 mile of distance over land. These tight turns create dozens of oxbows, side channels, and small ponds to paddle through. It is possible to spend all day paddling on the river and not make it more than a couple of miles downstream. While these diversions are welcome, they can be quite confusing at times. The best bet is to look to the river plants for direction: they will bend with the current and point downstream. Some intersections also have red and green buoys marking the way. In these cases, passing to the left of the red buoys will help paddlers stay on course.

The Raquette flows through a fairly wooded area for the first 1.5 miles or so from Axton Landing. Red maple and white pine trees dominate this stretch of river, with gray and paper birch trees marking the higher land

behind them. Soon after, the river enters a more open setting, more marsh than woodland. A few maple trees remain, although they now share the riverbanks with plants common to Adirondack wetlands such as cardinal flowers, cattails, alder, pickerelweed, and yellow pond lilies. A handful of primitive campsites can be found on the right-hand side of the river here as well. (*Note:* The land on the left-hand side is privately owned, and no camping is allowed.)

The Raquette continues curling its way to the west for 3.5 more miles until it begins a general turn to the north. The option for a short side trip exists here, as a small creek flowing out of nearby Follensby Pond can be found at the southern end of the large, shallow marsh on the left. Although paddling on the pond is prohibited, it is strongly recommended in the marsh and on the creek, where American black and wood ducks, great blue herons, kingfishers, cedar waxwings, and other marsh birds sometimes can be found in incredible numbers.

The Raquette continues flowing through extensive marshes and past many side creeks and coves, then makes a dozen or so more turns on its way north toward NY 3/30. As it does, it passes an attractive grove of birch trees to the left around mile 5, a pond filled almost to capacity with pickerelweed at mile 5.3, and a small island across from a classic Adirondack lean-to at mile 5.8. From there, it is only 1.25 miles to the boat access on NY 3/30. Many paddlers, happy with the 7 scenic miles they've traveled from Axton Landing, take out here instead of heading to Tupper Lake, although the river still has more to enjoy for those who have not yet had enough.

✧ **SHUTTLE DIRECTIONS** To get to the put-in at Axton Landing, take NY 30 from the south or NY 3 from the north into the town of Tupper Lake. Continue east on NY 3/30 5.5 miles, until NY 3 and NY 30 split. Stay on NY 3 an additional 2.4 miles before turning right onto Coreys Road. A sign pointing the way to the boat launch can be found after 1.75 miles.

To get to the takeout on NY 3/30, head back west on NY 3/30 4 miles. Look for the RAQUETTE RIVER FISHING ACCESS sign on the left side of the road.

✧ **GAUGE** Water conditions on the Raquette River can be checked visually at Axton Landing or by calling Raquette River Outfitters at (518) 359-3228.

NY 3/30 to Tupper Lake B

Class	I
Length	7 miles
Time	3 hours
Runnable Months	May–October
Hazards	None
Portages	None
Rescue Access	Easy
Gauge	Visual, phone
Level	N/A
Gradient	1
Scenery	B

DESCRIPTION The Raquette bends away from the highway and starts heading southwest after the NY 3/30 access, almost directly toward Tupper Lake. Unlike the more pristine section between the highway and Axton Landing, this stretch is more developed. In fact, a few houses appear on the right just 2 miles downstream. Despite their presence, the river still maintains its beauty, with alder and other lower shrubs and bushes replacing the larger trees found earlier. American black and wood ducks can be found here, as well as beavers, deer, and other small woodland creatures.

An unusual, perhaps even infamous, natural feature can also be found on this stretch of river. The Raquette flows through an area aptly known as the Oxbow around mile 3.5. Local stories tell of this corkscrew-shaped stretch of river and how it has been known to confuse and turn boaters so many times that they lose

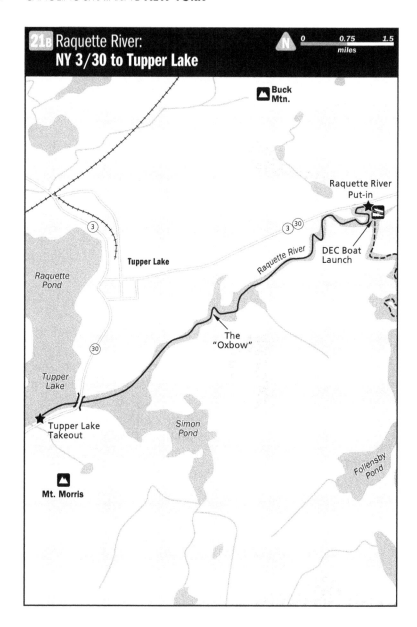

Buck
Mtn.

Raquette River
Put-in

DEC Boat
Launch

③ ㉚

Raquette River

③

Tupper Lake

Raquette
Pond

The
"Oxbow"

㉚

Tupper
Lake

Tupper Lake
Takeout

Simon
Pond

Follensby
Pond

Mt. Morris

GPS Coordinates (UTM Zone 18T, WGS84)

Put-in:		Takeout:	
Easting	548936	Easting	541248
Northing	4898622	Northing	4893750
Latitude	N 44° 14' 21.07"	Latitude	N 44° 11' 44.88"
Longitude	W 74° 23' 13.79"	Longitude	W 74° 29' 01.74"

all sense of bearing. In fact, Paul F. Jamieson writes in his book on Adirondack waters of one such story about a few men who were headed to Tupper Lake by canoe on a cloudy day. Apparently they got lost in the Oxbow and ended up back at Axton Landing before they knew what had happened. Although this legend seems a bit far-fetched, the spot can be tricky to navigate. Staying to the left when heading through should help paddlers avoid ending up back in Axton.

After the Oxbow, the Raquette flows beneath a low bridge at mile 4.6 and makes a straight run for Simon Pond. From the pond, the entrance to Tupper Lake underneath the NY 30 bridge is only 1 mile farther. The takeout on Tupper Lake is just 0.5 miles south from the bridge.

✧ **SHUTTLE DIRECTIONS** To get to the put-in on NY 3/30, pick up NY 3/30 in Tupper Lake and head east for 4.1 miles. Look for the Raquette River Fishing Access sign on the right side of the road.

The takeout on Tupper Lake can be found on NY 30, 0.5 miles south of the NY 30 Bridge over the Raquette River.

✧ **GAUGE** Water conditions on the Raquette River can be checked visually at Axton Landing or by calling Raquette River Outfitters at (518) 359-3228.

---

22 BOG RIVER FLOW

The Bog River is a short but beautifully scenic stretch of water in the central Adirondacks. Writer Paul Jamieson recognized its unique qualities when he described the river as both a "prima donna" and a "maverick" in *Adirondack Canoe Waters: North Flow*. The first description refers to the way the Bog enters its final destination, Tupper Lake: instead of simply flowing into the lake and gently becoming one with its waters, the river cascades over a series of high rock ledges, crashing into the lake with much deliberation and fanfare. The second term stems from the Bog's unusual eastward direction of flow (other rivers in the area head west).

While different observers may describe the Bog River in different ways, none will deny its beauty and attraction. In fact, the upper part of the river, known as the Bog River Flow, is one of the prettiest places to paddle in the Adirondacks. It stretches from the western end of Lows Lake to Lows Lower Dam, including Lows Upper Dam, Hitchins Pond, and Horseshoe Lake, as well as numerous islands, bogs, hiking trails, and 39 designated campsites. In addition, beavers, black bears, river otters, bald eagles, largemouth bass, and large numbers of loons are commonly found alongside, above, or underneath water fringed with large granite outcroppings and white pine, balsam fir, and red maple trees. It's no wonder that paddling and camping along the flow are so popular.

Every canoeist and kayaker has A. Augustus Low to thank for this

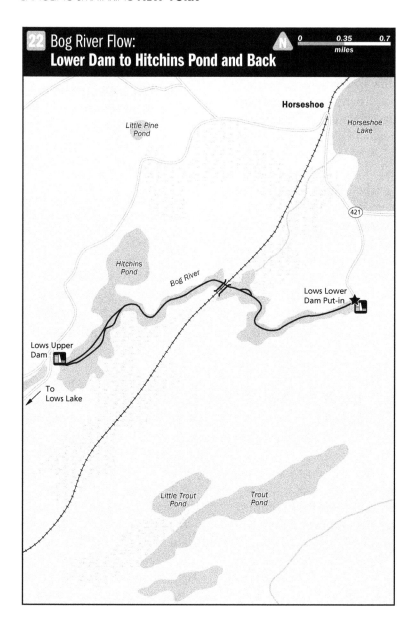

22 Bog River Flow:
Lower Dam to Hitchins Pond and Back

N

0   0.35   0.7
miles

Horseshoe

Little Pine
Pond

Horseshoe
Lake

421

Hitchins
Pond

Bog River

Lows Lower
Dam Put-in

Lows Upper
Dam

To
Lows Lake

Little Trout
Pond

Trout
Pond

GPS Coordinates (UTM Zone 18T, WGS84)

Put-in:		**Takeout:**	
Easting	529874	Easting	529874
Northing	4884766	Northing	4884766
Latitude	N 44° 06' 55.70"	Latitude	N 44° 06' 55.70"
Longitude	W 74° 37' 36.00"	Longitude	W 74° 37' 36.00"

wonderfully scenic location. Low purchased most of the land surrounding the Bog River Flow in the 1890s and proceeded to create a small empire for himself there. He built a small railroad station near Horseshoe Lake, started the Horseshoe Forestry Company to harvest lumber, bottled and sold Virgin Forest Springs water, and produced maple syrup. As one would expect, such enterprises required a significant amount of electricity to run, obliging Low to build two power-generating dams. When Low died in 1912, his land was split among many different owners and remained mostly off-limits until 1985, when New York state purchased more than 9,000 acres of the Bog River Flow and opened them to paddlers. This effectively saved much of the area from further development and preserved its natural beauty for future generations.

USGS Quadrangles
LITTLE TUPPER LAKE (NY)

DESCRIPTION The beauty that is synonymous with the Bog River Flow becomes immediately obvious upon launching in front of Lows Lower Dam. Just upstream of the dam lies a narrow channel that is lined with outcroppings of granite whose shades of gray stand in striking contrast to the greens of the pine, fir, and spruce trees that have taken hold in the loose soil in between. This stunning scene continues for about 0.75 miles until the river curves to the north and enters an area that is more marsh than woodland. While the predominant plant life changes here (grasses and pond lilies emerge), the area's beauty does not fade.

Lower Dam to Hitchins Pond and Back

Class	I
Length	5.6 miles (round-trip)
Time	2.5–3 hours
Runnable Months	May–October
Hazards	None
Portages	None
Rescue Access	Limited
Gauge	Visual
Level	N/A
Gradient	2.1
Scenery	A++

After 1 mile, the Bog River flows past a small creek on the right that leads to Horseshoe Lake, a worthy paddling destination in itself. Just 1 mile farther, the river flows into Hitchins Pond. Here, among the low-lying plants of the marsh and the taller evergreen trees standing beyond, lies an excellent habitat for bald eagles. Indeed, a pair of these majestic birds is frequently seen over and about the pond's waters. Likewise, another member of the animal kingdom has established itself in the area in such huge numbers that it may very well be the most common animal in the flow, if not the entire Adirondack Park. Yes, the infamous blackfly, the scourge of the Adirondacks, resides along the Bog River and stands ready to sink its teeth into any paddler who happens to pass by. Thus all visitors to the Bog River Flow should remember to bring both binoculars and bug spray.

Once on Hitchins Pond, paddlers can head north for about 0.5 miles and explore the Hitchins Pond Primitive Area or turn to the south and head for Lows Upper Dam. The dam, along with a small boat landing, is 0.5 miles south on the western shore of the pond. Also found here is one of the shortest carries in the Adirondacks, which provides a way around Lows Upper Dam and gives paddlers the option of continuing their trip on Lows Lake. Before reaching the main body of the lake, however, paddlers must travel down a narrow 3-mile-long stretch of river. Depending on water levels, a second short carry may be made about 0.5 miles along this stretch, where a low-lying bog blocks most of the river's span. At higher water levels, this bog can be easily avoided and feet can remain dry.

On Lows Lake, you can spend hours or even days exploring its roughly 20 miles of shoreline. Paddlers can also settle down into one of more than 30 backcountry campsites that ring the lake. The significant loon population of the western end of the lake can be sought out and admired. Largemouth bass and brook trout can be fished for. Adventure seekers can also head down the 3.5-mile carry that leads from the western shore of Lows Lake to the Oswegatchie River and continue their paddle there. Still others may simply decide to turn around and follow the gentle current of the Bog River back to the Lower Dam.

✧ **SHUTTLE DIRECTIONS** To get to the put-in at Lows Lower Dam, take NY 30 south from Tupper Lake or north from Long Lake until you reach NY 421. Head west on NY 421 5.8 miles and follow the signs showing the way to the canoe access.

✧ **GAUGE** Water conditions on the Bog River Flow are best determined visually from Lows Lower Dam.

23   CEDAR RIVER FLOW

As development continues to seek out more waterfront space in the Adirondacks, it has become harder to find natural, pristine paddling destinations. Luckily, the Cedar River Flow has remained an untouched gem among Adirondack Park's rivers and lakes. The flow, accessible only by a dirt road, fed by a mountain river, and set among stunning mountains, gives visitors a sense of remoteness, even though it is located about 11 miles from the village of Indian Lake.

Although the Cedar River Flow extends only 3 miles south from Wakely Dam, numerous paddling opportunities can be experienced almost all year long. The main body of the flow is surrounded by balsam fir, birch, and maple trees and harbors many small coves that yearn to be examined more closely. The flow also has three primitive campsites scattered along its shores for those looking to spend more time in the area. Closer to its southern end, the Cedar River Flow becomes inundated with marsh grasses and alder bushes, with numerous narrow channels in between. While most of these routes lead to dead ends, one channel opens into the actual Cedar River. The

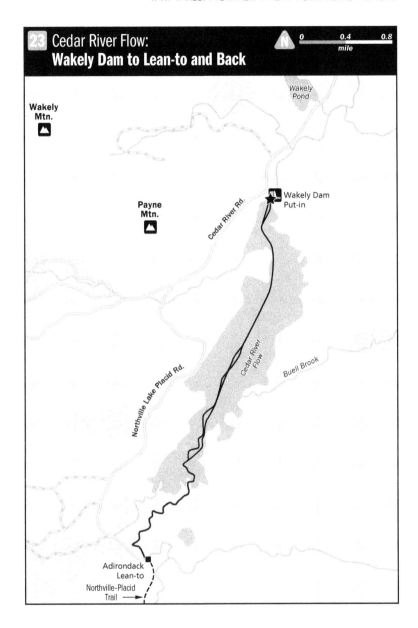

23 Cedar River Flow: Wakely Dam to Lean-to and Back

0   0.4   0.8
mile

Wakely
Pond

Wakely
Mtn.

Payne
Mtn.

Cedar River Rd.

Wakely Dam
Put-in

Cedar River
Flow

Buell Brook

Northville Lake Placid Rd.

Adirondack
Lean-to

Northville-Placid
Trail

GPS Coordinates (UTM Zone 18T, WGS84)

Put-in:		**Takeout:**	
Easting	542447	Easting	542447
Northing	4841572	Northing	4841572
Latitude	N 43° 43' 33.46"	Latitude	N 43° 43' 33.46"
Longitude	W 74° 28' 22.73"	Longitude	W 74° 28' 22.73"

most popular paddling trip on the flow includes heading up the river to a lean-to and, perhaps, a hike on the nearby Northville–Placid Trail.

USGS Quadrangles
INDIAN LAKE (NY)

DESCRIPTION Although the water downstream of the Wakely Dam is mostly unnavigable, putting in upstream of the dam and heading south on the Cedar River puts you on a wide, vast stretch of flat water perfectly suited for paddling. After you've launched there, a small island and a fairly large cove come into view to the left and right, respectively, both providing ample space for many balsam fir trees to grow and thrive. In fact, the entire perimeter of the Cedar River Flow seems to be dominated by balsam fir trees, a sight that becomes incredibly obvious once you paddle around the small island and enter the main flow 0.3 miles south of the dam.

Wakely Dam to Lean-to and Back

Class	I
Length	8.5m iles (round-trip)
Time	4 hours
Runnable Months	Late April– November
Hazards	None
Portages	None
Rescue Access	Difficult
Gauge	Visual
Level	N/A
Gradient	1.7
Scenery	A+

After 0.5 miles or so, the Cedar River Flow begins to widen a bit more, now about 1,000 feet across. The shore to the east is marked by a few primitive campsites, beaver dams, small coves, and protected inlets, making it a bit more interesting to paddle along than the western shore, which runs fairly straight and even. This shore also harbors the mouth to tiny Buell Brook, found 2 miles south of the Wakely Dam. The entrance to the brook is very well hidden from view by dense plant growth. Those who take the time to search it out will be rewarded with a pleasant, scenic paddle upstream.

The flow becomes more inundated by grasses and alder bushes toward its southern tip, and remains that way for its remaining mile. While the plant growth can be so thick at times as to completely halt any forward progress, the outflow of the Cedar River hides among its confines. The easiest way to find the river is to hug the eastern shore and look to the water plants for guidance. Head in the direction opposite the way they are bending.

The actual Cedar River is completely different from the flow before it, being quite narrow with a slow-flowing current. It twists and winds its way south, amid thick alder bushes, swamp milkweed plants, and bur reed. A beaver dam or fallen tree branch occasionally interrupts the river, although it is never completely blocked. An Adirondack lean-to, on the right-hand side just 1 mile after you've entered the river, is the usual turnaround spot for day paddlers.

CEDAR RIVER

◇ **SHUTTLE DIRECTIONS** To get to the put-in at the Wakely Dam, take NY 28/30 into Indian Lake. Turn left onto Cedar River Road (2.2 miles north of Indian Lake) and travel 12 miles west to the Cedar River Campground. Follow the signs for the canoe launch.

◇ **GAUGE** Conditions on the Cedar River Flow are best checked visually from Wakely Dam.

24 MARION RIVER

Raquette Lake, the largest natural lake in the Adirondacks, has always been a popular destination for people looking to get away from it all. With natural beauty, a convenient location, and advocates like William West Durant, it is easy to understand why. It was Durant, in fact, who designed and built many luxurious "camps" around the lake during the 1800s in what became known as the Great Camp style. These destinations, and the roads and rail lines they required, helped turn Raquette Lake into the bustling lake it is today.

No longer the playground of the rich and famous, Raquette Lake is a part of the vast system of canoe routes that run throughout the Adirondack Park. From its waters, one can travel to Old Forge along the Fulton Chain

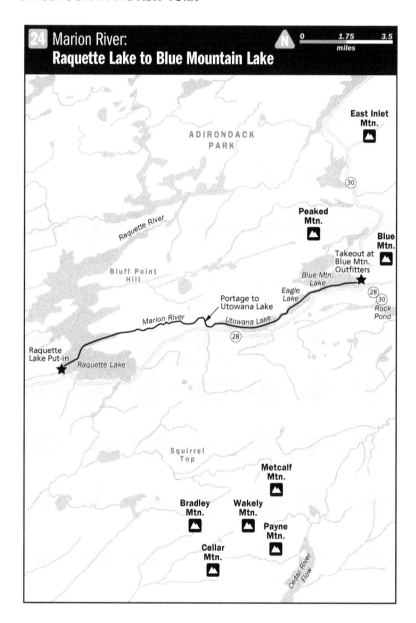

24 Marion River:
Raquette Lake to Blue Mountain Lake

N   0   1.75   3.5
miles

East Inlet
Mtn.

ADIRONDACK
PARK

30

Peaked
Mtn.

Blue
Mtn.

Raquette River

Takeout at
Blue Mtn.
Outfitters

Bluff Point
Hill

Blue Mtn.
Lake

Eagle
Lake

28
30
Rock
Pond

Portage to
Utowana Lake

Marion River

Utowana Lake

28

Raquette
Lake Put-in

Raquette Lake

Squirrel
Top

Metcalf
Mtn.

Bradley
Mtn.

Wakely
Mtn.

Payne
Mtn.

Cellar
Mtn.

Cedar River
Flow

GPS COORDINATES (UTM ZONE 18T, WGS84)

Put-in:		Takeout:	
Easting	527642	Easting	545653
Northing	4851200	Northing	4856380
Latitude	N 43° 48' 48.06"	Latitude	N 43° 51' 32.76"
Longitude	W 74° 39' 22.68"	Longitude	W 74° 25' 54.90"

of Lakes or head north to Long Lake and beyond. One can also pick up the Marion River from its eastern shore and follow the river to Utowana Lake, Eagle Lake, and ultimately Blue Mountain Lake (another series of lakes known as the Eckford Chain).

Like Raquette Lake, Blue Mountain Lake also served as a vacation destination for people in search of a bit of the outdoors. Instead of Great Camps, though, Blue Mountain Lake was known for its lavish hotels, one of which was the first in the world to have electricity in every room (thanks to one of Thomas Edison's generators). Most of these hotels are gone today and, although much of the southern shore of the lake is developed, the remainder of the lake has remained relatively unspoiled (even though electricity has become more widespread).

Paddling to Blue Mountain Lake along the scenic route from Raquette Lake through the Eckford Chain has become immensely popular among canoeists. The extensive shoreline of Raquette Lake, the twisting turns and extensive marshes of the Marion, the wilderness of Utowana and Eagle lakes, and the stunningly beautiful landscape of Blue Mountain Lake all add to its appeal. Even the short carry between the Marion and Utowana Lake is easy enough that it only adds a bit of charm to the paddle. Of course, there are no longer extravagant camps or hotels to stay in along the way. But I'm sure most paddlers won't mind.

USGS Quadrangles
RAQUETTE LAKE (NY),
BLUE MOUNTAIN LAKE (NY)

Raquette Lake to Blue Mountain Lake

Class	I
Length	13 miles
Time	5–6 hours
Runnable Months	May–November
Hazards	Boat traffic
Portages	1
Rescue Access	Easy
Gauge	Visual, phone
Level	N/A
Gradient	2.3
Scenery	A++

24 DESCRIPTION Although it is easy to paddle in either direction along the Marion River, most locals recommend paddling upstream from Raquette Lake to Blue Mountain Lake because of the prevailing winds from the west. Those wishing to embark on such a trip will find no better spot to launch from than the public boat launch in the village of Raquette Lake.

Once on the water, you'll find the shores of Raquette Lake lined with vacation homes, camps, and boathouses. Despite this development, however, there is little boat traffic to contend with. Even on busy days, the lake is big enough that there is more than enough room for powerboaters and paddlers to coexist peaceably. One could easily spend a full day, or many days, exploring the lake's islands, coves, and miles of shoreline. For those ultimately headed to Blue Mountain Lake, though, the mouth of the Marion River lies 3 miles from the

WHITE PINE TREE ON
THE MARION RIVER

village, north of the first big point of land on the lake's eastern shore.

While the lake's shores are lined with cedar, fir, and hemlock trees, the land around the Marion River is something quite different. Along its narrow, sinuous route are huge clusters of bright purple pickerelweed flowers, vast marshes of cattails and alder bushes, and wide floating mats of both yellow pond and fragrant water lilies. Also obvious are the blossoms of the beautiful cardinal flower, lending their vibrant red color to the green of the marsh, stately great blue herons hunting the shallows, and raucous kingfishers patrolling the shores. All the while, views of Blue Mountain pop up whenever the river turns to the east and the sky is clear.

The navigable portion of the Marion ends 3.5 miles later, necessitating a portage. Thankfully, the carry is quite short (0.3 miles) and very easy (it is along a wide and smooth trail). At its eastern end waits a small dock and the scenic Utowana Lake. Ringed with maple, birch, balsam fir, and white pine trees, Utowana also holds some marshy environs within its banks, which contain most of the same vegetation as the Marion. Heading 2.5 miles farther east leads to a narrow channel that empties into 1-mile-long Eagle Lake.

Once you've crossed Eagle Lake, a beautiful and rustic bridge comes into view on the left. This wood-and-stone bridge was built by William West Durant, famed designer and builder of camps in the Adirondack Great Camp style. A large plaque under its span tells the story of how Durant built this bridge, known as the Pioneer Bridge, in memory of his father, Dr. Thomas Clark Durant. Dr. Durant was well known himself as the man who developed the idea for and built the first transcontinental railroad and the Adirondack Railroad.

Once you've headed past the Pioneer Bridge and through the channel after it, you can finally experience the sheer beauty of Blue Mountain Lake. It may be tempting to paddle along the south shore of the lake and take the quickest route to the takeout, especially after paddling more than 10 miles from Raquette Lake. Nevertheless, you should explore at least a small part of the lake. With dozens of granite islands, verdant shorelines, beautiful camps, and scenic mountain vistas in every direction, even the weariest paddler will have trouble leaving this natural wonder. But every trip must finally come to an end, and the best places to end this one are at the public boat launch on the southeast corner of the lake or at the Blue Mountain Outfitters dock just a bit farther north.

✧ **SHUTTLE DIRECTIONS** To get to the put-in at the village of Raquette Lake, take NY 28/30 from the south or NY 30 from the north into the town of Blue Mountain Lake. Take NY 28 west from Blue Mountain Lake 13 miles into Raquette Lake. Turn right onto NY 2 and follow the signs for Raquette Lake. The boat launch is 0.5 miles down the road.

To get to the takeout in Blue Mountain Lake, head back east along NY 28 to the junction of NY 28 and NY 30. Continue heading north on NY 30 for

PICKERELWEED ON UTOWANA LAKE

a few hundred feet, looking for Blue Mountain Outfitters on the left. If you don't want to pay to use Blue Mountain's facilities, there is also a public boat launch just south of the store.

✧ **GAUGE** Water conditions on Raquette Lake, Blue Mountain Lake, and the Marion River can be checked visually or by calling Blue Mountain Outfitters at (518) 352-7306.

25 MOOSE RIVER, MIDDLE BRANCH

In the heart of the Adirondacks lies a well-known waterway called the Moose River. The Moose is made up of three separate branches—North, Middle, and South—that are favorites among whitewater kayakers. It is the Middle Branch, however, that is held back by a dam in Old Forge before completely falling victim to gravity, thus forming the famous Fulton Chain of Lakes. This particular stretch of water has been used for travel for centuries, from the earliest Native Americans in the area to European settlers, hunters and trappers, adventurers, and vacationers. In fact, the name *Fulton* was given to the lakes in recognition of the man who dreamed of using them as a corridor for steamboat travel, Robert Fulton. While his plans never materialized, the chain has long remained a

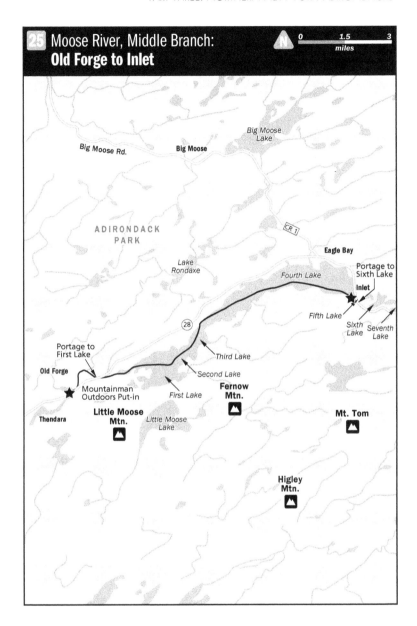

25 Moose River, Middle Branch: Old Forge to Inlet

GPS COORDINATES (UTM ZONE 18T, WGS84)

Put-in:		Takeout:	
Easting	501074	Easting	516887
Northing	4838990	Northing	4843747
Latitude	N 43° 42' 14.16"	Latitude	N 43° 44' 47.64"
Longitude	W 74° 59' 12.00"	Longitude	W 74° 47' 24.96"

popular waterway into the Adirondack region. Indeed, the 18-mile stretch of lakes connects to Raquette Lake with a carry a little more than 1 mile long. From there, one can travel to Forked Lake, Long Lake, Blue Mountain Lake, or beyond. Unbelievably, one can also paddle to Maine from Old Forge (the 740-mile-long Northern Forest Canoe Trail begins here as well). There is even an annual canoe race highlighting this navigability, the 90-mile-long Adirondack Canoe Classic, which runs from Old Forge to Saranac Lake.

While all eight lakes share a certain beauty and charm, each has its own distinct characteristics: Fourth Lake is the largest and most developed, for example, while Fifth is the smallest and Seventh and Eighth the most pristine. Likewise, camping is only allowed on Fourth and Eighth lakes, a carry is necessary to access Sixth and Eighth lakes, and the only town along the way (Inlet) is between Fourth and Fifth lakes. All

Old Forge to Inlet

Class	I
Length	12 miles
Time	5–6 hours
Runnable Months	LateA pril–November
Hazards	Boatt raffic
Portages	1
Rescue Access	Easy
Gauge	Visual, phone
Level	N/A
Gradient	N/A
Scenery	B+

eight are suitable for canoeing and kayaking, though, and should be experienced by Adirondack paddlers.

USGS Quadrangles
OLD FORGE (NY), EAGLE BAY (NY)

25 DESCRIPTION While most paddlers begin their trip on the Fulton Chain of Lakes from the canoe launch in Old Forge, the dock at the Mountainman Outdoor Supply Company offers another great put-in, complete with restrooms, ample parking, canoe and kayak gear, and boat rentals. The town beach is only a 1.5-mile upstream paddle from this dock, along the slow-moving Middle Branch of the Moose River. After a short portage around the dam under NY 28 (cross by the State Trooper barracks), boats can be relaunched on Old Forge Pond at the start of the famous chain.

Old Forge Pond is an extremely busy place where paddlers will share the water with fishermen, water skiers, and pontoon boaters. Everyone I met here was extremely friendly and willing to slow down and pass far enough away from me so that there was never a danger of swamping bow waves or large wakes. Likewise, the dozens of vacationers sitting on the decks of their camps along the shoreline were courteous, affable, and genuinely happy to share this beautiful spot with me.

After paddling through a 1-mile-long channel, you'll reach First Lake. Like the pond and channel before it, the shores of First Lake are lined with cabins and vacation homes. Gone, however, is the no-wake restriction on powerboats, which may cause a bit of

PFDs DRYING ON THE MOOSE RIVER

anxiety in some paddlers. Those not wishing to try their luck in these conditions can simply hug the shoreline instead of braving more-open waters. Thankfully, courtesy to others on the water does seem to be the norm here. I felt perfectly safe paddling across this lake, making sure to stay out of the boat channel, of course.

It is roughly 1 mile across from the start of First Lake to the narrow point of land that marks the beginning of Second Lake. This lake is smaller than First Lake and is not as populated. As such, it is a more tranquil place to paddle, although it tends to pass by quickly. In fact, the entrance to Third Lake lies just 0.2 miles beyond Second Lake's entrance. Like the first lake in the chain, Third Lake has quite a few

homes along its shores, especially to the north. To the southeast, though, a large side creek can be paddled as a welcome diversion to the goings-on along the lakes.

The narrow channel leading to Fourth Lake is reached 1 mile to the northeast of the start of Third Lake. The famous Adirondack paddler George Washington Sears once referred to Fourth Lake as the "Stormy Fourth" because of the way the weather on it can worsen and create treacherous paddling conditions in an instant. Although I did not experience the same kind of worsening weather that Sears did, the wind was obviously stronger on Fourth Lake than it had been on the previous three lakes. Staying close to the southern shore helped greatly and allowed me to continue my trip without much added effort.

Fourth Lake is the most populated lake of the chain and, at almost 6 miles in length, is also the longest. At its eastern end is the town of Inlet, where another narrow channel leads to tiny Fifth Lake. It can be found by heading just to the right of the large flagpole on the beach in Inlet. After 0.5 miles, the channel opens up to Fifth Lake, directly across from the start of the portage to Sixth Lake. The eastern shore of Fifth Lake is also the pickup spot for paddlers using the shuttle provided by Mountainman Outdoor Supply Company.

✧ **SHUTTLE DIRECTIONS** To get to the put-in at the Old Forge Town Beach, take NY 28/30 from the south or NY 30 from the north into the town of Blue Mountain Lake. Take NY 28

west from Blue Mountain Lake 35 miles into the town of Old Forge. The launch is just before the visitor center. If you're putting in at Mountainman Outdoor Supply Company, head 1 additional mile west along NY 28.

To get to the takeout in Inlet from Old Forge, head east along NY 28 for 11.5 miles and look for the brown-and-yellow sign just before you reach the Citgo gas station. This same spot is 23 miles west of Blue Mountain Lake.

✧ **GAUGE** It is best way to check water levels visually from the launch on Old Forge Pond. Mountainman Outdoor Supply Company can also provide updated water conditions at (315) 369-6672. Water levels are dam-regulated and should be suitable for paddling during most of the spring, summer, and early fall.

---

26 SCHROON RIVER

The Schroon is one of those special rivers that prove it is possible to exhibit stunning natural beauty and provide many paddling opportunities despite being less than two hours away from the city of Albany. It offers more than 50 miles of navigable water in a variety of habitats (farmland, evergreen forest, freshwater wetland, and so on) and also provides a home to deer, mink, beavers, and river otters, along with dozens of bird species. The Schroon is stocked with large numbers of rainbow, brown, and brook trout each year

and also boasts six campgrounds along its lower stretches.

USGS Quadrangles
CHESTERTOWN (NY)

26 **DESCRIPTION** One of the best spots to launch on the lower Schroon River is at the fishing access lot at the southern tip of Schroon Lake. From there, it is possible to head north onto the lake itself and enjoy its pine-rimmed shores or to head south on the actual river and marvel at its beauty and grace.

It is quite hard to discern the actual riverbanks in the first 0.25 miles or so of the river's flow below Schroon Lake. Instead of running directly out of the lake, the Schroon seems to spill out and spread itself over a wide and

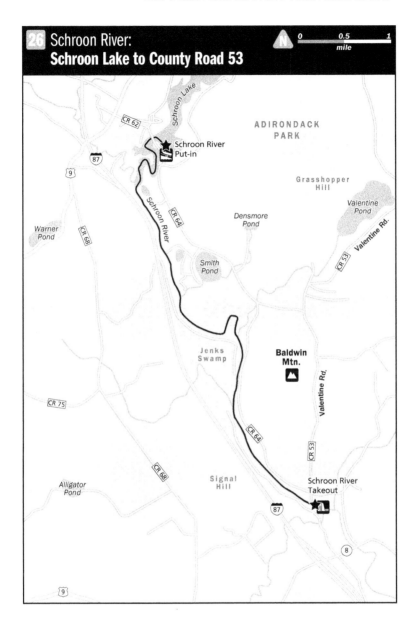

26 Schroon River: Schroon Lake to County Road 53

ADIRONDACK PARK

Schroon Lake

CR 62

Schroon River Put-in

87

9

Grasshopper Hill

Valentine Pond

Densmore Pond

Warner Pond

CR 68

CR 64

Schroon River

Smith Pond

CR 53

Valentine Rd.

Jenks Swamp

Baldwin Mtn.

Valentine Rd.

CR 75

CR 68

Alligator Pond

Signal Hill

CR 64

CR 53

87

Schroon River Takeout

9

8

GPS Coordinates (UTM Zone 18T, WGS84)

	Put-in:		Takeout:	
Easting	595930		Easting	598413
Northing	4842210		Northing	4836672
Latitude	N 43° 43' 36.20"		Latitude	N 43° 40' 35.53"
Longitude	W 73° 48' 32.17"		Longitude	W73° 46' 44.86"

Schroon Lake to County Road 53

Class	I
Length	5.3 miles
Time	2 hours
Runnable Months	April–November
Hazards	None
Portages	None
Rescue Access	Easy
Gauge	Web
Level	2 feet
Gradient	2.5
Scenery	A

curving area. This makes for good paddling, however, as the wide twists and turns and the low-lying clumps of land provide a pleasant warm-up for the rest of the trip downstream. White cedar, red maple, and birch trees dominate the drier land here, while scores of alder bushes inhabit the more moist soil below. Wherever the river's current slows (around the inside corners of turns, for example), large floating mats of fragrant white water lilies abound.

Once through the slow, wider section of the river, paddlers will encounter a narrower, more contained Schroon. Despite its close proximity to Interstate 87 and the sporadic development along its banks, the river maintains its sense of peace and solitude. Instead of crowds, noise, and car exhaust, paddlers will encounter chickadees, goldfinches, American black ducks, great blue herons, painted turtles, and dozens of other species common to freshwater environs.

A small marsh worth exploring can be found to the left about 1 mile south of the put-in. The Schroon then turns sharply to the north 3 miles south of the lake, marking its entrance into Jenks Swamp. The swamp is home to an amazing variety of plant and wildlife, providing shelter for beavers, river otters, many different kinds of waterfowl, pickerelweed, buttonbush, and cattails, to name a few. Unfortunately, the beauty of the swamp does not last forever, as the Schroon leaves its confines after 1 mile and begins to run near the Interstate once again. Houses also intrude on the river's banks below the swamp and continue for most of the way until the dam north of NY 8. Still, the Schroon's natural beauty is somehow preserved, often making paddlers reluctant to end their trip. If you wish to keep going, you can do a short carry around the left side of the dam and extend your trip farther south toward South Horicon or Warrensburg.

✧ **SHUTTLE DIRECTIONS** To get to the put-in at Pottersville, take I-87 to Exit 26 (US 9). Follow the signs to US 9 and take it north 0.8 miles before turning right onto Glendale Road (County Road 62). Look for the boat ramp on the left-hand side after 0.6 miles.

To get to the takeout in Starbuckville, head south from the put-in and pick up East Schroon River Road (CR 64) after 0.1 mile. Follow it south 4 miles and turn right onto Valentine Road (CR 53). The takeout can be found by the dirt parking area on the left, 0.2 miles later.

◇ **GAUGE** Water levels on the Schroon River are best determined at the gauge on the Schroon River at Riverbank (visit **waterdata.usgs.gov/ nwis/rt** to check these water levels online).

27 KUNJAMUK CREEK

Although many of the best Adirondack canoe routes are deep within the park, Kunjamuk Creek is a true classic that happens to be near its southernmost border. Like those scenic rivers farther to the north, the Kunjamuk offers flat water, natural beauty, and a bit of adventure, all less than a two-hour drive from the city of Albany.

The most popular trip on the Kunjamuk starts on the Sacandaga River, east of the town of Speculator. The mouth of the creek is only a short paddle along the Sacandaga, in a wider portion known as Kunjamuk Bay. From there, it slowly winds its way north through extensive marshes and boggy areas, ultimately reaching Elm Lake 3.5 miles later, although it is often interrupted by beaver dams and deadfall. In fact, depending on the time of year, you can spend almost as much time out of your boat climbing over obstacles as in your boat paddling the creek. Those willing to put up with such conditions, though, are often treated to scenery so beautiful that all difficulties are quickly forgotten.

USGS Quadrangles
PAGE MOUNTAIN (NY)

DESCRIPTION It is possible, and common, to begin a trip on Kunjamuk Creek by launching on the Sacandaga River from the boat launch near the firehouse in Speculator. Kunjamuk Bay and the mouth of Kunjamuk Creek are only 1.5 miles away. Another popular option is to put in directly on Kunjamuk Bay from the launch on NY 8/30, directly across from the mouth of the creek.

Although there is a definite current on the creek, it is slow enough that paddling upstream is quite easy to do. From its mouth, the creek twists and winds its way north to Elm Lake, sometimes turning almost 180 degrees on itself. With these turns come many surprises, for one never knows what will be found just around the next bend. Will it be a beaver dam backing up the creek's flow? Or will it be a great blue heron hunting for small fish along the banks? Might it be a large

NY 8/30 to Elm Lake and Back

Class	I
Length	7m iles (round-trip)
Time	3 hours
Runnable Months	May–October
Hazards	Beaver dams
Portages	None
Rescue Access	Limited
Gauge	Web, visual
Level	400 cfs
Gradient	0.3
Scenery	A+

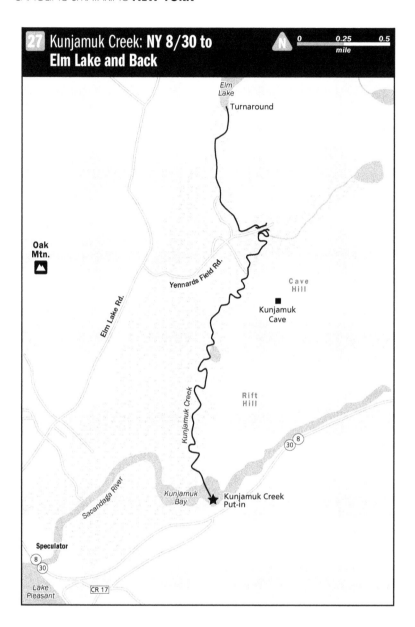

27 Kunjamuk Creek: **NY 8/30 to Elm Lake and Back**

GPS Coordinates (UTM Zone 18T, WGS84)

Put-in:		**Takeout:**	
Easting	553646	Easting	553646
Northing	4816698	Northing	4816698
Latitude	N 43° 30' 04.62"	Latitude	N 43° 30' 04.62"
Longitude	W 74° 20' 11.10"	Longitude	W 74° 20' 11.10"

grove of alder bushes and water willows growing to the water's edge? Or possibly a stand of tall balsam fir, red maple, and birch trees leaning over the creek? All are possible, and likely.

Quite a few other plants live along the lush banks of the Kunjamuk. Cardinal flowers are common during summer months, as are swamp milkweed, buttonbush, bur reed, yellow pond lilies, and fragrant water lilies. The creek is also home to a large variety of wildlife, including beavers, kingfishers, cedar waxwings, bald eagles, and many different kinds of waterfowl. I was even lucky enough to spot a pileated woodpecker flying from tree to tree here and witnessed the biggest group of blue jays I have ever encountered (at least a dozen in one tree). Combine all this nature with the scenic beauty of nearby Rift Hill and Cave Hill, and it's easy to see why the Kunjamuk is considered a classic Adirondack paddle.

The creek passes under a small bridge 2 miles upstream from the put-in and another one just under a mile upstream of that. There is access to the creek at this second bridge on Yennards Field Road, although parking is limited (the bridge serves better as a drop-off or pick-up point instead). There is also a trail on the eastern side of this bridge that leads to a cave between Rift and Cave hills. From the same bridge, Elm Lake lies 1 mile farther upstream, although progress may be checked by a beaver dam just before it. Depending on water levels, this dam may need to be carried over to continue to the lake. From Elm Lake, the takeout is an easy return trip downstream.

✧ **SHUTTLE DIRECTION** The put-in for Kunjamuk Creek is located on the north side of NY 30, 2 miles beyond the junction of NY 30 and NY 8 in the town of Speculator.

✧ **GAUGE** The gauge most useful in determining water levels on Kunjamuk Creek is on the Sacandaga River in the town of Hope (visit **waterdata .usgs.gov/nwis/rt** to check online). Conditions can also be checked visually at the NY 8/30 put-in.

---

28 SACANDAGA RIVER, UPPER WEST BRANCH

The Upper West Branch of the Sacandaga River is one of the most beautiful, and thus most popular, paddling destinations in the southern Adirondack Park. A tributary of the Main Branch of the Sacandaga, the West Branch helps drain water from a portion of the Adirondacks before it joins the Main Branch near the town of Wells. While the other branches of the Sacandaga are well known for their spirited whitewater, the Upper West Branch provides some of the best flatwater paddling in the Adirondacks and possibly the state.

To the Iroquois, *Sacandaga* means "cedar in water-drowned lands," and it is easy to see why they chose that name for this river. For most of its

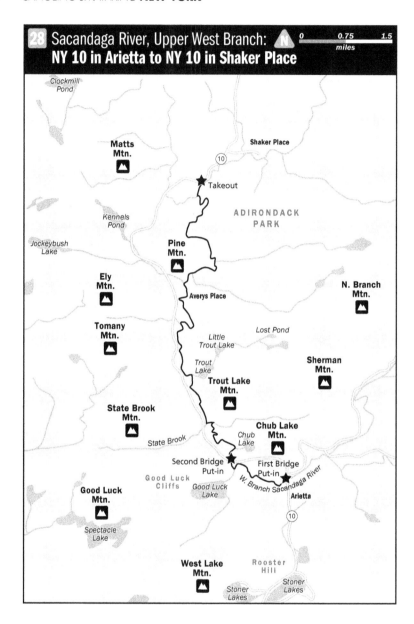

28 Sacandaga River, Upper West Branch: NY 10 in Arietta to NY 10 in Shaker Place

GPS Coordinates (UTM Zone 18T, WGS84)		
Put-in:		**Takeout:**
Easting	537686	Easting	536992
Northing	4789219	Northing	4796187
Latitude	N 43° 15' 17.4"	Latitude	N 43° 19' 03.4"
Longitude	W 74° 32' 08.6"	Longitude	W 74° 32' 37.7"

length, the Upper West Branch of the Sacandaga passes through marshland teeming with grasses, deciduous trees, and conifers. Indeed, cedar, hemlock, and pine trees abound along the river's course. Playful river otters and beavers also have been known to call the Sacandaga home. Anyone spending the day in this paddlers' paradise should keep his or her eyes open and camera at the ready. Stunning scenes and picturesque views lie around every corner.

USGS Quadrangles
MOREHOUSE LAKE (NY)

28 DESCRIPTION Access to the Upper West Branch of the Sacandaga is easily obtained at two places just north of the town of Arietta. These put-ins, both near bridges, are found where NY 10 crosses over the river and are about 1.25 miles apart. Both sites have a short trail leading to the water and room to park a few cars.

Paddlers starting their trip from the first bridge on NY 10 need head only 1 mile downstream before finding a narrow channel on the left that leads to Good Luck Lake. Paddling to this scenic lake, and possibly hiking up the trail to the Good Luck Cliffs, can make for a great side trip. From there, the second bridge lies just 0.25 miles farther downstream.

After passing the second bridge, the Upper West Branch continues its slow flow, gracefully winding its way through low-lying marshes as it seems to head straight for a small mountain in the distance. The river pools right before this mountain, however, and branches off in two directions.

NY 10 in Arietta to NY 10 in Shaker Place

Class	I
Length	7.6 miles
Time	4–5 hours
Runnable Months	April–October
Hazards	Beaver dams
Portages	None
Rescue Access	Difficult
Gauge	Web
Level	1,000 cfs
Gradient	0.1
Scenery	A+

Heading left takes paddlers farther downstream, while heading right leads to Chub Lake. Although smaller than Good Luck Lake, Chub Lake is just as beautiful, especially with Chub Lake Mountain standing proud watch over it. In addition, the small campsite on its eastern shore is a great place to spend a night.

A small beaver dam to the left of the Chub Lake channel partially blocks the way downstream. Luckily, though, much of the debris making up this dam has been cut away, making it wide enough to fit a canoe through. The same cannot be said of the three remaining dams, however. While these dams are not very large, they do require paddlers to drag their boats over or around them.

Beavers are truly amazing creatures. They gnaw on small trees growing near waterways until the trees fall, and then they use those trees to construct dams that ultimately raise water levels. As a result, the beavers can

UPPER WEST BRANCH
SACANDAGA RIVER

then reach food supplies growing at a greater distance. While paddlers often find these dams hard to miss, other signs of beaver activity (tooth marks on branches or slightly worn paths through marsh grass) are sometimes harder to find. Harder to find still are the beavers themselves. Increasingly, they are reacting to man's encroachment on their habitats by becoming more active at night. It is usually only the lucky paddler who sees a beaver during the day.

The Upper West Branch turns sharply to the north 1.5 miles from the second bridge and begins to parallel NY 10 for a bit. The road sits a bit higher than the river, however, so most of its noise is lost to paddlers. One mile later, you'll reach a T whose left branch leads farther downstream and right branch leads to Trout Lake. Like Chub Lake, Trout Lake sports a campsite, on its southern shore. It also shares the beauty that is the norm for lakes in the Adirondack Park. Paddling the 1,400 feet across to the eastern shore leads to another small channel that, if water levels are high enough, will bring paddlers to Little Trout Lake. Truly adventurous souls may choose to head even farther east from Little Trout Lake, leaving their boats behind to hike up the small stream at its northeastern shore. The trail leads to Lost Pond after 0.5 miles.

The Upper West Branch continues its slow course north after passing

Trout Lake and reaches the base of Pine Mountain 2.5 miles later. The river turns sharply to the east at this point and runs directly below the mountain for 0.5 miles or so. It then turns north again, passing some stunning areas as it winds its way near NY 10 once more. Two miles later the river comes its closest to the road, making a takeout possible. The best spot for doing so is where the marsh grass on the left bank is replaced by large rocks. A short, steep trail leads from this point to a section of NY 10 with a shoulder wide enough to fit a few cars. The river then flows into an impassable gorge just downstream of this spot, preventing paddlers from going any farther.

✧ **SHUTTLE DIRECTIONS** To get to the NY 10 put-in, take Interstate 90 to Exit 29 (NY 10). Follow the signs to NY 10, heading north over the Mohawk River. Continue north on NY 10 for 29 miles. Look for a sign reading WEST BRANCH SACANDAGA RIVER and a small parking area just north of the bridge.

To get to the takeout, simply head north on NY 10 7 miles. The takeout is on NY 10 where the river comes very close to the road. Look for a spot on the road with a fairly wide shoulder.

✧ **GAUGE** The gauge most useful in determining water levels on the West Branch of the Sacandaga River is the Sacandaga at Hope (visit **waterdata .usgs.gov/nwis/rt** to check online).

29 FISH CREEK (SARATOGA LAKE)

Fish Creek is an excellent paddling destination for those not interested in battling the crowds on Saratoga Lake. It flows out of the northern tip of Saratoga Lake, winding its way 13 miles to the Hudson River near Schuylerville. Along the way it passes vacation homes, marshlands, and woodlands, flowing over a few small sections of whitewater, past a dam, and underneath a few downed trees. In short, it allows you to experience a little bit of everything as you explore its length.

The creek is home to a great variety of birds, including wood ducks, American black ducks, egrets, great blue herons, and belted kingfishers, to name a few. It also harbors many species of plant life such as purple loosestrife, arrow arum, orange-spotted touch-me-nots, and buttonbush, as well as red

maple, ash, and oak trees commonly found in wetland areas. In addition, fishermen commonly ply the creek's shores looking for the numerous yet elusive bass hiding in the weeds.

As if the beauty of Fish Creek and its resident species weren't enough to attract paddlers, the creek's proximity to historic Saratoga (4 miles), its location in the foothills of the Adirondack Park, and its ease of accessibility make it the perfect spot for families and vacationers to spend an afternoon on the water. Beginners and expert paddlers, bird-watchers and wildflower collectors, young and old—Fish Creek has something for everyone.

USGS Quadrangles
QUAKER SPRINGS (NY)

29 **DESCRIPTION** The put-in on NY 9P puts boaters in the water just north of a fairly large bridge, next to a popular RV park and campground. Fish Creek is fairly wide at this point as it flows past numerous homes on its northern shore and extensive marshes to the south. The number of houses dwindles after the first mile, though, leaving paddlers in a quiet and serene setting. This is in stark contrast to Saratoga Lake and the hordes of powerboaters who cruise its length.

Fish Creek begins to narrow after the last of the houses have been left behind, and passes between even more low-lying marshland, now on both sides. These marshes are predominantly made up of red maple and small ash trees, with cattails growing as far as the eye can see. The creek then runs under Staffords Bridge on

Saratoga Lake to NY 29

Class	I–II
Length	7.3 miles
Time	2.5 hours
Runnable Months	April–October
Hazards	Downedt rees, rapids
Portages	1
Rescue Access	Easy
Gauge	Visual, Web
Level	4.5
Gradient	1.4
Scenery	B

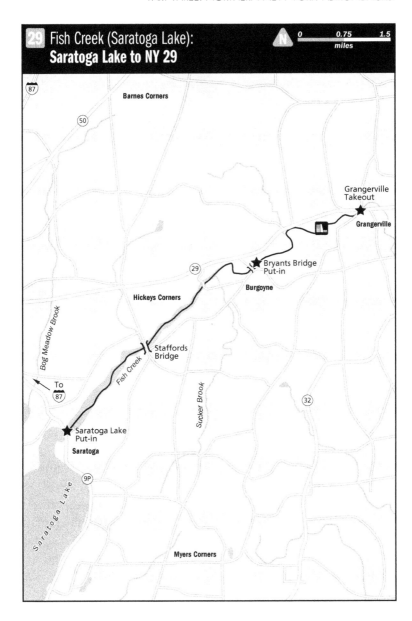

GPS Coordinates (UTM Zone 18T, WGS84)

Put-in:		Takeout:	
Easting	604143	Easting	611858
Northing	4767553	Northing	4773417
Latitude	N 43° 03' 12.7"	Latitude	N 43° 06' 18.8"
Longitude	W 73° 43' 16.3"	Longitude	W 73° 37' 31.1"

SPATTERDOCK ON FISH CREEK

County Road 67 1 mile after the last house is passed, bringing paddlers to the Fish Creek Marina. This small facility boasts a boat marina, a quaint restaurant, a boat launch, and kayak rentals. The last time I paddled Fish Creek, I ran into 10 or 12 kayakers, all sporting orange blades on their paddles. Thinking I had missed a memo or had not been invited to an exclusive party, I was relieved to discover that those were the paddles the marina rents. Obviously, the marina runs a very successful business. Its Web site, **www.saratogaoutdoorcenter.com**, offers a wealth of information on services, menus, rental rates for kayaks, and, of course, orange paddles.

Fish Creek continues to wind its way through marshland for another mile before reaching an old, abandoned brown house on its southern bank. The creek beyond this house is more developed than its earlier portions. Nevertheless, few powerboats are seen on this and the remaining portions of the creek. A second bridge, Bryants Bridge, crosses the creek after a series of S-turns at mile 5. Canoes and kayaks can be launched at the foot of this bridge instead of upstream by Saratoga Lake, making it a good alternative put-in to the one closer to Saratoga Lake.

Beyond the bridge, Fish Creek meanders through wooded areas and more marshland and past summer cottages, eventually reaching a small dam after 6.5 miles of paddling. There is no easy way around this dam, although a small trail on the left bank leads downstream of it. This trail is on private property, however. I was lucky enough to meet the woman who lives there one day on the creek, and she gave me permission to use the trail so I could continue on past the dam. This may not always be possible, though, so you should keep other options open (returning to Bryant's Bridge or Saratoga Lake).

Paddlers able to make it past the dam will soon encounter a few more obstacles between themselves and the takeout in Grangerville—namely, rapids and three downed trees. The rapids are lively (up to Class II) and can give paddlers a pretty good ride. The trees lie across the creek after the rapids and can prove problematic with higher water levels. If the creek is running low enough, you may be able to paddle under the first and third of these trees, although the middle tree will most likely force you to climb over its top. Paddlers will reach their take-out on the right riverbank immediately after going under the last tree.

✧ **SHUTTLE DIRECTIONS** To get to the put-in on Saratoga Lake, take Interstate 87 to the Saratoga exit (Exit 14E). The exit ramp will end at NY 9P, where you should turn left. NY 9P will cross over the northern tip of Saratoga Lake after 2 miles and lead right to the Saratoga Lake Boat Launch. Be sure to have $6 handy for the parking fee.

To get to the takeout in Grangerville, head back north over the NY 9P Bridge and take the second right onto Dyer Switch Road. A small intersection will be reached after 1.5 miles. Veer left at this intersection onto Dyer Circle, then quickly right onto Meadow Brook Road. Meadow Brook Road will end in 3 miles at Staffords Bridge Road. Turn left onto Staffords Bridge Road and take it north 3.5 miles until it reaches NY 29 (Lake Avenue). Turn right onto NY 29 and continue east 8 miles. After 8 miles, Hayes Road will appear on the right. The takeout spot and a fairly large dirt parking area can be found on Hayes Road a few feet south of NY 29.

✧ **GAUGE** The best way to determine water level on Fish Creek is in person. The river gauge nearest the creek is the Batten Kill below the mill in Battenville (visit **waterdata.usgs.gov/ nwis/rt** to check online).

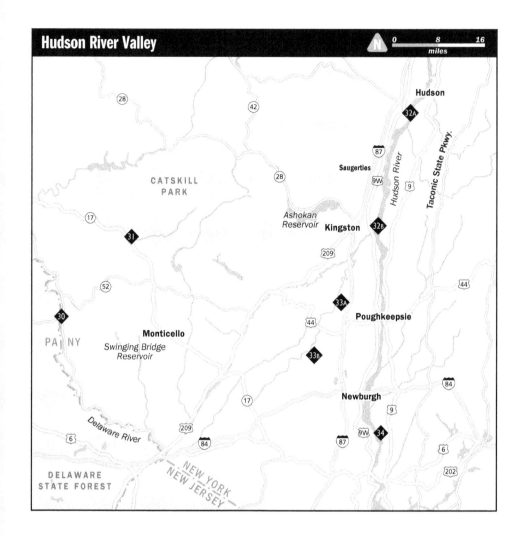

Hudson River Valley

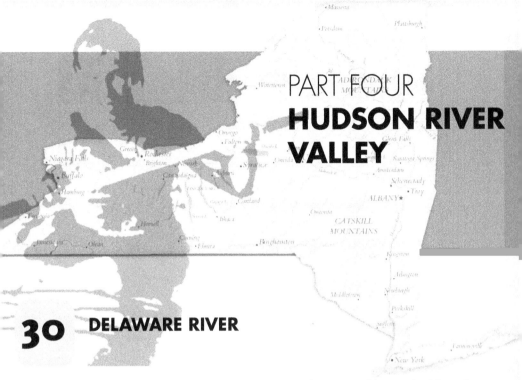

30 DELAWARE RIVER

The Delaware is a very well-known river in New York state and beyond, although it is difficult to pinpoint why. It is named after Lord Delaware, a former governor of Virginia, but that is not likely why many people are familiar with it. The river was the site of George Washington's famous crossing during the Revolutionary War, which may have something to do with its fame. It also forms part of the border between New York and Pennsylvania, all of the border between Pennsylvania and New Jersey, and much of the border between New Jersey and Delaware, facts which very well may have something to do with the river's household-name status. Then again, perhaps people simply appreciate its natural beauty and recreation activities. Whatever the reason (or reasons) may be, the Delaware has become the most popular and well-used river in the state.

The Main Branch of the Delaware begins in Hancock, New York, at the confluence of its East and West branches, and continues to flow south for about 200 miles before it enters a wide tidal estuary below Trenton, New Jersey. This lengthy run makes the Delaware the longest undammed river east of the Mississippi. Luckily for canoeists and kayakers, the Main Branch is navigable for most of this stretch, with river-access points spaced anywhere from 3 to 20 miles along its length. There are also quite a few significant rapids between Hancock and Trenton, making it a rafter's and whitewater paddler's paradise. In fact, more than 1,000 canoes, kayaks, and rafts can be found on the Delaware during an average spring weekend.

For those wishing to experience the excitement and beauty of the Delaware for themselves, there is perhaps no better portion to paddle than the stretch between Callicoon and Mongaup. Moderate rapids, long pools of calm water,

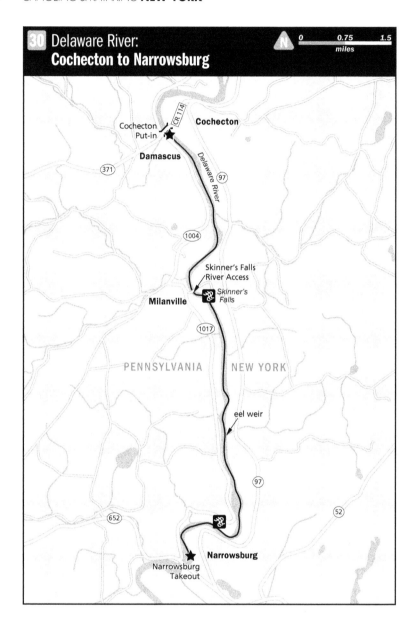

30 Delaware River:
Cochecton to Narrowsburg

N   0   0.75   1.5
              miles

Cochecton
Put-in

CR 114

Cochecton

Damascus

371

Delaware River

97

1004

Skinner's Falls
River Access

Skinner's
Falls

Milanville

1017

PENNSYLVANIA   NEW YORK

eel weir

97

652

52

Narrowsburg

Narrowsburg
Takeout

GPS Coordinates (UTM Zone 18T, WGS84)

Put-in:		Takeout:	
Easting	494483	Easting	495121
Northing	4617023	Northing	4606661
Latitude	N 41° 42' 17.92"	Latitude	N 41° 36' 41.94"
Longitude	75° 03' 58.71"	Longitude	W 75° 03' 30.79"

mountain views, abundant wildlife, and convenient river accesses are just a few of its draws. Consider too that water levels are maintained by periodic dam releases (making the river runnable through most of the summer and fall), and it is easy to see why everyone loves the Delaware.

USGS Quadrangles DAMASCUS (NY), NARROWSBURG (NY)

DESCRIPTION Located about 4 miles south of the well-used boat launch in Callicoon, the put-in underneath the County Road 114 bridge in Cochecton is a popular spot to begin a trip on the Delaware River. Launching there, surrounded by low-lying mountains and fast moving water, gives you a sense that this is an exciting stretch of river, and it truly is. In fact, just a few hundred feet downstream of the put-in, some riffles run across the width of the river. Neither difficult nor dangerous to navigate, these little features provide just enough stimulation to get the heart beating a bit faster.

Aside from a few houses that sit on the Pennsylvania side of the river and some road noise from the highway nearby, little else in the way of civilization can be seen or heard from the river in this stretch. Instead, the lush deciduous trees lining the river's edges and the wildlife they harbor are the only things that may grab your attention from the water. Tulip, white ash, red maple, locust, and willow trees seem to be everywhere along the banks, with great blue herons, kingfishers, common mergansers, and other species of birds making good use of the rocks and shallows in between. Observant eyes may

Cochecton to Narrowsburg

Class	II+
Length	8.2 miles
Time	3 hours
Runnable Months	April–October
Hazards	Rapids, Eel weir
Portages	None
Rescue Access	Easy
Gauge	Visual, Web
Level	3 feet
Gradient	3.4
Scenery	A

even be able to spot red foxes, deer, and bald eagles along this stretch as well.

A few more riffles emerge after 0.5 miles of paddling, and again 1.5 miles after that. As is the case in a good portion of the Delaware in this part of the state, riffles and rapids appear and are separated by long stretches of flat water. Long Eddy, named after a section of calm water a bit north of here, is one such example. The largest rapids along this stretch of river come only 1 mile after these last riffles, just under the CR 44 bridge. Known as Skinner's Falls, these rapids are the most difficult in the area (Class II+) and the most popular. In fact, in the spring and early summer, the picnic

MEAN WATER TEMPERATURES BY MONTH (Degrees Fahrenheit)					
	JAN	FEB	MAR	APR	MAY	JUN
MEAN	N/A	N/A	N/A	51	61	72
	JUL	AUG	SEP	OCT	NOV	DEC
MEAN	75	73	67	51	N/A	N/A

KAYAKING THE DELAWARE RIVER

area on the left side of the river is often filled with spectators watching all of us crazy paddlers navigate the whitewater. A sign on the upstream bridge says that the right side of the rapids is the easiest route to take, and this is true. However, those with more whitewater experience will surely want to run the falls down the more exciting middle. Either way, scouting the rapids from the riverbanks is highly recommended. And anyone who does not wish to attempt the middle, right, or any side of Skinner's Falls can simply portage around them on the right side.

Although there is nothing farther on the river that will create as much excitement as the rapids of Skinner's Falls, the remainder of the run to Narrowsburg is still scenic, swift, and enjoyable. A few low-lying islands barely rise

above the river's surface along these last 4 miles, a handful of houses sit along its banks, and two or three more sets of riffles sporadically break up its calm flow. An eel weir constricts the river into a narrowing chute 2 miles south of Skinner's Falls, but even this structure is easily bypassed by following the signs around to the right side.

As if it were attempting to provide paddlers with just one more thrill on the river, the Delaware begins a wide S-turn 1.5 miles downstream of the eel weir, with a small set of rapids in its center. This whitewater is smaller in size and scale than Skinner's Falls, but it does quicken the pulse one last time before taking out in Narrowsburg.

✧ **SHUTTLE DIRECTIONS** To get to the put-in at Cochecton, take NY 17 to Exit 87 in Hancock. Pick up NY 97 in

Hancock and head south 28.5 miles into the town of Cochecton. Bear right onto CR 114 and continue 0.5 miles, following the signs for the Department of Environmental Conservation fishing-access site, where a short trail leads to the river.

To get to the takeout in Narrowsburg from Cochecton, head south on NY 97 7.3 miles and turn right onto Kirks Road. Continue on Kirks Road 0.4 miles, turn right onto DeMauro Lane, and turn right once again at the sign for the Narrowsburg Campground. Look for the Department of Environmental Conservation fishing-access site on your left just before the campground.

✧ **GAUGE** The gauge most useful in determining water levels on the Delaware is on the Delaware in Callicoon (visit **waterdata.usgs.gov/nwis/rt** to check online). Water levels can also be checked visually from the CR 114 bridge in Cochecton.

---

31 WILLOWEMOC CREEK

Willowemoc Creek is considered by many, including myself, to be one of the most beautiful stretches of water in New York state. It runs for more than 26 miles, starting deep within the Catskill Park, near the village of Willowemoc, and eventually joins the Beaver Kill in the aptly named Junction Pool in Roscoe. Together, the Willowemoc and Beaver Kill are renowned for their trout fishing and draw fishermen from all over the world wishing to try their luck in these magnificent waters.

There are many access points suitable for both boaters and fishermen along the creek's length, although much of the upper Willowemoc has restrictions on access and fishing. The lower section, from Livingston Manor to Roscoe, is completely open to the public. Because of this accessibility and the perfect water conditions, many people believe this stretch of river is the best part of the Willowemoc.

Kayakers and canoeists on the creek will find fairly swift-moving water, frequent eddies, swirls, small rocks, and light whitewater to contend with. None of these characteristics deter from the joy of paddling the Willowemoc, however. Rather, they simply add to its appeal. Furthermore, with its proximity to the Catskill Fly Fishing Center and Museum, numerous public campgrounds, and the famous Roscoe Diner, Willowemoc Creek is the perfect spot for a day paddle or an extended weekend trip.

USGS Quadrangles LIVINGSTON MANOR (NY), ROSCOE (NY)

DESCRIPTION Although numerous access points exist along Willowemoc Creek, one of the most easily reached is in the Livingston Manor Town Park. Boaters will find ample parking there as well as gently sloped

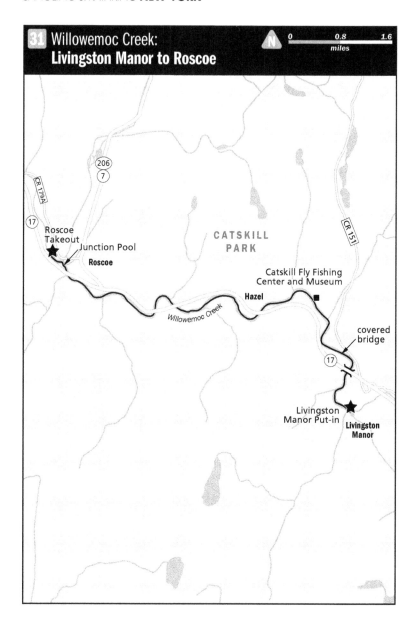

GPS Coordinates (UTM Zone 18T, WGS84)

Put-in:		Takeout:	
Easting	514186	Easting	506229
Northing	4638844	Northing	4642793
Latitude	N 41° 54' 05.1"	Latitude	N 41° 56' 13.5"
Longitude	W 74° 49' 44.3"	Longitude	W 74° 55' 29.5"

riverbanks that lead right down to the creek. The Willowemoc is not very wide at this point but does move fairly quickly, enough to make upstream paddling difficult, if not impossible. This portion of the creek also seems to be littered with trash and debris, though just a brief paddle downstream leads to much cleaner water.

The Willowemoc passes under the NY 17 Bridge 1 mile downstream of Livingston Manor, then begins flowing through stands of sycamore and chestnut trees and past bunches of wild sunflowers and joe-pye weed. Paddlers enjoying the beauty of the river at this point will also enjoy floating under the lovely century-old covered bridge 0.5 miles after the NY 17 Bridge.

The creek then passes two access points maintained by the Department of Conservation for fishermen and canoeists at mile 2, and flows under the walkway leading to the Catskill Fly Fishing Center and Museum after 2.5 miles. Die-hard fly-fishermen or anyone interested in learning more about the sport of fly-fishing should definitely stop here. Check the center's Web site (**www.cffcm.net**) for more information about its incredible programs and exhibits.

The creek again passes under NY 17 1 mile past the museum and enters what I've found to be one of the most

Livingston Manor to Roscoe

Class	I+–II
Length	8 miles
Time	2 hours
Runnable Months	April–May (later depending on rainfall)
Hazards	Rapids
Portages	None
Rescue Access	Limited
Gauge	Visual, Web
Level	4.0
Gradient	16.0
Scenery	A–A+

beautiful sections of water between Livingston Manor and Roscoe. The water's depth drops dramatically here as the creek flows over and around large granite outcroppings covered in moss and lichens. Eastern hemlock trees and rhododendron provide enough cover to block out most of the sun, while ferns and other small ground cover have sprung up in between. My wife, Laura, having grown up upstate, has always treasured this kind of environment. In her words, "it smells like the outdoors to me." Those accustomed to hiking or paddling in the Adirondacks or other parts of northern New York will agree with my wife and appreciate the beauty of this particular part of the Willowemoc.

The creek then runs parallel to NY 17 for the next 2 miles before crossing under it once more. In fact, it will cross under NY 17 two additional times, once in 0.5 miles and again, 2 miles later, in the town of Roscoe.

MEAN WATER TEMPERATURES BY MONTH (Degrees Fahrenheit)					
	JAN	FEB	MAR	APR	MAY	JUN
MEAN	33	33	37	45	55	64
	JUL	AUG	SEP	OCT	NOV	DEC
MEAN	68	69	61	50	41	30

There, the Willowemoc joins the Beaver Kill and continues flowing to the west. A very convenient takeout is just 1,000 feet downstream of where the Willowemoc and Beaver Kill meet.

✧ **SHUTTLE DIRECTIONS** To get to the put-in at Livingston Manor, take NY 17 west to Exit 96 (Livingston Manor). Exit there and turn right onto County Road 81 (Debruce Road). Turn left at the bottom of the hill onto CR 178. Take CR 178, cross over Willowemoc Creek, and turn right onto CR 149 (Main Street). You should reach a stoplight in less than 0.25 miles. The entrance to Livingston Manor Park and the put-in will be on the right, immediately after the stoplight.

To get to the takeout in Roscoe, take NY 17 west to Exit 94 (Roscoe). Exit there and turn left onto CR 179. Continue west on CR 179 0.5 miles, passing through the town of Roscoe. After 0.5 miles you will reach CR 179A. Turn left onto CR 179A and you will reach the Department of Environmental Conservation boat launch area after 0.5 miles.

✧ **GAUGE** The best way to determine water levels on the Willowemoc is in person. The gauge nearest the Willowemoc is the Beaver Kill at Cooks Falls (visit **waterdata.usgs.gov/nwis/rt** to check online).

COVERED BRIDGE ON THE
WILLOWEMOC

32   HUDSON RIVER, PART ONE

The Hudson is perhaps New York's most well-known river, named after Henry Hudson, who explored it in the 1600s. It is fitting that New York's longest river begins flowing on New York's highest mountain, Mount Marcy. From there it flows south for 315 miles, passes through 17 counties, is fed by 24 tributaries, and eventually empties into New York Harbor between Manhattan and New Jersey.

The river can be separated into two sections by a dam found just a bit north of Albany in the town of Troy. The northern portion of the river is known as the Upper Hudson River Valley, while the southern portion is simply called the Hudson River Valley. This portion of the river can actually be considered an estuary acted on by both high and low tides. In fact, the Native Americans called the Hudson *Muh-he-kun-ne-tuk,* meaning "the river that flows both ways."

Since people first settled along its banks, the Hudson River has witnessed a great deal of history. The Hudson River Valley is where the Algonquin, Mohican, and Iroquois Indian tribes first developed their civilizations and where they thrived until Europeans, following in Henry Hudson's footsteps, colonized the area. The river valley is also where many strategic battles of the Revolutionary War were fought, where many of the nation's first steamships were used, and where the United States Military Academy at West Point was founded. The Hudson has also welcomed great numbers of immigrants at Ellis Island and helped create a more industrialized America when it became a part of the Erie Canal system.

Just as diverse as the river's history are the areas it flows through. The Hudson begins its life flowing slowly through the Adirondacks, eventually becoming both wider and faster while creating some first-class whitewater sections in the Upper Hudson River Valley. It joins the Erie Canal System in Troy, flows south through a series of locks, and enters the Hudson River Valley. Vast marshes and numerous islands abound in this part of the Hudson but eventually give way to rolling hills and farms in the Newburgh area. From there the river flows past Sleepy Hollow and other beautifully wooded towns that inspired some of Washington Irving's stories. The Hudson then passes the towering vertical cliffs of the Palisades, the skyscrapers of Manhattan, and the iconic Statue of Liberty, finally flowing into New York Harbor and the Atlantic Ocean.

The majestic Hudson does not flow without problems, however. Hazards such as pollution and overdevelopment plague its waters. Power plants, factories, and housing projects continuously colonize its shores. Overuse and abuse stretch its resources. And as if all this weren't enough, invasive species, including water chestnut, Eurasian watermilfoil, phragmites, and zebra mussels, threaten to take over river ecosystems, altering them forever. Thankfully, though, the New York State Department of Environmental

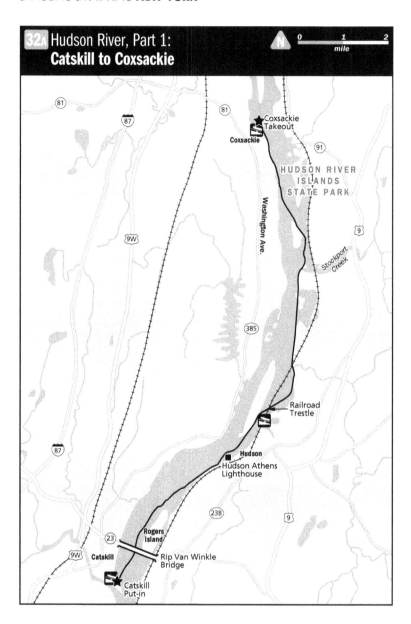

32A Hudson River, Part 1:
Catskill to Coxsackie

N   0   1   2
        mile

Coxsackie
Takeout

Coxsackie

HUDSON RIVER
ISLANDS
STATE PARK

Stockport Creek

Washington Ave.

Railroad
Trestle

Hudson

Hudson Athens
Lighthouse

Rogers
Island

Catskill   Rip Van Winkle
            Bridge

Catskill
Put-in

GPS Coordinates (UTM Zone 18T, WGS84)

Put-in:		Takeout:	
Easting	594528	Easting	599186
Northing	4674085	Northing	4689696
Latitude	N 42° 12' 47.6"	Latitude	N 42° 21' 11.6"
Longitude	W 73° 51' 17.2"	Longitude	W 73° 47' 44.5"

Conservation and conservation groups such as Scenic Hudson and the Hudson River Sloop *Clearwater* are constantly working to protect the river and the environment around it. Their respective Web sites, **www.scenichudson.org** and **www.clearwater.org**, tell of this struggle and what you can do to help.

Although the conservation groups' tasks may seem endless, great progress has been made. New construction projects have been fought off. Legal and illegal dumping has been limited and in many cases stopped altogether. Programs to control and remove invasives have been implemented throughout the entire river valley. Many riverside towns have undergone revitalization projects that have made themselves and the river more beautiful than ever. All of these improvements have helped to make the Hudson River a natural treasure to be enjoyed by all.

Various opportunities have recently been created in response to the river's new and improved reputation. Many farms and wineries have opened their doors to the public, museums and historic sites have developed exhibits showcasing the river's history, and tour companies have created hiking and cycling tours, all of which allow visitors a chance to experience the river's natural beauty. In addition, a large number of paddling groups have organized guided paddling tours throughout the river's length. While these guided tours are extremely popular, a large number of people also paddle the Hudson on their own. Recently, the Hudson River Greenway Water Trail was created to improve public access on the river.

Catskill to Coxsackie	**A**

Class	I
Length	12.2 miles
Time	4 hours
Runnable Months	Year-round
Hazards	Boat traffic
Portages	None
Rescue Access	Easy
Gauge	Web
Level	Tidal
Gradient	Tidal
Scenery	A–

The Web site **www.hrwa.org** identifies a total of 67 launch sites paddlers may use when exploring this trail. There is even a summer camp of sorts for adults wishing to paddle from Albany to Manhattan on the Hudson.

Note: Because the Hudson traverses so much of the state, I've included three run profiles later in the book in addition to the two that follow. For the Cold Spring to Peekskill run, see page 157; for the Yonkers to Tarrytown and West 79th Street to Brooklyn Bridge runs, see pages 163 and 166.

USGS Quadrangles
RUN 32A: HUDSON SOUTH (NY), HUDSON NORTH (NY);
RUN 32B: KINGSTON EAST (NY), SAUGERTIES (NY)

DESCRIPTION Although tides affect the Hudson River as far north as Troy, their effect diminishes the farther one travels from the Atlantic Ocean. As a result, paddlers may head either north or south on the river in the Catskills region, regardless of incoming or outgoing tides. A great place to start a trip heading north is in the town of Catskill at a public park named Dutchman's Landing. There's free parking, a convenient boat ramp, bathrooms, a playground, and a snack bar, making this an ideal put-in spot.

Paddlers taking to the river in Catskill will find themselves just south of the Rip Van Winkle Bridge and Rogers Island. Shallow water and large clusters of spatterdock (yellow pond lily) lurk near the southern tip of the island and may prevent paddlers from reaching the east side, especially during low tide. However, the west side of the island is pristine and beautiful, with views of elm, maple, oak, and birch groves broken up by the occasional

clearing. These spots are perfect for landing boats and allowing access into the interior of Rogers Island.

The northern tip of Rogers Island lies 2 miles beyond the Rip Van Winkle Bridge. Anyone paddling there during late spring or summer months will definitely encounter the scourge of the Hudson River, the water chestnut. Native to Europe and Asia, this invasive aquatic plant has begun to spread throughout the Hudson River Valley, altering ecosystems and outcompeting native species for oxygen and sunlight. Water chestnut favors slow-moving water, taking root and spreading uncontrollably. In fact, despite being nonnative, it is the second most abundant plant in the Hudson River, only

HUDSON-ATHENS LIGHTHOUSE

MEAN WATER TEMPERATURES BY MONTH (Degrees Fahrenheit)					
	JAN	FEB	MAR	APR	MAY	JUN
MEAN	34	34	37	46	59	70
	JUL	AUG	SEP	OCT	NOV	DEC
MEAN	75	76	72	61	48	37

slightly less common than the native water celery.

Paddlers need only cruise 2 miles past Rogers Island to reach the small town of Hudson. Well known as a whaling port during the 18th and 19th centuries, Hudson soon became infamous as a center for gambling and other nefarious pastimes. The town has recently undergone a tremendous transformation, though, and is now a quaint, charming riverside hamlet worth spending a day or a weekend in. Hudson also boasts a boat ramp, which may be of great interest to paddlers looking to explore the Middle Ground Flats or the two bays directly to the north.

Paddlers may pass under the small railroad overpasses 0.5 miles and 1 mile north of the Hudson boat ramp to gain access to these bays. Cattail, pickerelweed, spatterdock, and water chestnut seem to grow there as far as the eye can see. I was also lucky enough to see four bald eagles the last time I paddled these bays. Wildlife is easy to find in the abundance of small channels and side creeks. Many of these channels have dead ends, however, so care should be used when exploring them. I actually got lost going down one such dead end on the same day I saw the bald eagles. Unable to turn around or retrace my steps, I was forced to wade through knee-deep mud to the railroad

right-of-way and drag my boat over the tracks back to the river—obviously neither a very safe nor a highly recommended thing to do.

There is another river access point on Stockport Creek, just upriver of the northern bay. Many kayakers choose to enter the water there, just as many tour companies begin their guided trips there. The benefit is its proximity to Hudson River Islands State Park. This beautiful park is only accessible by boat, making it the perfect getaway spot for paddlers. It boasts hiking trails, campsites, and picnic areas, nestled among forests of red and silver maple, birch, and cottonwood trees. It seems a shame that this gem of a park is only open from Memorial Day to Columbus Day.

The town of Coxsackie and its boat ramp lie 1 mile north of Hudson River Islands State Park. Paddlers can find this ramp in the Coxsackie Riverside Park, a very convenient spot with bathrooms, playground, beach, ample parking, and close proximity to the New York State Thruway.

✧ **SHUTTLE DIRECTIONS** To get to the put-in at the town of Catskill, take the New York State Thruway (Interstate 87) to Exit 21. Follow this exit east toward Catskill. The exit ramp will curve around to the south and intersect County Road 23B at a fork. Take the left fork onto CR 23B and follow it south 3 miles. After 3 miles you will see a sign on your left for Dutchman's Landing, a waterfront park. There you'll find ample parking and a boat ramp.

To get to the takeout in the town of Coxsackie, pick up NY 385 in Catskill and head north 10 miles. Turn right onto Ely Street and continue north 0.75 miles. Turn left onto Mansion Street and make a quick right onto Betke Boulevard. Coxsackie Riverside Park will be on your left.

✧ **GAUGE** The best way to determine water levels is in person. You may also check the currents and tide levels at **tidesandcurrents.noaa.gov**. However, the river is usually runnable year-round.

DESCRIPTION Paddlers using the Kingston Point Park put-in will enter the water about 3.5 miles south of the Kingston–Rhinecliff Bridge and 6 miles south of the Tivoli Bays. The river at this point is pretty wide (1 mile across) with a fair amount of boat traffic. In fact, the last time I happened to be paddling this section of the Hudson there was a large bass-fishing tournament going on. Anyone who's shared a stretch of water with bass boats knows how exciting, yet nerve-wracking, it can be. Care should

be taken any time the marked boat channel is crossed, whether or not a tournament is being held.

After paddling less than a mile up the western side of the river, paddlers will be able to see the remains of the Hudson Cement Company, a plant built in the 1950s to manufacture bricks and cement. Its silos, a few large buildings, dozens of abandoned concrete slabs, and one broken-up barge are clearly visible onshore. One-half mile farther north lies Robert E. Post County Park. This park packs a lot of amenities into a small space, including a beach and boat launch. Charles Rider Town Park, 1 additional mile upstream, provides paddlers with many of the same conveniences. A third park, named Ulster Landing, is 3 miles farther up. Like the previous two, this park boasts a beach perfect for landing a boat or taking a break from paddling.

The beautiful Tivoli Bays Wildlife Management Area is just 1 mile north of Ulster Landing on the opposite (eastern) shore. This amazing piece of land contains a good deal of paddle-able water, more than 4 miles of scenic nature trails, and ample parking for visitors. There is even a canoe/kayak launch located in the back marsh for anyone wishing to explore the area's two bays without having to paddle on the Hudson. Those coming off the Hudson can pass under any one of five railroad trestles that lead to both South and North bays.

While the Tivoli Bays are located in a beautiful area, paddlers should be forewarned. Unfortunately, like many places along the Hudson River, South

B Kingston to Saugerties

Class	I
Length	12.1 miles
Time	4–5 hours
Runnable Months	Year-round
Hazards	Boat traffic, strong currents
Portages	None
Rescue Access	Easy
Gauge	Visual, Web
Level	Tidal
Gradient	Tidal
Scenery	A

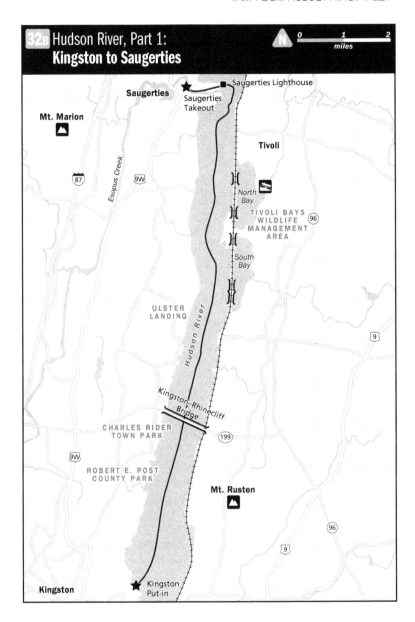

32B Hudson River, Part 1:
Kingston to Saugerties

GPS Coordinates (UTM Zone 18T, WGS84)

Put-in:		**Takeout:**	
Easting	585789	Easting	587268
Northing	4642608	Northing	4658250
Latitude	N 41° 55' 50.80"	Latitude	N 42° 04' 17.30"
Longitude	W 73° 57' 54.90"	Longitude	W 73° 56' 42.28"

MEAN WATER TEMPERATURES BY MONTH (Degrees Fahrenheit)					
JAN	FEB	MAR	APR	MAY	JUN
MEAN 34	34	37	46	59	70
JUL	AUG	SEP	OCT	NOV	DEC
MEAN 75	76	72	61	48	37

Bay becomes inundated with water chestnut during the warm summer months. Native to Europe and Asia, this invasive aquatic plant has begun to spread throughout the Hudson River Valley, altering ecosystems and outcompeting native species for oxygen and sunlight. In fact, I last visited Tivoli in early September and found South Bay to be impenetrable due to the chestnut growth. Thankfully, North Bay usually does not succumb to such an invasion.

Passing under the trestles north of Cruger Island brings paddlers into North Bay, a wild and beautiful marsh dominated by spatterdock, narrow-leaf cattail, and pickerelweed. Great blue herons, egrets, and red-winged blackbirds are found there as well. Exploring the many channels, mazes, and dead ends that exist in the marsh can take hours and is best done two hours or so before high tide.

After leaving the Tivoli Bays, paddlers must head 2 more miles upstream before reaching Esopus Creek.

The mouth of the creek lies between a large brown house with a blue roof and the Saugerties Lighthouse, on the western side of the river. From there, the takeout is only 1 mile upstream at the Saugerties Waterfront Park.

◌ **SHUTTLE DIRECTIONS** To get to the put-in at Kingston, take Interstate 87 to Exit 19 and follow the signs for Interstate 587. Stay on I-587 for 1.25 miles, until it intersects with NY 32. Bear left at this point onto Broadway and continue east for another mile. Turn left onto Delaware Avenue, continuing to head east. The entrance to Kingston Point Park and its boat ramp will be found 1.5 miles later.

To get to the takeout in Saugerties, head back west on Delaware Avenue 1.25 miles, until you reach US 9W. Head north on US 9W 1 mile, but turn right onto NY 32 when it intersects US 9W. After heading north 8 miles, SR 32 joins US 9W once again. Continue north on US 9W 1.7 miles and turn right onto East Bridge Street. The takeout is in the Saugerties Waterfront Park, 0.25 miles down East Bridge Street.

◌ **GAUGE** The best way to determine water levels is in person. You may also check the currents and tide levels at **tidesandcurrents.noaa.gov**. However, the river is usually runnable year-round.

33 WALLKILL RIVER

New Paltz to
Interstate 87

Class	I
Length	8.3 miles
Time	2.5 hours
Runnable Months	April–Oct.
Hazards	None
Portages	None
Rescue Access	Easy
Gauge	Web, visual
Level	2.5–3
Gradient	0.7
Scenery	A

For many, the Wallkill River is a favorite place to paddle because of its beautiful scenery, proximity to New York City, and miles of navigable water. It starts at Lake Mohawk in Sparta, New Jersey, and flows north for 96 miles before combining with Rondout Creek and emptying into the Hudson River. On its way it crosses a state line, passes through a national wildlife refuge, is diverted for agricultural uses, backs up behind two dams, and, most unusual, empties into a creek (the Rondout). In short, the Wallkill leads a varied life.

Native Americans named the river *Twischsawkin*, or "the land where plums abound"; later on, Dutch settlers renamed it the Waal Kill, in honor of the Waal River in their homeland (*kill* means "stream"). It was these settlers who first realized the Wallkill's value in irrigating their farms and powering their mills. In fact, the town of Walden is named after Jacob Walden, who built the first mill on the river. This mill stood close to where the dam in Walden is located today.

Most of the Wallkill is paddleable. However, one of the best spots to enter the water is just downstream of the Walden dam, in the town of Wallkill. From there, canoers and kayakers can travel the full 24 miles to Rondout Creek or break the trip into shorter sections—Wallkill to New Paltz, for example. Either way, the Wallkill River is a pleasure to paddle.

USGS Quadrangles WALDEN (NY), GARDINER (NY), CLINTONDALE (NY), AND ROSENDALE (NY)

DESCRIPTION The lower section of the Wallkill River provides paddlers with miles of flat, calm water, unlike the small rapids on the upper section of the Wallkill. In fact, because it flows so slowly, the river can be paddled either upstream or down from New Paltz. Paddlers can head upstream for about 3 miles or so before turning back, whereas 8 miles of river lie before them downstream.

After the put-in, the Wallkill flows behind some of the quaint but eclectic shops of New Paltz on its eastern bank and past farmland on its western bank. Some rough concrete steps can be found on the eastern bank after almost a mile of paddling, leading to the New Paltz Community Gardens. These beautiful flower and vegetable gardens are worth checking out. In addition, public restrooms are available for those who did not plan ahead.

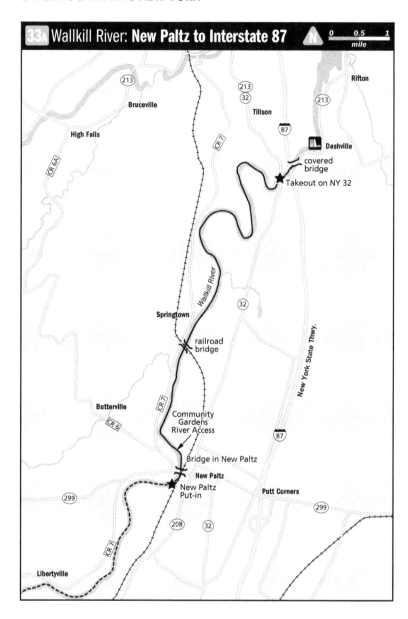

33A Wallkill River: **New Paltz to Interstate 87**

GPS Coordinates (UTM Zone 18T, WGS84)

Put-in:		Takeout:	
Easting	575363	Easting	578242
Northing	4621750	Northing	4629659
Latitude	N 41° 44' 38.4"	Latitude	N 41° 48' 53.8"
Longitude	W 74° 05' 37.1"	Longitude	W 74° 03' 28.7"

SHAWANGUNK MOUNTAINS

As the Wallkill continues flowing north, paddlers won't be able to miss the many trees growing down to the water's edge. While elm, silver maple, hickory, and oak trees are the most common species seen, observant paddlers may notice the occasional European linden tree or Northern catalpa tree in between. They may also notice many small side creeks on either side of the river worth checking out. While most of these creeks dead-end, paddlers can spend hours exploring their reaches during periods of high water.

The lower Wallkill remains wild and scenic for much of its length, with occasional views of the beautiful Shawangunk Mountains. Houses begin to pop up after 5 miles of paddling,

though, and the river begins to open up a bit as well. Most of the trees that grew down to the water's edge are gone by mile 6, and roads begin to come ever closer to the river's banks. The takeout spot can be found at mile 8 in a small park on the eastern bank of the river, just past the bridge on NY 32. Paddlers may exit the water there or head a bit downstream to the covered bridge. Beyond that bridge looms a dam, however, preventing further travel on the Wallkill.

✧ **SHUTTLE DIRECTIONS** To get to the put-in at New Paltz, take Interstate 87 to Exit 18 (New Paltz). Once you're past the tolls, the exit ramp will end at an intersection with NY 299 (Main

MEAN WATER TEMPERATURES BY MONTH (Degrees Fahrenheit)					
	JAN	FEB	MAR	APR	MAY	JUN
MEAN	N/A	N/A	N/A	51	61	72
	JUL	AUG	SEP	OCT	NOV	DEC
MEAN	75	73	67	52	N/A	N/A

Street). Turn left onto Main Street, head west down the hill 0.75 miles, and you will enter the town of New Paltz. Continue west through the town, heading straight for the bridge crossing the Wallkill River. Do not cross it, though. Instead, turn left before the bridge onto Water Street. You will reach Sojourner Truth Park and its boat launch in 0.4 miles.

To get to the takeout on NY 32, follow the directions to the town of New Paltz and head for the river again. However, rather than turning left onto Water Street, you should turn right a bit earlier onto NY 32 (North Chestnut Street). Head north 5 miles until you reach a fork in the road where NY 32

B Wallkill to New Paltz

Class	II
Length	13.3 miles
Time	4 hours
Runnable Months	April–Oct.
Hazards	Rapids
Portages	None
Rescue Access	Somewhat easy
Gauge	Web, visual
Level	2.5–3
Gradient	4.9
Scenery	A

continues north but NY 213 heads east. Head to the right and the takeout will be located in the small park on the left.

✧ **GAUGE** The river gauge most useful for determining water levels is the Wallkill River at Gardiner (visit **waterdata.usgs.gov/nwis/rt** to check online). Water levels can also be easily determined in person.

33B DESCRIPTION Although some paddlers may choose to begin their trip on the Wallkill River in the town of Walden, an excellent put-in spot exists in the town of Wallkill, just north of the dam off CR 18. A small dirt clearing on the side of the road, just five feet from the river's western bank, is big enough for a car or two. The Wallkill is about 100 feet wide at this point and is bordered mostly by houses and private property. Most of the river's banks there are dominated by a small plant called lizard's tail, easily identified by its heart-shaped leaves, orangelike scent, and long, narrow spikes resembling a lizard's tail.

Paddlers will face a fun set of light rapids soon after hitting the water in Wallkill. While not very large, the rapids do require your attention. In addition, a few submerged logs and rocks may impede progress on the river during times of very low water levels. Nevertheless, these obstacles can provide you with a chance to brush up on your whitewater skills and get your trip off to an exciting start.

Once past the faster moving water, paddlers can sit back a bit and enjoy the beautiful scenery on the slower sections of the river. Most of

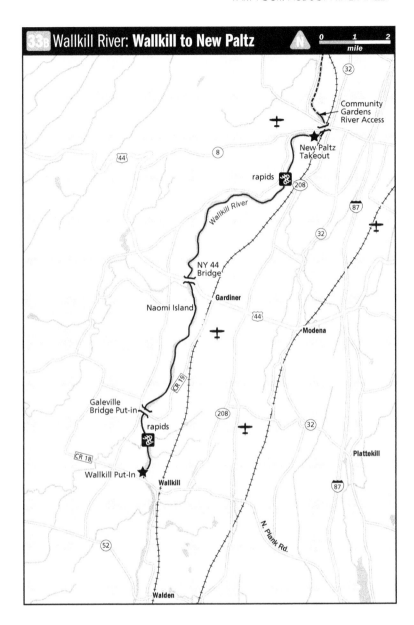

33B Wallkill River: **Wallkill to New Paltz**

GPS Coordinates (UTM Zone 18T, WGS84)

Put-in:		Takeout:	
Easting	567520	Easting	575363
Northing	4606821	Northing	4621750
Latitude	N 41° 36' 36.9"	Latitude	N 41° 44' 38.4"
Longitude	W 74° 11' 22.7"	Longitude	74° 05' 37.1"

the houses have been passed at this point, and the more natural side of the Wallkill starts to show itself. Paddlers skirting the shore may find themselves flushing wood ducks hiding in the brush or stirring up catfish resting on the muddy river bottom. In fact, many people take to the Wallkill to reel in these catfish, as well as the bass and walleye that call the river home. Still others enjoy watching the aerial antics of cedar waxwings and belted kingfishers.

A small island sits in the center of the river about 1 mile downriver of the put-in, followed by the Galeville Bridge at mile 2. There is access to the river from County Road 19 on the east side of this bridge, although there is not much room for parking. Paddlers putting in here should get dropped off by a friend instead. Some fairly large rocks rise up from the river bottom about 1 mile past the Galeville Bridge,

accompanied by another stretch of light whitewater. Just as before, these rapids are fairly easy to negotiate but can keep paddlers on their toes.

Observant paddlers may be able to catch glimpses of the Shawangunk Mountain Ridge on their left soon after passing under the Galeville Bridge. The "Gunks" have long been a favorite playground of mine, and my heart quickens every time I see the bare cliffs or Skytop Tower. The view from the Wallkill is superb on clear days and begs for a picture stop or two.

A fairly large island, Naomi Island, will appear 6 miles downriver of Wallkill, and not a moment too soon. A very large and oftentimes crowded RV campground lies on the western riverbank, intruding on the natural beauty of the river. However, paddling around the eastern side of Naomi Island skirts most of the noise and distractions from this eyesore.

GREAT BLUE HERON ON THE WALLKILL

The NY 44 Bridge crosses the Wallkill about 0.5 miles past Naomi Island, marking the approximate halfway point of the trip. Some small, bubbling rapids churn up the water immediately after the bridge but soon give way to flatter water. However, one final whitewater section must be paddled before you reach the takeout in New Paltz. It is similar to the earlier sections and does not require a great deal of maneuvering. Care should be exercised, though, just as before. The takeout can be found after about 13 miles of paddling, where the town of New Paltz has constructed a boat launch in its beautiful Sojourner Truth Park.

✧ **SHUTTLE DIRECTIONS** To get to the put-in at Wallkill, take Interstate 84 to Exit 5N (NY 208). Head north on NY 208 for 4 miles, and you will be in the town of Walden. Continue north an additional 3.5 miles to the town of Wallkill. Once here you will reach

CR 18. Turn left onto CR 18 heading west, cross over the Wallkill River, and follow the road to the right. You will see a small dirt turnoff 0.25 miles up the road after crossing the river. You may leave your car there if there is room. If not, drop off your boat and park in Wallkill.

To get to the takeout in New Paltz, head north on NY 208 from Wallkill. Twelve miles later, you will enter the town of New Paltz and reach NY 299. Turn left onto NY 299, heading toward the river. Do not cross it, though. Instead, turn left just before the bridge onto Water Street. You will reach Sojourner Truth Park and its boat launch in 0.4 miles.

✧ **GAUGE** The river gauge most useful for determining water levels is the Wallkill River at Gardiner (visit **waterdata.usgs.gov/nwis/rt** to check online). Water levels can also be easily determined in person.

34 HUDSON RIVER, PART TWO

Although the entire area around Cold Spring is stunning, two landmarks along this section of the Hudson stand out as exceptionally beautiful: the United States Military Academy at West Point and the mountain named Crows Nest. West Point and its impressive fortlike structures stand overlooking the river just beyond Constitution Island, while Crows Nest looms large on the horizon directly across the river.

These two views are visually pleasing throughout the year and are truly exceptional during autumn months.

USGS Quadrangles PEEKSKILL (NY), WEST POINT (NY)

DESCRIPTION The Constitution Marsh area is probably one of the most beautiful stretches of water on the Hudson River. It is possible to launch canoes and kayaks from the Audubon Nature Sanctuary in Constitution Marsh, but it is not recommended. Doing so obliges boaters to carry their boats the 0.5 miles from the parking

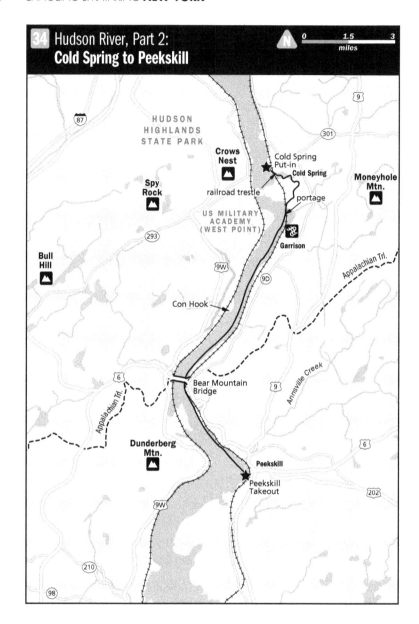

34 Hudson River, Part 2:
Cold Spring to Peekskill

0   1.5   3
miles

HUDSON
HIGHLANDS
STATE PARK

Crows
Nest

Cold Spring
Put-in

Cold Spring

Moneyhole
Mtn.

Spy
Rock

railroad trestle

portage

US MILITARY
ACADEMY
(WEST POINT)

Garrison

Bull
Hill

Appalachian Trl.

Con Hook

Annsville Creek

Bear Mountain
Bridge

Dunderberg
Mtn.

Appalachian Trl.

Peekskill

Peekskill
Takeout

GPS Coordinates (UTM Zone 18T, WGS84)

Put-in:		Takeout:	
Easting	587061	Easting	589454
Northing	4585263	Northing	4571143
Latitude	N 41° 24' 51.1"	Latitude	N 41° 17' 12.4"
Longitude	W 73° 57' 29.8"	Longitude	W 73° 55' 54.2"

lot to the water, which can be too shal-low to even float a boat. A much better spot to launch from is in the town of Cold Spring. A boat launch adjacent to the town's train station puts paddlers on the river just a bit north of Consti-tution Island and its marsh.

Access to Constitution Marsh is possible by paddling under the rail-road trestle to the southeast of the boat ramp. The fairly wide-open body of water on the other side of this trestle is named Foundry Cove. As expected from its name, this cove was the loca-tion of a large military foundry during the Civil War. In fact, it supplied the majority of cannons and other artillery pieces for the Union Army. Today it has a more environmentally friendly use, at least for the many species of waterfowl that enjoy its nature-preserve designation and boaters who appreciate its beauty.

Directly south of Foundry Cove lies Constitution Island. As its name implies, this island played a fairly large part in American history. It is perhaps best known as the eastern anchoring point for the "Great Chain" during the American Revolution. This chain, strung across the river from West Point to Constitution Island, was set up to stop British warships and put them within easy reach of the artillery at West Point. Apparently the British Navy feared this trap enough that they never attempted to run the blockade. As a result, the strength of the chain's links was never tested. One of the links now rests in the West Point Military Museum, though. The island, or at least one of its previous inhabitants, is also famous, though not for anything

Cold Spring to Peekskill	
Class	I
Length	13.5 miles
Time	4–5 hours
Runnable Months	Year-round
Hazards	Boatt raffic, strong currents
Portages	I
Rescue Access	Easy
Gauge	Visual, Web
Level	Tidal
Gradient	Tidal
Scenery	A+

war-related. Anna Warner, who lived on the island until her death in 1915, wrote the lyrics to the well-known children's hymn "Jesus Loves Me."

Once through Foundry Cove and around Constitution Island, you will enter the marsh proper. There you will find acres upon acres of cattails grow-ing tall, with the smaller arrow arum growing at their base. With a keen eye you may also spot muskrat dens scat-tered throughout the marsh. Muskrats build these domelike structures out of reeds when there are no steep, muddy banks into which they can burrow. While I didn't see any muskrats the last time I paddled the marsh, I was able to find three or four of their dens.

It is quite easy to spend hours exploring the maze of channels within Constitution Marsh. The variety of birdlife calling it home (swans, geese, mallards, American black ducks, mer-gansers, kingfishers, and so on) is cer-tainly astounding. The mountains in the distance are incredibly impressive.

KAYAKING NEAR WEST POINT

The quiet is welcoming. There is even a waterfall that you can paddle right up to, supposedly anyway. I say "supposedly" because I've never seen it. I have read of it, and I met a fellow paddler in the marsh who gave me somewhat questionable directions to it. Nevertheless, its location still eludes me. I will divulge all that I know for anyone interested in seeking this waterfall: it is found in the southeasternmost corner of the marsh, at the end of a channel that is hidden behind a large stand of phragmites.

A very short portage is needed to leave the southern part of the marsh, because the railroad trestle there hangs too low to allow paddling underneath. When asked if the water is ever low enough for paddling, a local paddler replied that he has never seen it.

However, this was the same local who led me astray in my waterfall hunt. Thus, it may be possible to fit under the bridge, perhaps during extreme low tides. I recommend simply crossing over the right-of-way just to the right of the bridge, though, where a gentle slope comes out of and leads back into the water.

Paddlers can continue their trip south once back on the water and marvel at the West Point campus directly across the river. Although it currently serves as a military academy, West Point was originally built as an American fort during the Revolutionary War. In fact, it is the oldest continuously occupied fort in American history.

The quaint town of Garrison lies just 0.5 miles south of West Point on the east side of the river and can provide paddlers with a welcome rest stop if needed. The eastern shoreline south of Garrison is mostly wild, with little in the way of civilization except for a few scattered houses and the Metro North railroad tracks that run parallel to the river. The western shore is more developed, lined with dozens of homes, private docks, and some railroad tracks of its own. It also sports a small piece of land named Con Hook, located 3 miles south of West Point. Maps show Con Hook to be firmly attached to the mainland, but in reality it is only tenuously attached by a small finger of marshland. Nevertheless, it's an interesting place to check out by kayak.

The river turns to the east and passes under the Bear Mountain Bridge after 10 miles, with the city of Peekskill in the distance. Paddling an additional 2.5 miles past the bridge will bring boaters to Annsville Creek. The creek is a very popular paddling destination in itself and boasts its own kayaking center. Its Web site, **www .atlantickayaktours.com**, provides a wealth of information about the area, guided tours, hours, rates, and so on. Access to Annsville Creek and the kayaking center can be gained by paddling under a railroad trestle. The takeout at Peekskill Landing is only 0.5 miles beyond Annsville Creek. This beautiful park contains a huge playground, some bathrooms, picnic tables, a beach, and a boat ramp. Look for it next to the Peekskill Train Station.

✧ **SHUTTLE DIRECTIONS** To get to the put-in at Cold Spring, take the Palisades Interstate Parkway north to US 6 and the Bear Mountain Bridge. Cross over the Hudson and turn left onto NY 9D once on the eastern side of the river. Head north on NY 9D for 8.5 miles into the town of Cold Spring. Turn left onto Wall Street, take your first right onto Furnace Street, and finally take the first left onto Main Street. Main Street will end after 0.25 miles, at which point you should turn left onto Market Street, following the signs for the train station and the town boat launch.

To get to the takeout in Peekskill, pick up NY 301 in Cold Spring and head north 2.5 miles until you reach US 9. Take US 9 south for 10.5 miles and exit onto Main Street (US 6) in Peekskill. Take Main Street to North Water Street and turn left. North Water Street will lead directly to Peekskill Landing and its boat ramp.

✧ **GAUGE** You may check water levels in person (the best method) or online at **tidesandcurrents.noaa.gov**. However, the river is usually runnable year-round.

MEAN WATER TEMPERATURES BY MONTH (Degrees Fahrenheit)					
	JAN	FEB	MAR	APR	MAY	JUN
MEAN	34	34	37	46	59	70
	JUL	AUG	SEP	OCT	NOV	DEC
MEAN	75	76	72	61	48	37

SOUTHEASTERN NEW YORK–LONG ISLAND

35 HUDSON RIVER, PART THREE

After flowing through the fjordlike Hudson River Valley south of Albany, the Hudson River enters an area much more urbanized as it nears its finish in New York Harbor. While such environments do not normally provide much of a draw, this is not so in the case of the Hudson. Instead, these locales have become extremely popular paddling destinations, offering opportunities to view the New York City region from a unique perspective—the water.

One of the most dramatic views in this portion of the state lies a bit south of the Tappan Zee Bridge, as the Hudson flows past the 200-million-year-old cliffs of the Palisades. These sheer rock walls run about 20 miles down the western bank of the Hudson and can only be truly appreciated from a boat on the river. Likewise, the world-famous New York City skyline is of another class altogether when seen from a boat on the Hudson.

Those wishing to explore the lower Hudson River for themselves need only look to the New York City Parks Department for help. Its water trail, containing access sites across the entire metropolitan area, features seven locations along the river where boats can be launched; access requires the purchase of an inexpensive annual permit. More information and an excellent interactive map are available at the department's Web site, **www.nycgovparks.org/sub_things_to_do/facilities/kayak**.

USGS Quadrangles
Run 35A: Mount Vernon (NY), Flushing (NY), Central Park (NY);
Run 35B: Central Park (NY), Weehawken (NJ), Jersey City (NJ/NY)

DESCRIPTION The Hudson River is greatly affected by tides in its lower sections, making it possible for paddlers to head either upstream or down, depending on conditions. The best place to put in near the Palisades section of

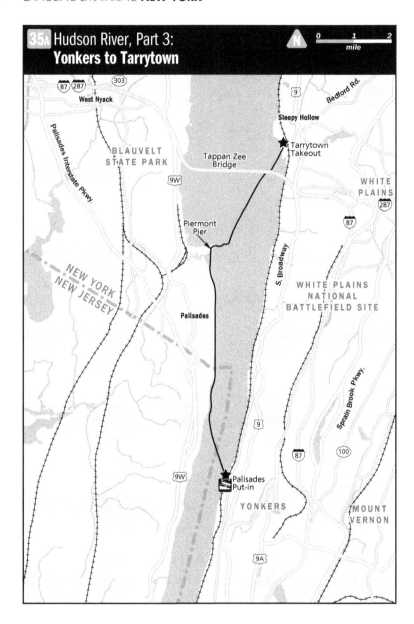

35A Hudson River, Part 3:
Yonkers to Tarrytown

GPS Coordinates (UTM Zone 18T, WGS84)

Put-in:		**Takeout:**	
Easting	592793	Easting	594990
Northing	4534526	Northing	4547936
Latitude	N 40° 57' 23.8"	Latitude	N 41° 04' 37.7"
Longitude	W 73° 53' 50.6"	Longitude	W 73° 52' 09.2"

the river with an incoming tide is at the town boat ramp in Kennedy Marina Park in Yonkers. This ramp puts paddlers on the river directly across from the New Jersey shoreline, Palisades Interstate Park, and the dramatic Palisades cliffs for a small ($5) fee.

It is hard to ignore the amazing vertical rise of the Palisades when on the water. These cliffs seem to rise directly from the Hudson's waters, towering more than 500 feet in some places. In fact, their Native American name, *We-awk-en*, means "rocks that look like rows of trees." Although they have been eroded in spots, quarried for rocks and gravel, and altered for roads and bridges, the Palisades still remain an impressive sight. Thankfully, the National Park Service designated them a National Natural Landmark in 1983, protecting them for generations to come.

The New York side of the Hudson near Yonkers is very developed, with boatyards, industrial plants, and apartment buildings taking up every inch of available space. It is only a 1-mile paddle across the river to the New Jersey side, though, where the riverside is more pristine in nature. Both the George Washington Bridge and the Tappan Zee Bridge are visible from this vantage point to the south and north, respectively. Also visible to the north is the pier at Piermont, about

Yonkers to Tarrytown

Class	I
Length	9.4 miles
Time	2.5 hours
Runnable Months	Year-round
Hazards	Boat traffic
Portages	None
Rescue Access	Limited
Gauge	Visual, Web
Level	Tidal
Gradient	Tidal
Scenery	B+

2.5 miles from the takeout in Tarrytown. The land on the western side of the Hudson is part of the Palisades Interstate Park, where a vast array of hiking trails, cycling paths, and picnic areas exist. While accessing this park from the water is a bit tough, it is well worth visiting by car or foot.

The sheer rock walls of the Palisades are truly amazing to behold. Their geologic history is just as amazing. The cliffs were formed about 200 million years ago, when molten magma rose upward through the earth's crust and intruded into the sandstone that was originally in the area. After erosion from wind and rain, the sandstone was completely removed, leaving the harder rock behind in the large columnlike formations we know today.

In between these dramatic cliffs and the river live an abundance of oak, maple, and locust trees, with some fairly large stands of phragmites growing everywhere else. The cliffs drop down to sea level after 3 miles of paddling, marking the New Jersey–New York state

MEAN WATER TEMPERATURES BY MONTH (Degrees Fahrenheit)					
	JAN	FEB	MAR	APR	MAY	JUN
MEAN	34	34	37	46	59	70
	JUL	AUG	SEP	OCT	NOV	DEC
MEAN	75	76	72	61	48	37

line and the location of Tallman Mountain State Park. Paddling 1 mile farther north leads to an extensive freshwater marsh in this state park. Numerous channels and small coves can be found everywhere in this marsh, begging paddlers to explore their depths. I always make it a point to stop and play here whenever I have the time.

The Piermont pier lies immediately to the north of the large marsh, sticking out a few hundred feet into the Hudson. Its location is perfect for a rest stop, lunch break, or midafternoon swim. The pier is often used by fishermen as well as boaters, though, so keep an eye out for fishing lines and flying lures. Takeouts exist north of Piermont on the western side of the river in the town of Nyack and again in Upper Nyack in Nyack Beach State Park. A third takeout can be found in Tarrytown at the Tarrytown Marina. This marina is on the eastern side of the river, just north of the Tappan Zee Bridge. Its sloped, rocky landing is easy to see just to the south of the yellow-colored condos and small, white lighthouse. There is four-hour parking in the marina lot, which is more than enough time for car shuttling and completing a 9- or 10-mile paddle.

✧ **SHUTTLE DIRECTIONS** To get to the put-in at Yonkers, take the Saw Mill River Parkway (NY 9A) to Exit 9 (Executive Boulevard). Take Executive Boulevard west until it ends in 1 mile. Turn left at this intersection onto US 9 (North Broadway). Take North Broadway south, taking your first right onto Odell Avenue. Odell Avenue will end at Warburton Avenue in 0.75 miles.

Turn left onto Warburton Avenue at this point. You will see a sign for the Hudson River Museum after 1.25 miles. Follow the sign to John F. Kennedy Memorial Drive, where you should turn right. Go down the hill and past the school, and you will reach the John F. Kennedy Memorial Park. The boat ramp is located on the far northern end of this park, next to the fire station.

To get to the takeout in Tarrytown, take US 9 north from Yonkers 9 miles to the town of Tarrytown. Turn left onto Wildey Street, head west 0.3 miles, and turn left once again onto River Plaza. Head south but take the first right turn onto Railroad Avenue. Take the quick left onto West Main Street and head south 500 feet before continuing right on West Main Street. There is free four-hour parking along the road near the water.

✧ **GAUGE** The best way to determine water levels is in person. You may also check the currents and tide levels at **tidesandcurrents.noaa.gov**. However, the river is usually runnable year-round.

35B **DESCRIPTION** Kayaking has become a very popular activity around Manhattan Island in recent years. Although water access around the city is limited, the New York City Water Trail was created recently to make paddling in this area much easier. A total of 30 sites in each of the city's five boroughs are included in the trail and can be found on an interactive map at **www .nycgovparks.org/facilities/kayak**. The Downtown Boathouse (**www.downtown boathouse.org**) operates a few of these sites around the island. The New York

The Palisades

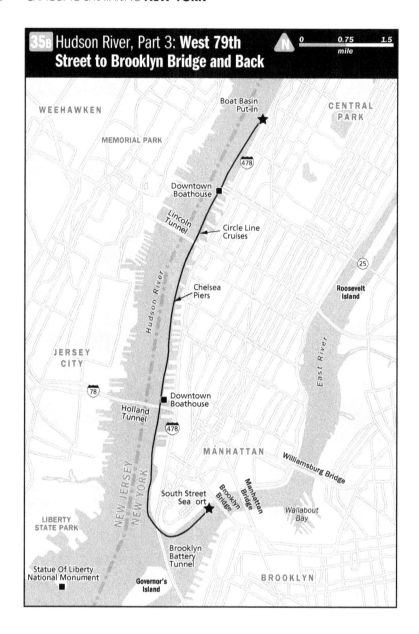

GPS Coordinates (UTM Zone 18T, WGS84)

Put-in:		**Takeout:**	
Easting	585657	Easting	5855657
Northing	4515574	Northing	4515574
Latitude	N 40° 47' 12.1"	Latitude	N 40° 47' 12.1"
Longitude	W 73° 59' 05.2"	Longitude	W 73° 59' 05.2"

City Parks Department also maintains a few, such as the launch at the West 79th Street Boat Basin. The Boat Basin's amenities also include inexpensive parking and kayak-storage facilities for paddlers unable to store their boats in their tiny Manhattan apartments. In addition to all of these benefits, the Boat Basin puts paddlers on the Hudson, poised perfectly for a trip north toward the George Washington Bridge and the New York–New Jersey Palisades. It is also useful for starting a trip south toward Battery Park, the Statue of Liberty, or the Brooklyn Bridge. An annual permit from the parks department is all you need to launch there. These permits, available at **www.nycgovparks.org**, cost $15.

Upon entering the water at the 79th Street Boat Basin, paddlers will be faced with a decision: whether to head north toward the George Washington Bridge or south toward the Statue of Liberty and Brooklyn. I believe the trip south affords better views and experiences than heading north. Keep in mind that the Hudson River is greatly affected by tides as it flows past Manhattan. It is best to travel south during the last hour of the outgoing tide. This allows boaters to paddle easily to the southern tip of the island, rest during the slack tide, and return north with the newly changed incoming tide.

W. 79th St. to Brooklyn Bridge and Back B

Class	I
Length	16 miles (round-trip)
Time	4 hours
Runnable Months	Year-round
Hazards	Boatt raffic, currents
Portages	None
Rescue Access	Limited
Gauge	Visual, Web
Level	Tidal
Gradient	Tidal
Scenery	A

Heading south, paddlers will likely pass dozens of joggers and dog walkers on the riverside path, tugboats pushing or pulling cargo ships in the boat channel, and an occasional cruise ship or two heading upriver. The remains of an old pier jut out 1 mile south of the boat basin, as does a large gray building used by the sanitation department. Beyond those structures, numerous concrete or wood piers jut out into the Hudson. These piers are all numbered, easily identifying them and one's progress on the river. For example, the aircraft carrier *Intrepid* is docked at Pier 86, the famous Circle Line cruise ships board at Pier 83, the historic lightship *Frying Pan* floats patiently at Pier 63, and the massive Chelsea Piers Sports Complex spans Piers 61 to 59.

You'll reach the financial district of Manhattan after 5 miles of paddling and the southernmost tip of Manhattan, known as Battery Park, 1 additional mile after that. Once off Battery Park, paddlers again have a decision to

MEAN WATER TEMPERATURES BY MONTH (Degrees Fahrenheit)					
	JAN	FEB	MAR	APR	MAY	JUN
MEAN	34	34	37	46	59	70
	JUL	AUG	SEP	OCT	NOV	DEC
MEAN	75	76	72	61	48	37

BROOKLYN BRIDGE

make. Continuing around Battery Park to the east will bring you into the East River and lead to South Street Seaport 1 mile later. Anyone choosing this option should take care when paddling past Battery Park, however, as the orange boats of the Staten Island Ferry system are constantly zooming between Battery Park and Staten Island. Likewise, the restaurants and shops of South Street Seaport may be alluring, but there is no safe or legal access to them by kayak. A small, rocky shoreline a bit north of the seaport is sometimes exposed during low tides. It lies under the beautifully intricate Brooklyn Bridge. Kayaks can be landed there, and paddlers can rest a bit and stretch their legs while snapping a few photos. Once again, though, there is no safe or legal access to Manhattan from this point.

If contending with hurried ferryboats isn't that appealing, Governors Island lies 0.5 miles south of Battery Park, the Brooklyn dockyards lie 1 mile to the southeast, and the Statue of Liberty National Monument lies 1.5 miles to the west across New York Harbor. There are a couple of problems with these options, however: the Brooklyn docks provide paddlers with very few landing sites, while Governors Island and the Statue of Liberty National Monument prohibit landing altogether. Those intent on landing in this area

must instead head for Louis J. Valentino Memorial Park in Brooklyn, which is south of Governors Island and part of the water trail. The park provides paddlers with a convenient boat ramp and street parking, making it the perfect stopping point for trips south.

As a final option, paddlers may wait for the tide to change and ride it back north to the West 79th Street Boat Basin. It is worth noting, however, that tides in this portion of the Hudson can actually lag behind the posted times by up to two hours. This fact, plus the obvious doubling of trip mileage, may deter some from returning to their starting point. For those unsure if the return trip is worth the effort, the incredibly delicious food at the 79th Street Boat Basin Café should be enough motivation to urge them on.

✧ **SHUTTLE DIRECTIONS** To get to the West 79th Street Boat Basin in Riverside Park, take the Henry Hudson Parkway to the West 79th Street exit. Turn left (west) onto West 79th Street and go around the traffic circle. Take the small road at the southwestern corner of the circle down the hill to the Boat Basin's parking garage.

✧ **GAUGE** The best way to determine water levels is in person. You may also check the currents and tide levels at **tidesandcurrents.noaa.gov.** However, the river is usually runnable year-round.

36   EAST RIVER

Once a polluted, unwelcoming stretch of New York City water, the East River has recently taken on new life as an immensely popular metropolitan paddling destination. Truth be told, it is not really a river at all, but a tidal strait connecting the Hudson River and New York Harbor to Long Island Sound. Nevertheless, the East flows past some of New York City's prime real estate—LaGuardia Airport, Rikers Island, Roosevelt Island, the United Nations Building, South Street Seaport, and the Brooklyn Bridge—giving all who ply its waters a lot to look at.

With the river's ever-increasing popularity among kayakers and the launching of the New York City Water Trail, gaining access to the East has never been easier. In fact, there are at least nine different launch sites associated with the water trail. These sites are all shown on a very user-friendly interactive map at **www.nycgovparks.org/sub_things_to_do/facilities/kayak** and are available for all to use with the purchase of an inexpensive annual permit. The Long Island City Community Boathouse (**www.licboathouse.org**), at the Hallets Cove boat launch, runs group paddles and organized events, giving everyone a chance to get out and enjoy the river.

Although paddling on the East River has become easier than ever, it is still not without its dangers. Bustling boat traffic, strong tidal currents, and the infamous waters of Hell Gate can combine to make navigating the river quite an adventure. To make the most of your trip, keep the following in mind: stay out of the boat channel and you will avoid most, if not all, powerboats; follow the tidal flow to avoid paddling against the strong current; the treacherous waters of Hell Gate calm down enough during the slack between high and low tides to make paddling through them easier and safer. The tide and current predictions listed at **tidesandcurrents.noaa.gov/currents08** show exactly when such opportune conditions occur. So whether you're participating in one of the LIC Community Boathouse's organized paddles or going it alone, the East River is one paddling destination not to be missed.

Flushing Bay to Brooklyn Bridge

Class	I (Hell Gate is sometimes rated Class II)
Length	13 miles
Time	3–4 hours
Runnable Months	Year-round
Hazards	Strong currents, boatt raffic
Portages	None
Rescue Access	Limited
Gauge	Visual, Web
Level	Tidal
Gradient	Tidal
Scenery	D

USGS Quadrangles

FLUSHING (NY), CENTRAL PARK (NY), BROOKLYN (NY), JERSEY CITY (NJ/NY)

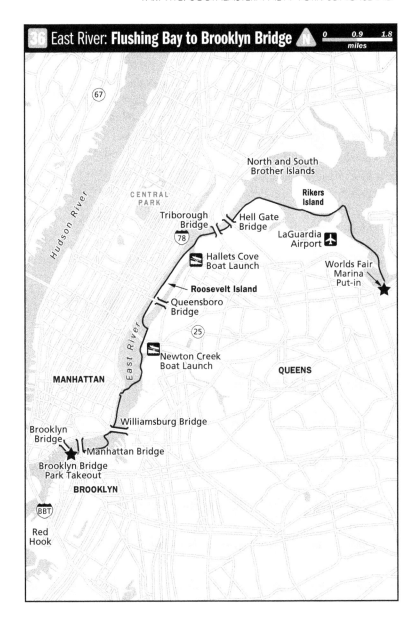

36 East River: **Flushing Bay to Brooklyn Bridge**

GPS Coordinates (UTM Zone 18T, WGS84)

Put-in:		Takeout:	
Easting	597112	Easting	585286
Northing	4512801	Northing	4506445
Latitude	N 40° 45' 37.60"	Latitude	N 40° 42' 16.20"
Longitude	W 73° 50' 58.10"	Longitude	W 73° 59' 25.50"

DESCRIPTION While not the most scenic stretch, the first few miles of a paddle down the East River are arguably unique. Indeed, the first mile of paddling is spent skirting the 100-yard security zone of LaGuardia Airport, with passenger jets zooming overhead. Paddlers must then turn to the west after heading north for a mile and cruise between the airport and Rikers Island, immediately north of it. Alternately, the island can be circumnavigated. Either way, keep in mind that Rikers Island houses a very large jail (hence the barbed-wire fences and security cameras). Obviously, no landing of any kind is permitted anywhere on the island, even if you do happen to know someone who calls Rikers home.

Both the airport and the jail will be left behind by mile 4, while two smaller islands come into view immediately to the north (0.5 miles away). These islands, North and South Brother Island, are both uninhabited, although North Brother Island once housed a hospital where patients suffering from typhoid fever were quarantined (the infamous "Typhoid Mary" Mallon was a patient there in the early 1900s). North Brother Island is currently off-limits to boaters, although South Brother Island sports a small beach on its south shore that's perfect for a paddle break or lunch stop.

The East River continues to flow west past ten large smokestacks on the Queens shore leading to Hell Gate 0.5 miles later. This notorious stretch of water is known for its swift, treacherous currents and dangerous water conditions that result from the confluence of three major bodies of water: the East River, the Harlem River, and Long Island Sound. As a result, only experienced and competent paddlers should attempt to navigate it, especially during its peak flow. I highly recommend paddling it only during periods of slack water. The beautiful Hell Gate Bridge comes into view soon after you enter the waters of Hell Gate, with the classic Triborough Bridge spanning the East River 0.5 miles after that. Next on the river is Roosevelt Island, a 2-mile-long piece of land that splits the river down the middle.

Anyone who wants to stop and take a break from paddling, or who is ready to call it a day altogether, can land just opposite the northern tip of Roosevelt Island on the Queens side of the river. The Hallets Cove boat landing (part of the New York City Water Trail) is just in front of the old Adirondack Furniture building. Those wishing to continue farther may head down either the east or west sides of the island, although the west side offers better views of the New York City skyline. This side also runs underneath the famous Roosevelt Island Tramway about three quarters of the way down, just north of the Queensboro Bridge.

Like Hallets Cove, there is yet another Water Trail site along the

MEAN WATER TEMPERATURES BY MONTH (Degrees Fahrenheit)					
	JAN	FEB	MAR	APR	MAY	JUN
MEAN	34	34	37	46	59	70
	JUL	AUG	SEP	OCT	NOV	DEC
MEAN	75	76	72	61	48	37

HELL GATE BRIDGE

East River to aid anyone who has had enough paddling for one day. This one is on Newton Creek, about 1 mile south of Roosevelt Island, on the Brooklyn side of the river. Beyond the creek, the East River gradually turns to the left and passes under the Williamsburg Bridge before it turns sharply to the right along Manhattan's Lower East Side. Paddlers are graced with an amazing view out into New York Harbor when heading around this right turn, with the Statue of Liberty showcased under the beautiful Manhattan and Brooklyn bridges.

The East River supplies paddlers with a surprising number of options at this point. Some may choose to continue around the southern tip of Manhattan and then up the Hudson River, while others may opt to explore New York Harbor. Still others may want to head farther south and take out in Valentino Park in the Red Hook section of Brooklyn. Yet one more option is to land at the tiny city-park beach between the Manhattan and Brooklyn bridges. This beach is an extremely safe and convenient spot to use; however, its approval as a landing site is as of yet unofficial. (I haven't had any problems taking my boat out there, but perhaps I've just been in the right place at the right time.) The state park immediately south of the city park prohibits boat landing of any sort, though, so either try the city park or head elsewhere.

✧ **SHUTTLE DIRECTIONS** To get to the put-in on Flushing Bay, take the Grand Central Parkway to Exit 9E (Shea Stadium). From there follow the signs for the World's Fair Marina. The canoe and kayak launch are located in the parking lot farthest to the east.

To get to the takeout in Brooklyn Bridge City Park, take the Brooklyn–Queens Expressway to Exit 29 (Tillary Street). Head west on Tillary Street for 0.5 miles before turning right onto Cadman Plaza West. Take Cadman Plaza West another 0.5 miles and turn right into Front Street. Head east for two blocks, turning left onto Main Street. The park will be straight ahead.

✧ **GAUGE** Because the East River is tidal, water levels and current speeds can be checked at **tidesandcurrents .noaa.gov/tides08** and **tidesandcurrents .noaa.gov/currents08.**

37   BRONX RIVER

The Bronx River, New York City's only freshwater river, rises from the Kensico Reservoir, 24 miles north of New York City. From there it heads south, passing through a large variety of suburban and urban areas, eventually emptying into the East River. Despite its length and prominent location, the river is often overlooked by some residents and taken for granted by others.

Since Jonas Bronck, the river's namesake, began trapping beaver there in the 1600s, the Bronx River has been used and abused by humans. It has seen its share of hunting, fishing, dams, and mills. Its water has been diverted into aqueducts, its course has been straightened, and its banks have been hardened with rocks and concrete. Most detrimental, however, has been its use for carrying raw sewage. Thanks to the efforts of conservation groups like the Bronx River Alliance, though, the river has recently begun a dramatic recovery.

The Bronx's waters are now cleaner then they have been in years. Erosion-control measures are being put into place, invasive plants such as purple loosestrife and Japanese knotweed are being removed, and native plant and animal species are returning. In fact, paddling the river is like entering another world—an oasis in the middle of a city.

Beautiful red maple, red oak, and sycamore trees tower over the many ducks, turtles, and small baitfish swimming in the river. Alewives have been successfully reintroduced in the river and can also be seen swimming its waters. Recently, a beaver was sighted in the river for the first time in more than 200 years.

The natural diversity of life on the river is amazing. Furthermore, the chance to paddle through the New York Botanical Gardens and the Bronx Zoo makes the Bronx River a great destination. In fact, the Bronx River Alliance has started running kayak tours for all who want to experience it for themselves. Check the alliance's Web site (**www.bronxriver.org**) for more information.

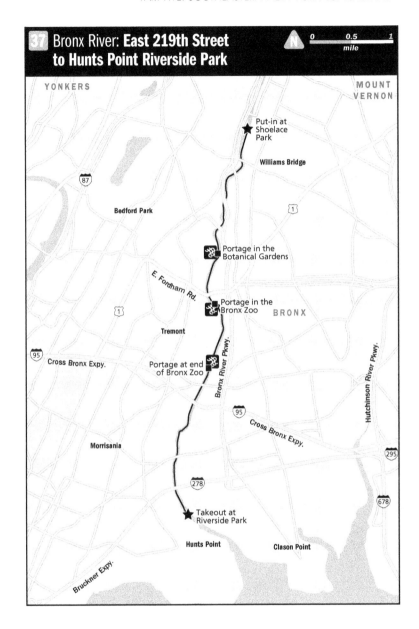

37 Bronx River: East 219th Street to Hunts Point Riverside Park

YONKERS

MOUNT VERNON

Put-in at Shoelace Park

Williams Bridge

87

Bedford Park

1

Portage in the Botanical Gardens

E. Fordham Rd.

1

Portage in the Bronx Zoo   BRONX

Tremont

95   Cross Bronx Expy.

Portage at end of Bronx Zoo

Bronx River Pkwy.

Hutchinson River Pkwy.

95   Cross Bronx Expy.

Morrisania

295

278

678

Takeout at Riverside Park

Hunts Point   Clason Point

Bruckner Expy.

GPS Coordinates (UTM Zone 18T, WGS84)

Put-in:		Takeout:	
Easting	595421	Easting	594334
Northing	4526544	Northing	4519145
Latitude	N 40° 53' 03.9"	Latitude	N 40° 49' 04.4"
Longitude	W 73° 52' 02.6"	Longitude	W 73° 52' 53.1"

USGS Quadrangles
MOUNT VERNON (NY),
FLUSHING, CENTRAL PARK (NY)

DESCRIPTION The northernmost put-in on the Bronx River is at Shoelace Park on East 219th Street. The river is very shallow at this point and only about 25 feet wide. It also runs very close to the Bronx River Parkway here, creating a noisy and somewhat distracting environment. This noise will be forgotten after a few paddle strokes, though, as the beauty of the river becomes apparent.

The river is also incredibly straight in this section as a result of decades-old attempts at controlling its flow. Large red maple and oak trees stand overhead filtering the sunlight and blocking out the sights and sounds of the city streets nearby. In fact, paddlers will feel as if they've left the city altogether. The river will then begin to twist and turn a bit as it continues

East 219th Street to Hunts Point Riverside Park

Class	I
Length	5.6 miles
Time	2.5 hours
Runnable Months	Year-round
Hazards	Underwater debris
Portages	3
Rescue Access	Easy
Gauge	Visual, Web
Level	Tidal
Gradient	9.1
Scenery	B–D

on its southward course, soon entering the New York Botanical Gardens. Although it is very tempting, landing boats within the garden's property is prohibited. The Bronx is perhaps its most beautiful at this point, though, so most paddlers would not want to leave it anyway.

The first portage will be reached after 1.7 miles of paddling. The Botanical Gardens staff has created a short marked trail to help paddlers circumvent the waterfall there. The trail starts on the left riverbank, immediately before the signs warning of the falls, and leads to a spot downriver that is perfect for reentering the water near where the Bronx Zoo property begins. As with the Botanical Gardens, the zoo does not permit visitors by water. Paddlers who disregard this rule may find themselves in trouble with zoo staff and perhaps some angry animals. However, paddling through the middle of the zoo is an experience not soon forgotten.

A second waterfall will be reached after 2.8 miles of paddling, requiring another portage. It can be found near the zoo's bison exhibit. In fact, the smell of the bison will tip boaters off to the portage before the sight or sound of the falls will. The small island in the center of the river is the best place to land boats and carry them downriver of the waterfall. The river then passes under the zoo's monorail after another 0.5 miles, where paddlers can wave to its passengers as they pass overhead.

The Bronx flows through more-developed areas once it leaves the zoo property. One final waterfall must be dealt with before entering this new stretch of river, though. Boats can be

AUTHOR ON THE BRONX RIVER

landed on the right riverbank soon after passing under the second monorail track, where a rockslide helps lower paddlers and their boats to the base of the falls. From this point on, the river passes large buildings, flows under railroad and subway overpasses, and runs next to highways. It also provides one final surprise to paddlers accustomed to more-pristine environments: a floating garbage boom. This plastic-and-rubber barrier prevents garbage on the river from flowing any farther downstream. Although there may be a fairly large backup of floating debris behind it, the boom is quite easy to paddle over. It also makes for a unique photo opportunity and some good paddling stories.

The river then continues south for an additional 0.5 miles before reaching Hunts Point Riverside Park. Boaters may choose to end their trip at this point or continue paddling south toward the East River. In doing so, they will have views of New York's LaGuardia Airport, the jail at Rikers Island, and Shea Stadium. This option will add 2 additional miles to the trip.

✧ **SHUTTLE DIRECTIONS** To get to the put-in at Shoelace Park, take the Bronx River Parkway north to Exit 9 (Gunhill Road). Head east on Gunhill Road, turning left onto Olinville Avenue after 0.1 mile. Olinville Avenue will take you to East 211th Street and a stop sign. Turn right at this stop sign onto Bronx Boulevard, and head north to East 219th Street. Shoelace Park's boat

MEAN WATER TEMPERATURES BY MONTH (Degrees Fahrenheit)					
JAN	FEB	MAR	APR	MAY	JUN
MEAN 42	47	54	59	63	73
JUL	AUG	SEP	OCT	NOV	DEC
MEAN 75	75	71	60	50	41

launch is on the river directly across from East 219th Street.

To get to the takeout at Hunts Point Riverside Park, take the Bronx River Parkway south to Exit 2W. Turn left onto Morrison Avenue, which will quickly lead to Bruckner Boulevard. Turn right onto Bruckner Boulevard and head west 1 mile, turning left onto Hunts Point Avenue. Hunts Point Avenue will reach Lafayette Avenue in 0.25 miles. Turn left onto Lafayette Avenue and head straight for the river. Hunts Point Riverside Park will be straight ahead.

Paddlers can also use the New York City subway system to bring them to their put-in or takeout locations. Stops very near Shoelace Park on East 219th Street and on Hunts Point Avenue can make shuttling to either end of the river easy. Subway maps and information are available at **www.mta.info**.

✧ **GAUGE** The USGS gauge showing flow rates for this river is Bronx River at New York Botanical Garden at Bronx. You may also check the tide levels for the lower Bronx River at **www.tidesonline.com**.

38 CONNETQUOT RIVER

Known to Native Americans as "The Great River," the Connetquot is the most pristine and protected of Long Island's four rivers. It originates from a freshwater spring near the center of the island in the town of Islandia. It then flows south for 6 miles, almost entirely within the boundaries of the Connetquot River State Park, before finally emptying into the Great South Bay. Unfortunately, boating of any kind is prohibited on the river while it flows through state-park property. Such a prohibition limits paddlers to the lower, estuarine portion of the river, south of NY 27 (Sunrise Highway).

More limitations exist on the lower portion of the Connetquot. Although paddling on this portion of the river is permitted, access is severely limited. Most of the river's shores are lined with homes and private property. The Department of Environmental Conservation maintains a few fishing-access points near Sunrise Highway but does not permit boat launching from any of them. This leaves paddlers with a single launching site on the Connetquot: Timber Point County Park.

Timber Point's amenities include ample parking, picnic tables, and a sandy beach for launching. In addition, its location, near the mouth of the Connetquot, puts boaters on the river poised for a trip north toward Sunrise Highway or south to the Great South Bay and Heckscher State Park. Although these are its only two paddling options, the Connetquot has always been, and will likely remain, a local favorite.

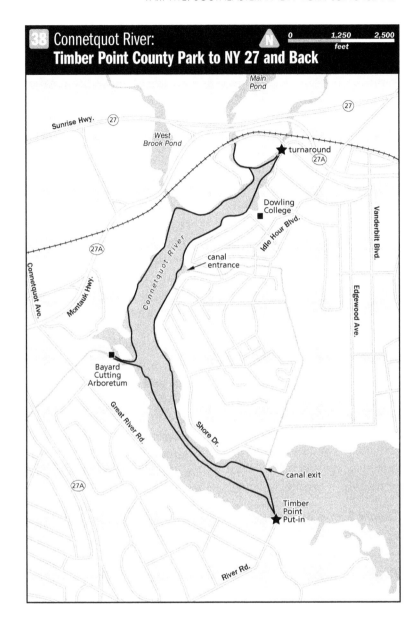

38 Connetquot River:
Timber Point County Park to NY 27 and Back

| | 0 | 1,250 | 2,500 |
feet

Main Pond

Sunrise Hwy. 27

27

West Brook Pond

turnaround
27A

Dowling College

Idle Hour Blvd.

canal entrance

Connetquot River

Vanderbilt Blvd.

27A

Connetquot Ave.

Montauk Hwy.

Edgewood Ave.

Bayard Cutting Arboretum

Great River Rd.

Shore Dr.

27A

canal exit

Timber Point Put-in

River Rd.

GPS Coordinates (UTM Zone 18T, WGS84)

Put-in:		Takeout:	
Easting	656430	Easting	656430
Northing	4509657	Northing	4509657
Latitude	N 40° 43' 22.8"	Latitude	N 40° 43' 22.8"
Longitude	W 73° 08' 51.9"	Longitude	W 73° 08' 51.9"

USGS Quadrangles
Bay Shore East (NY)

DESCRIPTION Paddling options are limited on the Connetquot River due to the scarcity of access points along its length. Entering the water from the Timber Point put-in allows paddlers to choose from two different trips. One can head south toward the Great South Bay and its salt marshes, ultimately traveling 6 miles to a take-out in Heckscher State Park. While very scenic, this trip obliges boaters to travel on more-open water and is not recommended for boaters with limited skills or during windy conditions. The second option, a round-trip paddle to the north, is better suited for all boaters and can be done during most weather conditions.

The Connetquot is quite wide near the put-in at Timber Point, with both shores being extensively developed. The eastern shore contains some fairly large boatyards and yacht clubs, while the western shore is lined with houses.

Timber Point County Park to NY 27 and Back

Class	I
Length	5.4 miles (round-trip)
Time	2 hours
Runnable Months	Year-round
Hazards	Boatt raffic
Portages	None
Rescue Access	Easy
Gauge	Visual, Web
Level	Tidal
Gradient	Tidal
Scenery	B–C+

These houses eventually give way to a pristine, scenic shoreline 1 mile north of Timber Point. At this point you will reach the Bayard Cutting Arboretum's southernmost boundary. Considering the lack of open space on the river's shores, the natural beauty of the arboretum is welcoming.

Since it was laid out in 1887, this arboretum has, according to its benefactor, Mrs. William Bayard Cutting, served to "provide an oasis of beauty and quiet for the pleasure, rest, and refreshment of those who delight in outdoor beauty." Anyone with time on his or her hands should definitely pay this amazing park a visit. Please note, though, that landing boats is not permitted along any part of the arboretum's shoreline. Its small coves, inlets, and tiny islands are a pleasure to paddle among, however.

The arboretum's northern terminus is reached after 2.5 miles, and houses dominate the shoreline once again. The Dowling College campus can be seen directly across from the river at this point. First a Vanderbilt family mansion, the property was also home to a group of metaphysicians, the site of the National Dairy Research Lab, and part of Adelphi University. Since 1968, it has been known as Dowling College. Lucky paddlers may be able to share the river with Dowling's crew teams as they scull along its length during their workouts.

A fork in the river is reached just north of the Dowling campus at mile 2.3. Here paddlers can head left, straight ahead, or right. The left branch takes paddlers through a narrow canal lined with private homes

THE AUTHOR ON THE CONNETQUOT

before it dead-ends at a low-hanging railroad trestle after about 2,000 feet of paddling. Heading straight or right leads around either side of a small island with a large cedar-shingled house situated firmly in its center. This portion of the Connetquot also dead-ends just south of NY 27 (Sunrise Highway).

After turning around, paddlers may head back to Timber Point County Park the way they came or take a slightly different path, through a canal that joins the eastern shore of the Connetquot 0.5 miles south of the turnaround. This route leads past numerous homes, boat ramps, and docks before bringing paddlers back to the river 1.5 miles later, directly across

from the Timber Point County Park. From there, you may simply head due south to reach the takeout.

✧ **SHUTTLE DIRECTIONS** To get to Timber Point County Park, take NY 27 (Sunrise Highway) to Exit 46 (Connetquot Avenue). Head south on Connetquot Avenue for 0.75 miles, cross over Montauk Highway, and continue heading south on Great River Road. Look for the entrance to Timber Point County Park after 1.5 miles, just before the road turns sharply to the right.

✧ **GAUGE** The best way to determine water levels is in person. Check the river gauge on the Connetquot in Central Islip, or on the Web at **www .tidesonline.com.**

39 NISSEQUOGUE RIVER

The Nissequogue is Long Island's third-longest river, flowing for 8 miles from its source in the center of the island to its mouth at the Long Island Sound. Roughly 6 miles of the river are navigable and will take paddlers through many different habitats, including freshwater ponds, river tributaries, freshwater wetlands, brackish waters, and marine estuaries.

Red maple, tulip, and locust trees dominate the banks of the Nissequogue's upper portion, while spartina grasses and phragmites characterize the marshes of the lower river. Numerous species of birds, reptiles, and other animals also call the river home. Expect to see Canada geese, mute swans, and mallard ducks swimming along the water's surface, with snapping turtles and many species of crabs

cruising below. Muskrats are very common along the river's muddy banks, just as terns, ospreys, and red-winged blackbirds sometimes fill the sky. The Nissequogue's clean water, combined with its gravel riverbed, makes it a great place for fishing. The river is naturally home to brown trout, bluefish, and striped bass and is stocked weekly during the spring and summer with rainbow and brook trout as well.

Because the Nissequogue is a tidal river, it can be run upstream or down, depending on the tides. The last four hours of a rising tide are perfect for a trip north, while the first four hours of a falling tide are great for a paddle south. Paddling during low tide is not recommended, though. (*Nissequogue* is a Native American word meaning "clay banks"—a fitting description of the river at low tide.)

USGS Quadrangles
SAINT JAMES (NY)

DESCRIPTION When beginning your run from Smithtown, head south after entering the water and you will quickly reach a fork in the river. Taking either branch will lead you to a dam, built in the early 1800s to power the local gristmill. After exploring this small section of river, turn around and head north, paddling under the concrete overpass for NY 25A. Noise from the traffic will soon fade and leave you with only the sounds of the wildlife on the river.

As you continue north, the shoreline changes from tree-lined to being bordered by phragmites. If you look at the riverbanks wherever there are breaks in the reeds, you'll notice that the majority

NY 25A to Old Dock Road

Class	I
Length	6.5 miles
Time	3 hours
Runnable Months	Year-round
Hazards	Someb oat traffic near northern end
Portages	None
Rescue Access	Easy
Gauge	Visual, Web
Level	Tidal
Gradient	Tidal
Scenery	B+

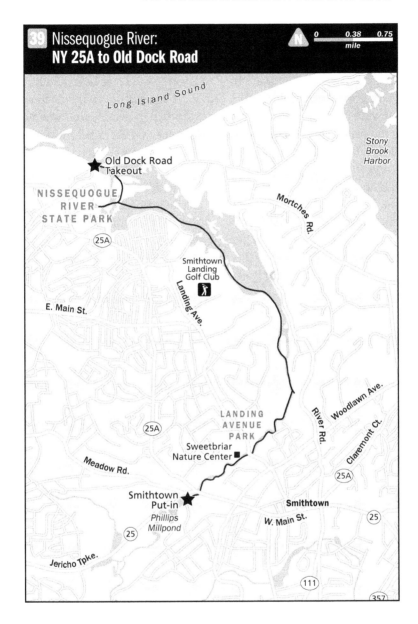

39 Nissequogue River:
NY 25A to Old Dock Road

GPS Coordinates (UTM Zone 18T, WGS84)

Put-in:		**Takeout:**	
Easting	650784	Easting	649047
Northing	4524534	Northing	4529706
Latitude	N 40° 51' 28.8"	Latitude	N 40° 54' 17.6"
Longitude	W 73° 12' 39.6"	Longitude	W 73° 13' 49.3"

of the eastern bank is filled with private homes while most of the western bank is undeveloped. In fact, a section of this bank borders Sweetbriar Nature Center, a 54-acre park containing nature exhibits, a butterfly house, rehabilitated wildlife, and miles of hiking trails. Paddle down the small creek shown on the map and you'll be able to land your boat and hike on the nature center's trails. You may also get out of your boat a bit farther north on the east side of the river at Landing Avenue Park. There is a playground there, as well as picnic tables and another short hiking trail to check out.

After paddling for another mile or so, you should start to notice a few changes on the river. On shore, cattails and phragmites of freshwater wetlands give way to the cordgrasses of salt marshes. Likewise, the ducks and swans of the lower river are soon replaced by the seagulls, herons, and egrets of the salt marsh.

The Smithtown Landing Golf Club should come into view on your left as the river widens. A small beach on the western bank, after the large wooden bulkhead, is a perfect spot to take a break. You can land there and follow the trail to the country club for restrooms and water or just sit on the beach, eat a snack, and relax a bit.

The river will then turn west after the golf club, where the old Kings Park Psychiatric Hospital looms over the horizon. New York state has taken over this huge property and developed it into a state park. If you head for the small boat docks on shore, look for a small, navigable creek called Sand Creek. The Nissequogue River State Park canoe

and kayak launch is at its end. You may choose to end your trip there if you are not interested in continuing farther north to the Long Island Sound.

If you are not yet ready to end your trip, however, continue heading downriver. Pass the Smithtown boat ramps, follow the river to its mouth, and enter the sound. Once there, you can paddle west along the beaches of Sunken Meadow State Park or head east along Short Beach. Although both of these options are worthwhile, you may be tired, hungry, and ready to end your trip. Head back upriver to the town boat ramps or the state-park boat launch, land your boat, and end your journey.

✧ **SHUTTLE DIRECTIONS** To get to the put-in, take the Long Island Expressway (Interstate 495) to Exit 55N (Old Willets Path). Old Willets Path will take you 3 miles north to Jericho Turnpike (NY 25). Turn right onto NY 25. After 1.5 miles you will see the famous Smithtown Bull statue. Across from this statue, on your right, is Paul T. Given County Park. You can park anywhere in the dirt lot by the boat launch.

To get to the takeout, turn left after leaving Paul T. Given County Park and bear right onto NY 25A (St. Johnland Road) just before the Smithtown Bull statue. Continue north for 4 miles before turning right onto Old Dock Road. The takeout can be found at the end of Old Dock Road.

✧ **GAUGE** The best way to determine water levels is in person. You may also check the tide levels at **www.tidesonline.com**. However, the river is usually runnable year-round.

40   CARMANS RIVER

The Carmans is Long Island's most beautiful and perhaps most protected river. It originates as a freshwater stream, flowing out of a series of small ponds in the center of the island, and eventually turns into a saltwater estuary leading into the Great South Bay. The majority of land along its 10-mile length is designated parkland, and as such is scenic and pristine, making it an extremely popular paddling destination.

The upper freshwater portion of the Carmans River flows through land once owned by a hunting and fishing club. Suffolk County obtained the land decades ago and forever protected it by creating the 1,500-acre Southaven County Park. Red maple trees abound along this stretch of river, as do pepperidge trees, honeysuckle bushes, swamp rose bushes, and sprawling groves of bright blue forget-me-nots. Also common are muskrats, brook trout, wood ducks, and cedar waxwings.

The lower tidal portion of the Carmans River flows just south of NY 27. Vastly different from the upper river, this estuarine portion lies almost entirely within the bounds of the Wertheim National Wildlife Refuge, a 2,500-acre property designed to help protect the area for migrating birds. Huge stands of phragmites line most of the river in the refuge, augmented by spartina grasses and other salt-tolerant plant species. Great blue herons, great egrets, and ospreys are numerous on the lower Carmans, as are bluefish and striped bass.

Landing boats along the Carmans River is either difficult or completely prohibited. Southaven County Park does maintain a few spots where paddlers can get out of their boats and stretch their legs. Indian Landing and Squassux Landing are the only landing sites available along the lower river, though. The Wertheim refuge does not allow visitors to enter by water. Its hiking trails are worthy of a visit, however, and can be reached by paying an entrance fee and entering the park by land.

USGS Quadrangles BELLPORT (NY)

 DESCRIPTION The best place to begin your paddle on the upper Carmans River is just below Lower Lake in Yaphank (permits must first be obtained at the Southaven County Park office). The river is very shallow and narrow in these northern sections and contains submerged logs and fallen

Yaphank Avenue to Southaven County Park	**A**
Class	1+
Length	3.8 miles
Time	2 hours
Runnable Months	February–March, May–October (weekends only)
Hazards	Deadfall
Portages	2
Rescue Access	Easy
Gauge	Visual
Level	Spring-fed
Gradient	5.9
Scenery	A

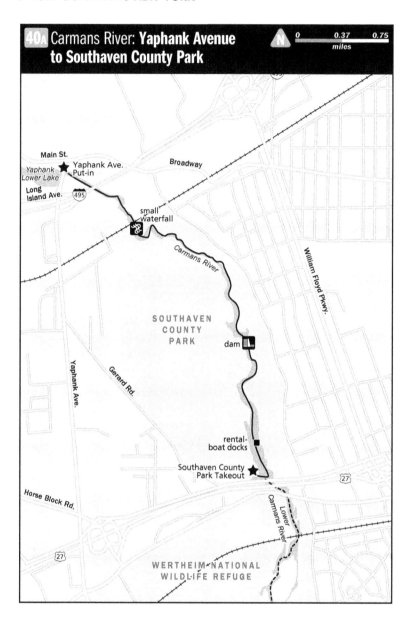

40A Carmans River: **Yaphank Avenue to Southaven County Park**

N   0   0.37   0.75
miles

Main St.

Yaphank
Lower Lake

Yaphank Ave.
Put-in

Broadway

Long
Island Ave.   495

small
waterfall

Carmans River

SOUTHAVEN
COUNTY
PARK

dam

William Floyd Pkwy.

Yaphank Ave.

Gerard Rd.

rental-
boat docks

Southaven County
Park Takeout

27

Horse Block Rd.

27

Lower
Carmans River

WERTHEIM NATIONAL
WILDLIFE REFUGE

GPS COORDINATES (UTM ZONE 18T, WGS84)

Put-in:		**Takeout:**	
Easting	675673	Easting	678120
Northing	4522601	Northing	4519065
Latitude	N 40° 50' 08.3"	Latitude	N 40° 48' 11.8"
Longitude	W 72° 54' 59.1"	Longitude	W 72° 53' 18.3"

tree limbs. While these conditions can make paddling this stretch of river a bit tricky, the exquisite scenery is well worth the patience required.

As the river winds its way south, it passes under the Long Island Expressway and widens a bit, making paddling easier. After another 0.5 miles, the river will lead to a small waterfall. This waterfall is visible directly under the concrete railroad trestle but can be heard much earlier. Daring paddlers may simply head straight over the two-foot drop, though the more cautious, and perhaps smarter, approach is to land your boat on the right bank before you reach the train trestle. From there you can easily walk your boat over the drop and resume paddling on the other side.

The river widens even more past the waterfall, entering Southaven County Park. You will reach a second dam that requires a short portage after 1.5 miles. Just as before, there is a small landing spot on the right riverbank before the dam. Land your boat there and carry it over to the other side of the drop. From this point on, you will be paddling in the section of the river used by rental boats from the park. The water can get very crowded here, especially during summer weekends. If you stay close to the left riverbank, though, you should be able to avoid most of the boat traffic.

You can end your trip at the takeout located at the small beach just a bit south of the rental boat docks. However, you may also continue farther south, paddling the lower Carmans River to its mouth in Bellport Bay. To do so, you must portage your boat around yet another waterfall. You should be cautious if this is your plan. The current is very swift on the other side of the portage, requiring strength and care when putting your boat back in the water. A better idea is to paddle to the takeout spot in Southaven County Park and simply drive your boat to the lower river put-in.

✧ **SHUTTLE DIRECTIONS** To get to the put-in, take the Long Island Expressway (Interstate 495) to Exit 67N (Yaphank Avenue). Turn right onto Yaphank Avenue and travel north approximately 0.3 miles. You will see the put-in on the east side of the road, across from the Yaphank Lower Lake. You should drop your boat off here but park down the road a bit. To do so, head back the way you came on Yaphank Avenue, taking your first right turn onto Long Island Avenue. There will be a small parking lot on the corner as you turn. Follow the signs and park your car in any available spot.

To get to the takeout from I-495, take Exit 68S (William Floyd Parkway). Travel south on William Floyd Parkway 2.7 miles until you reach Victory Drive. Turn right onto Victory Drive and follow the signs to Southaven County Park and the boat launch.

✧ **GAUGE** The best way to determine water levels is in person from the bridge on Yaphank Road. The river is usually runnable year-round, though.

B Montauk Highway to Squassux Landing

Class	I
Length	4.7 miles
Time	2 hours
Runnable Months	Year-round
Hazards	None
Portages	None
Rescue Access	Easy
Gauge	Web
Level	Tidal
Gradient	2.1
Scenery	A

40B **DESCRIPTION** You can reach the lower Carmans River by portaging your boat around the dam at the south end of Southaven County Park. The steep stairs and strong current make this a difficult maneuver, however. The best idea is to put your boat in at the river access on NY 27A (Montauk Highway).

You will enter the water just south of the NY 27 (Sunrise Highway) overpass and just north of NY 27A. Once under Montauk Highway you will be paddling in the Wertheim National Wildlife Refuge. The refuge's headquarters will come into view on the western bank as the river continues south. As it does, a large island will also appear in the center of the river. Both sides of the island are navigable, although the eastern shore is more protected and may provide a better chance of seeing wildlife. The island itself has a slightly barren appearance due to fire. In the spring of 2007, the U.S. Fish and Wildlife Service conducted a controlled burn on the island to rid it of an invasive plant known as phragmites. This plant is known to crowd out naturally occurring plants that are beneficial to local wildlife.

Past the island, the river takes on a different appearance. Gone are the red maple and birch trees that lined its shores, and now present are huge stands of cattails and phragmites. If you keep an eye out on the western riverbank for breaks in the reeds, you may discover some side creeks to explore. The northernmost creek, Yaphank Creek, is almost 3 miles south of your put-in. Follow it and you will be led as far north as Montauk Highway. Little Neck Run, another side creek, lies 0.5 miles south of Yaphank Creek. Between these two creeks, on the opposite riverbank, is Indian Landing. This small beach, once a meeting site for the Unkechaug Indians, is the perfect spot to beach your boat, have a snack, and stretch your legs. There is also a 0.8-mile nature trail to walk.

Many paddlers turn back around after leaving Indian Landing, paddling upstream to the put-in and their cars. The current is usually slow enough to make this an easy thing to do. Another option, though, is to continue south for another 0.5 miles to the takeout at Squassux Landing. You may also decide to head even farther downstream to Long Point, the last bit of land before the river drains into the Great South Bay. You'll still have to head back to Squassux Landing from there, however, as there is no good spot for a takeout.

✧ **SHUTTLE DIRECTIONS** To get to the put-in, take NY 27 (Sunrise Highway) to Exit 58S (William Floyd Parkway).

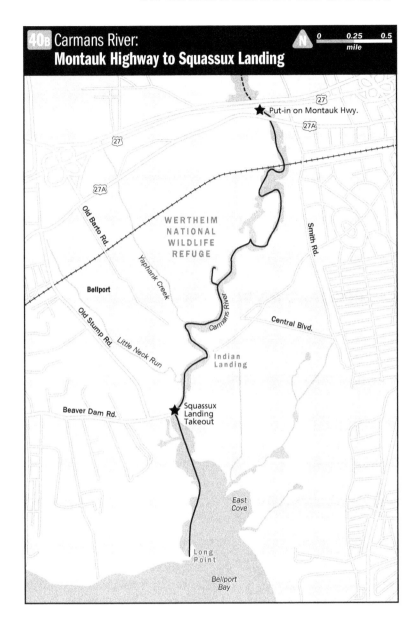

40B Carmans River: Montauk Highway to Squassux Landing

GPS COORDINATES (UTM ZONE 18T, WGS84)

Put-in:		**Takeout:**	
Easting	678429	Easting	677556
Northing	4518998	Northing	4515888
Latitude	N 40° 48' 9.4"	Latitude	N 40° 46' 29.3"
Longitude	W 72° 53' 5.2"	Longitude	W 72° 53' 45.6"

Travel south on William Floyd Parkway, turning right at the second intersection onto NY 27A (Montauk Highway). Stay on Montauk Highway 1 mile, and you will see the boat launch on your right.

To get to the takeout at Squassux Landing, take Sunrise Highway to Exit 57S (Old Horseblock Road). Old Horseblock Road will end at Montauk Highway, where you should turn right. Take Montauk Highway until you reach your second left turn, Yaphank Avenue. Yaphank Avenue eventually merges into Old Stump Road and leads you to Beaver Dam Road. Turn left on Beaver Dam Road, and the dock at Squassux Landing will be straight ahead.

✧ **GAUGE** You may check the tide levels for the lower Carmans River at **www.tidesonline.com**. The river is usually runnable year-round.

---

41 PECONIC RIVER

The Peconic is Long Island's longest river, flowing east 15 miles from swamps and bogs near the center of the island to its mouth at Peconic Bay. On its way, the river passes through such diverse habitats as freshwater swamps, farmland, and oak forests. In addition, it also flows through a portion of the Long Island Pine Barrens region, important for providing critical habitat for a variety of wildlife as well as providing clean, fresh drinking water for Long Island's residents.

The Peconic also passes through some historic areas where residents once farmed cranberries and forged iron. Cranberry farming was so successful on the Peconic that the area was once the third-largest cranberry producer in the nation. Likewise, the iron deposits in the Peconic's bogs were so vast that large anchors and metal hulls for Civil War–era ironclad ships were easily produced there.

These days the Peconic is most popular as a paddling destination. The iron forges and cranberry farms are gone, leaving a beautiful, scenic river in their place. The riverbanks are lined with red maples and willow trees, pitch pine and oak trees tower overhead, and water willows and phragmites dominate the water's edge. Paddlers can expect to see swans, wood ducks, cedar waxwings, ospreys, and kingfishers flying along the river's course, while muskrats, snapping turtles, bluegills, and largemouth bass swim its waters.

Because Long Island is limited in its paddling destinations, the river can get very crowded, especially during summer weekends. Be ready to share the water with other canoeists and kayakers, as well as local fishermen. Whether done alone or with a group, though, paddling the Peconic River is an incredibly enjoyable adventure.

USGS Quadrangles:
RIVERHEAD (NY)

41 DESCRIPTION Although there are numerous put-ins along the Peconic

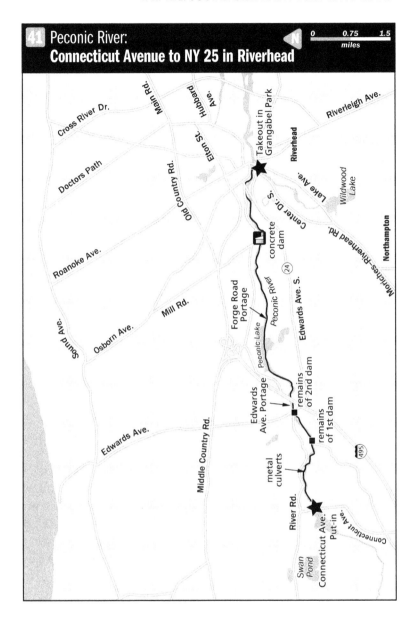

41 Peconic River:
Connecticut Avenue to NY 25 in Riverhead

0   0.75   1.5
miles

GPS COORDINATES (UTM ZONE 18T, WGS84)

Put-in:		**Takeout:**	
Easting	687541	Easting	696715
Northing	4530115	Northing	4532016
Latitude	N 40° 54' 02.4"	Latitude	N 40° 54' 56.2"
Longitude	W 72° 46' 24.6"	Longitude	W 72° 39' 50.6"

Connecticut Avenue to NY 25 in Riverhead

Class	I
Length	7 miles
Time	4 hours
Runnable Months	Year-round
Hazards	None
Portages	4
Rescue Access	Easy
Gauge	Visual, phone
Level	Spring-fed
Gradient	3
Scenery	B–

River, most paddlers begin their trip at Connecticut Avenue in Calverton. The river is very shallow and narrow there, but also wild and scenic. As you begin heading east, you will be paddling through part of Long Island's Pine Barrens region. Be wary of rubbing up against any low-lying bushes here— poison ivy abounds!

Four metal culverts will come into view after 0.5 miles of paddling. While the opening farthest to the left is almost completely blocked off, the remaining three are free and clear. The easiest path lies through the culvert farthest to the right. A beautiful yet tiny purple flower named bittersweet nightshade thrives in the portion of the river immediately after the culverts. It grows as a vine and produces a flower with five purple petals and a bright yellow stamen. The flower and its berries are poisonous if ingested. Ironically, though, nightshade can be used to treat certain skin conditions.

The river widens after a mile or so of paddling, eventually leading to a section of river that was once dammed for cranberry farming. The remains of the first dam can be seen about 1 mile past the culverts. Continue heading east, pass through the remnants of the second dam, and weave your way through the striking white flowers of the fragrant water lilies and the bulbous yellow flowers of the yellow pond lilies that inhabit the river here.

You will reach Edwards Avenue and your first portage after 2 miles of paddling. While the stairs and boat ramp there make maneuvering your boat easier, a certain amount of care must be used when reentering the water. Water currents at the bottom of the boat ramp can be swift and unpredictable.

The river will narrow again once you have crossed Edwards Avenue. It passes under Interstate 495 (Long Island Expressway) through two concrete culverts with low ceilings and eventually flows into Peconic Lake. You will reach the eastern shore of the lake after 4 miles of paddling, requiring yet another portage. You will need to cross Forge Road, named after an iron forge that existed there 200 years ago, and slide your boat down the wooden ramp on the other side. The river takes on a different feel from this point on, as natural wetlands give way to developed tracts of land. You will paddle past numerous houses, businesses, and side roads as you continue your trip east.

Your third portage occurs 1.5 miles past Forge Road. Head for the small landing and carry your boat across Mill Road and through a small dirt parking lot to reenter the water on the other side. A concrete dam immediately after the portage will require you to get out of your boat one more time. You can carry your boat over the waterfall quite easily on the right side of the river.

The sights and sounds of civilization will become more pronounced during your last mile of paddling on the Peconic. This section of the river will end at Grangabel Park. Look for your takeout at the Peconic Paddler canoe and kayak store on the far right side of the park.

✧ **SHUTTLE DIRECTIONS** To get to your put-in on Connecticut Avenue, take Interstate 495 (Long Island Expressway) to Exit 71N (NY 24). Travel north on NY 24, taking your third left onto River Road. Head west on River Road 1.8 miles and you will reach Connecticut Avenue on your left. You will see the sign for the Peconic River put-in on the left, 0.3 miles down the road.

To get to your takeout at Peconic Paddler in Riverhead, take I-495 to Exit 72S (NY 25). Travel east on SR 25 toward the town of Riverhead. You will reach a traffic light at Peconic Avenue after 3.5 miles. Turn right there and you will see Peconic Paddler on the right side of the road. You may pick up or drop off any boats and gear in front of the store, but you should park across the street in the public parking lot.

✧ **GAUGE** The best way to determine water levels is in person. You may also call Peconic Paddler at (631) 369-9500 or (631) 727-9895 for the latest river conditions. The river is usually runnable year-round, though.

FRAGRANT WATER LILY ON THE PECONIC

MORNING MIST ON GOODYEAR LAKE

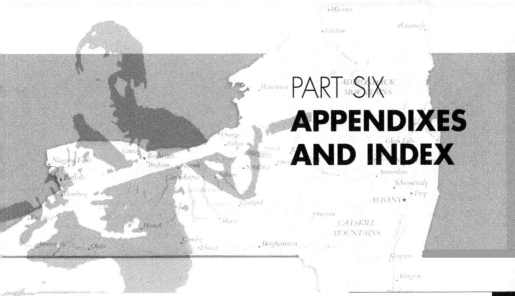

PART SIX
APPENDIXES
AND INDEX

APPENDIX A: PADDLING OUTFITTERS

WESTERN NEW YORK

Evergreen Outfitters
4845 NY 474
Ashville, NY 14710
(716) 763-2266
www.evergreen-outfitters.com

Canoe and kayak rentals and delivery service; retail store and online shopping for boats, paddling gear, and outdoor clothing; services southwestern New York.

Genesee Waterways Center
P.O. Box 18607
Rochester, NY 14618
(585) 328-3960
www.geneseewaterways.org

Runs New York's only permanent white-water facility. Offers boat rentals on weekends and on weekdays by appointment. Paddling instruction available.

Oak Orchard Canoe and Kayak
2133 Eagle Harbor–Waterport Road
Waterport, NY 14571
(585) 682-4849
www.oakorchardcanoe.com/rentals.php

Offers canoe and kayak rentals and shuttle service; canoes, kayaks, and paddling gear available for sale online and at retail store.

Paths, Peaks & Paddles
1000 Ellicott Creek Road
Tonawanda, NY 14150
(716) 213-0350
www.pathspeakspaddles.com

Provides canoe, kayak, and camping gear rentals; offers route planning services; boats and paddling gear available for sale online; operates in northwestern New York.

CENTRAL NEW YORK

Camillus Kayak Shop
24 Main Street
Camillus, NY 13031
(315) 672-8439
www.camilluskayak.com

Provides kayak sales and rentals; offers paddling instruction; sells boats, paddling gear, and clothing.

Chenango River Landing
315 NY 12B
Sherburne, NY 13460
(607) 674-5596
www.chenangoriver.com

Provides canoe and kayak rentals, shuttle services, and a campground on the Chenango River.

CENTRAL NEW YORK
[continued]

Reagan's Finger Lakes Canoe and Kayak Livery

440 Hall Road
Himrod, NY 14842
(607) 243-9100
www.reaganskayak.com

Rents canoes and kayaks and will deliver them to any part of the Finger Lakes region. Also offers online catalog shopping services.

Puddledockers Kayak Shop

704½ West Buffalo Street
Ithaca, NY 14842
(888) 273-0096
www.puddledockers.com

Canoe and kayak rentals; retail store and online shopping for boats, paddling gear, and camping gear; services Central New York and the Finger Lakes region.

Sam Smith's Boatyard

6098 NY 80
Cooperstown, NY 13326
(607) 547-2543
www.samsmithsboatyard.com

Rents canoes, kayaks, and fishing gear from May to October; located on shore of Otsego Lake.

NORTHERN NEW YORK– ADIRONDACKS

Adirondack Lakes and Trails Outfitters

541 Lake Flower Avenue
Saranac Lake, NY 12983
(518) 891-7450
www.adirondackoutfitters.com

Provides canoe, kayak, and camping gear rentals, guided trips, and instruction throughout the Adirondacks.

Blue Mountain Outfitters

144 Main Street
Blue Mountain Lake, NY 12812
(518) 352-7306
www.indian-lake.com/listingpics/
Blue Mountain Outfitters.html

Offers canoe and kayak rentals, boat deliveries, and shuttle services; retail store sells boats, paddling gear, and camping supplies; operates throughout the Adirondacks.

Lake George Kayak Company

Main Street
Bolton Landing, NY 12814
(518) 644-9366
www.lakegeorgekayak.com

Rents canoes and kayaks; offers both online and retail store shopping for boats, paddling gear, and clothing; operates in the southern Adirondacks.

Mac's Canoe Livery

5859 NY 30
Lake Clear, NY 12945
www.macscanoe.com

Canoe rental, livery, shuttle service, and guided trips available; services the St. Regis Canoe Area, Raquette River, Saranac Lakes Wild Forest, and most other waterways of the Adirondacks.

Mountain Air Adventures

1089 Main Street
Schroon Lake, NY 12870
(518) 532-9954
www.townestore.com/Mountain

Sells and rents canoes and kayaks in the Schroon Lake area.

Mountainman Outdoor Supply Company
2855 NY 28
Old Forge, NY 13420
(315) 369-6672
www.mountainmanoutdoors.com

Rents canoes and kayaks, offers shuttle services throughout the Adirondacks, and is the largest canoe and kayak dealer in New York. Online shopping available.

Raquette River Outfitters
1754 NY 30
P.O. Box 653
Tupper Lake, NY 12986
(518) 359-3228
www.raquetteriveroutfitters.com

List of services includes canoe, kayak, and camping gear rentals, route advice and planning, shuttles, and car deliveries; boat and paddling gear sales available; services most of the Adirondack region.

Route 96 Power & Paddle
1036 Owego Road
Candor, NY 13743
(866) 705-2925 or (607) 659-7693
www.powerandpaddle.com

Retailer of canoes and kayaks, but no rental services are available.

St. Regis Canoe Outfitters
73 Dorsey Street
Saranac Lake, NY 12983
(518) 891-1838
www.canoeoutfitters.com

Offers canoe, kayak, and camping gear rentals; trip planning services; runs guided paddling trips throughout the Adirondacks. Online and retail store shopping available.

Tickner's Canoe Rentals
Riverside Drive, Box 267
Old Forge, NY 14320
(315) 369-6286
www.ticknerscanoe.com

Offers canoe and kayak rentals on the Moose River and nearby Fulton Chain of Lakes, provides shuttle services for both customers and noncustomers.

HUDSON RIVER VALLEY

Hudson Valley Outfitters
63 Main Street
Cold Spring, NY 10516
(845) 265-0221
www.hudsonvalleyoutfitters.com

Offers kayak rentals, sales, instruction, paddling gear, and guided tours on the Hudson River.

Hudson Valley Pack & Paddle
45 Beekman Street
Beacon, NY 12508
(845) 831-1300
www.hvpackandpaddle.com

Rents and sells canoes and kayaks in the Hudson River Valley; offers delivery services; both online and store sales of boats and paddling gear; services the Hudson River, the Wallkill River, and other waters throughout the Hudson River Valley.

The River Connection
9 West Market Street
Hyde Park, NY 12538
(845) 229-0595
www.the-river-connection.com

Runs various guided paddling tours throughout the Hudson River Valley; retailer of canoes, kayaks, paddling gear, and outdoor clothing.

APPENDIX A: PADDLING OUTFITTERS
[continued]

SOUTHEASTERN NEW YORK–LONG ISLAND

Bob's Canoe Rental, Inc.
(631) 269-9761
www.canoerentalslongisland.com

Canoe and kayak rental and livery service on Long Island's Nissequogue River.

The Dinghy Shop
(631) 264-0005
334 South Bayview Ave
Amityville, New York 11701
www.dinghyshop.com

Provides kayak rentals and guided tours on Long Island's South Shore; sells boats, clothing, and paddling gear.

Glacier Bay Sports
(631) 262-9116
81-C Fort Salonga Road
Northport, NY 11768
www.glacierbaysports.com

Provides kayak and canoe rentals on the North Shore of Long Island; retailer of boats, paddling gear, and clothing.

Long Island City Community Boathouse
(718) 228-9214
www.licboathouse.org

Offers free walk-up paddling programs and runs guided tours in the New York City area.

Manhattan Kayak Company
The Boathouse, Pier 66
West 26th Street and 12th Avenue
New York, NY 10001
(212) 924-1788
www.manhattankayak.com

Provides kayak rentals, tours, and instruction in the New York City area.

New York City Downtown Boathouse
Box 20214, West Village Station
New York, NY 10014
www.downtownboathouse.org

Offers free walk-up kayaking programs and guided tours on the Hudson River; open weekends and holidays from May to October.

New York Kayak Company
Pier 40, South Side
West Houston and West streets
New York, NY 10014
(800) KAYAK-99
www.nykayak.com

Offers guided tours in the New York City area; online retailer of canoes, kayaks, paddling gear, and outdoor clothing.

Nissequogue River Canoe & Kayak Rentals
(631) 979-8244
www.canoerentals.com

Provides canoe and kayak rentals, guided tours, and instruction on Long Island's Nissequogue River.

Peconic Paddler
(631) 727-9895
89 Peconic Avenue
Riverhead, NY 11901
www.peconicpaddler.com

Offers canoe and kayak rentals and provides shuttle services for customers; sells boats and paddling gear.

APPENDIX B: PADDLING CLUBS

Adirondack Mountain Club, Genesee Valley Chapter
P.O. Box 18558
Rochester, NY 14618-0558
www.gvc-adk.org

Ahwaga Canoe and Kayak Club
P.O. Box 545
Johnson City, NY 13790
www.ahwagacanoeandkayak.org

Atlantic Sea Kayakers
www.atlanticseakayakers.org

CNY Kayakers
4661 Antoinette Drive
Marcellus, NY 13108
www.cnykayakclub.com

Cold Spring Kayak Club
www.cskc.org

Finger Lakes Ontario Watershed Paddlers' Club (FLOW)
43 Whelehan Drive
Rochester, NY 14616
www.flowpaddlers.org

Gowanus Dredgers Canoe Club
P.O. Box 22403
Brooklyn, NY 11202
www.gowanuscanal.org

Hackensack River Canoe and Kayak Club
P.O. Box 369
Bogota, NJ 07603
www.hrckc.org

The Hudson River Watertrail Association
Box 110
245 Eighth Avenue
New York, NY 10011
www.hrwa.org

Inwood Canoe Club
P.O. Box 562
New York, NY 10034
www.inwoodcanoeclub.org

Ithaca Kayak Club
www.ithacakayakclub.blogspot.com

Ka-Na-Wa-Ke Canoe & Kayak Club of Central New York
4166 St. John Drive
Syracuse, NY 13215
www.kanawakecanoe.org

Kayak and Canoe Club of New York
www.kccny.com

Long Island Paddlers
P.O. Box 115
West Sayville, NY 11796
www.lipaddlers.org

New York City Downtown Boathouse
Box 20214 West Village Station
New York, NY 10014
www.downtownboathouse.org

North Atlantic Canoe and Kayak–NACK, Inc.
www.getthenack.org

Sebago Canoe Club
Paerdegat Basin, Foot of Avenue N
Brooklyn, NY 11236
www.sebagocanoeclub.org

Storm Paddle
www.stormpaddle.com

Yonkers Paddling and Rowing Club
Alexander Street at Hudson River
Yonkers, NY 10701
www.yprc.org

APPENDIX C: INTERNET RESOURCES

Adirondack Mountains Official Recreation Guide
www.visitadirondacks.com/recreation/canoe-overview.cfm

Features an interactive map of canoeable waterways as well as listings of useful guidebooks, local outfitters, and route suggestions.

American Canoe Association (ACA)
www.americancanoe.org

Official Web site of the ACA. Provides information on skills, instruction, stewardship, and membership opportunities as well as lists of publications, outfitters, clubs, and other paddling resources.

American Whitewater
www.americanwhitewater.org

Provides news, discussion forums, and information on rivers across the United States.

Bronx River Alliance
www.bronxriver.org

Contains a good deal of information about the history and current conditions of the Bronx River. The site also lists valuable information on paddling the Bronx River, such as water conditions and wildlife to look out for.

Campground Owners of New York
www.nycampgrounds.com

Searchable database of privately owned campgrounds in New York state.

The Catskill Fly Fishing Center and Museum
www.cffcm.net

Gives information about the Fly Fishing Center and Willowemoc Creek.

Hudson River Sloop *Clearwater*
www.clearwater.org

Web site of the sloop *Clearwater* and the environmental advocacy and education group

that runs it. They are dedicated to protecting the Hudson River environment and teaching about its ecosystems. Event schedules and educational programs are listed.

Kampgrounds of America, Inc.
www.koa.com

Online directory of KOA campgrounds across the United States. Provides maps, directions, rates, and availability.

Marden E. Cobb Waterway Trail
co.chautauqua.ny.us/parks/trailslist/cobb

Provides some basic information about the Marden E. Cobb Waterway Trail and maps of Conewango Creek.

Metropolitan Transportation Authority
www.mta.info

Provides maps and schedules for bus and subway routes around New York City.

National Oceanic and Atmospheric Administration Tidal Current Predictions
tidesandcurrents.noaa.gov

Provides tidal and current predictions for a large number of locations across the United States.

New York City Water Trail
www.nycgovparks.org/sub_things_to_do/facilities/kayak

Gives links to applications for paddling permits and contains an interactive map of the entire NYC Water Trail.

New York State Department of Environmental Conservation
www.dec.ny.gov

Official Web site with information on rules and regulations regarding state lands, wildlife, recreation opportunities, maps and facilities, and applications and permits.

New York State Department of Environmental Conservation Campgrounds

www.dec-campgrounds.com

Searchable list of DEC campgrounds, containing schedules, maps, and reservation information.

New York State Parks

nysparks.state.ny.us/parks

List of state parks across New York, sorted by available recreational activities or location.

Northeast Paddlers Message Board

www.npmb.com

Online forum for anyone looking to discuss anything to do with paddling in the northeast United States.

Paddling.net

www.paddling.net

Online paddling resource containing everything from gear reviews, trip suggestions, dealer listings, and photo galleries to message boards.

ReserveAmerica

www.reserveamerica.com

Online campground finder and reservation service. Provides maps, rates, availability, and nearby attractions for most campgrounds across the United States.

Scenic Hudson

www.scenichudson.org

Advocacy group working to protect the Hudson River Valley. The site gives information about their work and how others can help.

Tides Online

www.tidesonline.com

Searchable database of tidal levels for all of the coastal United States.

Trails.com

www.trails.com

Online retailer of outdoor trail descriptions, topographic maps, and aerial photographs of the United States and Canada. Covers canoeing and kayaking, hiking and backpacking, mountain biking, and more.

United States Geological Survey

www.usgs.gov

Official site of the federal agency concerned with the natural and living resources of the earth, its environments, and nature. The site provides a great deal of scientific and reference information on latitude and longitude, maps, water conditions, and weather.

USGS Real-Time Water Data

waterdata.usgs.gov/nwis/rt

The go-to site for real-time and archived stream-flow data and water levels on rivers across the United States.

The USGS Store

store.usgs.gov

Government retailer of topographic maps.

Waterline

www.h2oline.com

Source of river-flow forecasts and water-level reports, available online and by telephone.

APPENDIX D:
Safety Code of American Whitewater

Eric Nise, *Safety Chairman* | Charlie Wbridge, *Safety Vice Chairman*

Mark Singleton, *Executive Director*

Adopted 1959, Revised 2005

© 2006 American Whitewater, P.O. Box 1540, Cullowhee, NC 28723; (866) BOAT-4-AW; info@amwhitewater.org.

INTRODUCTION

This code has been prepared using the best available information and has been reviewed by a broad cross section of whitewater experts. The code, however, is only a collection of guidelines; attempts to minimize risks should be flexible, not constrained by a rigid set of rules. Varying conditions and group goals may combine with unpredictable circumstances to require alternate procedures. This code is not intended to serve as a standard of care for commercial outfitters or guides.

I. PERSONAL PREPAREDNESS AND RESPONSIBILITY

1. Be a competent swimmer, with the ability to handle yourself under water.

2. Wear a life jacket. A snugly fitting vest-type life preserver offers back and shoulder protection as well as the flotation needed to swim safely in whitewater.

3. Wear a solid, correctly fitted helmet when upsets are likely. This is essential in kayaks or covered canoes, and recommended for open canoeists using thigh straps and rafters running steep drops.

4. Do not boat out of control. Your skills should be sufficient to stop or reach shore before reaching danger. Do not enter a rapid unless you are reasonably sure that you can run it safely or swim it without injury.

5. Whitewater rivers contain many hazards that are not always easily recognized. The following are the most frequent killers:

    a. *High water.* The river's speed and power increase tremendously as the flow increases, raising the difficulty of most rapids. Rescue becomes progressively harder as the water rises, adding to the danger. Floating debris and strainers make even an easy rapid quite hazardous. It is often misleading to judge the river level at the put-in, since a small rise in a wide, shallow place will be multiplied many times where the river narrows. Use reliable gauge information whenever possible, and be aware that sun on snowpack, hard rain, and upstream dam releases may greatly increase the flow.

    b. *Cold.* Cold drains your strength and robs you of the ability to make sound decisions on matters affecting your survival. Cold-water immersion, because of the initial shock and the rapid heat loss that follows, is especially dangerous. Dress appropriately for bad weather or sudden immersion in the water. When the water temperature is less than 50°F, a wetsuit or drysuit is essential for protection if you swim. Next best is wool or pile clothing under a waterproof shell. In this case, you should also carry waterproof matches and a change of clothing in a waterproof bag. If, after prolonged exposure, a person experiences uncontrollable shaking, loss of coordination, or difficulty speaking, he or she is hypothermic and needs your assistance.

c. *Strainers.* Brush, fallen trees, bridge pilings, undercut rocks, or anything else that allows river current to sweep through can pin boats and boaters against the obstacle. Water pressure on anything trapped this way can be overwhelming. Rescue is often extremely difficult. Pinning may occur in fast current, with little or no whitewater to warn of the danger.

d. *Dams, weirs, ledges, reversals, holes, and hydraulics.* When water drops over a obstacle, it curls back on itself, forming a strong upstream current that may be capable of holding a boat or swimmer. Some holes make for excellent sport; others are proven killers. Paddlers who cannot recognize the difference should avoid all but the smallest holes. Hydraulics around man-made dams must be treated with utmost respect regardless of their height or the level of the river. Despite their seemingly benign appearance, they can create an almost escape-proof trap. The swimmer's only exit from the "drowning machine" is to dive below the surface when the downstream current is flowing beneath the reversal.

e. *Broaching.* When a boat is pushed sideways against a rock by strong current, it may collapse and wrap. This is especially dangerous to kayak and decked-canoe paddlers; these boats will collapse, and the combination of indestructible hulls and tight outfitting may create a deadly trap. Even without entrapment, releasing pinned boats can be extremely time-consuming and dangerous. To avoid pinning, throw your weight downstream toward the rock. This allows the current to slide harmlessly underneath the hull.

6. Boating alone is discouraged. The minimum party is three people or two craft.

7. Have a frank knowledge of your boating ability, and don't attempt rivers or rapids that lie beyond that ability.

8. Be in good physical and mental condition, consistent with the difficulties that may be expected. Make adjustments for loss of skills due to age, health, fitness. Any health limitations must be explained to your fellow paddlers prior to starting the trip.

9. Be practiced in self-rescue, including escape from an overturned craft. The Eskimo roll is strongly recommended for decked boaters who run rapids Class IV or greater, or who paddle in cold environmental conditions.

10. Be trained in rescue skills, CPR, and first aid, with special emphasis on the recognizing and treating hypothermia. It may save your friend's life.

11. Carry equipment needed for unexpected emergencies, including footwear that will protect your feet when walking out, a throw rope, knife, whistle, and waterproof matches. If you wear eyeglasses, tie them on and carry a spare pair on long trips. Bring cloth repair tape on short runs and a full repair kit on isolated rivers. Do not wear bulky jackets, ponchos, heavy boots, or anything else that could reduce your ability to survive a swim.

12. Despite the mutually supportive group structure described in this code, individual paddlers are ultimately responsible for their own safety and must assume sole responsibility for the following decisions:

a. *The decision to participate on any trip.* This includes an evaluation of the expected difficulty of the rapids under the conditions existing at the time of the put-in.

b. *The selection of appropriate equipment,* including a boat design suited to their skills and the appropriate rescue and survival gear.

c. *The decision to scout any rapid, and to run or portage according to their best judgment.* Other members of the group may offer advice, but paddlers should resist pressure from anyone to paddle beyond their skills. It is also their responsibility to decide whether to pass up any walkout or takeout opportunity.

d. *All trip participants should consistently evaluate their own and their group's safety,* voicing their concerns when appropriate and following what they believe to be the best course of action. Paddlers are encouraged to speak with anyone whose actions on the water are dangerous, whether they are a part of your group or not.

II. BOAT AND EQUIPMENT PREPAREDNESS

1. Test new and different equipment under familiar conditions before relying on it for difficult runs. This is especially true when adopting a new boat design or outfitting system. Low-volume craft may present additional hazards to inexperienced or poorly conditioned paddlers.

2. Be sure your boat and gear are in good repair before starting a trip. The more isolated and difficult the run, the more rigorous this inspection should be.

3. Install flotation bags in noninflatable craft, securely fixed in each end and designed to displace as much water as possible. Inflatable boats should have multiple air chambers and be test-inflated before launching.

4. Have strong, properly sized paddles or oars for controlling your craft. Carry sufficient spares for the length and difficulty of the trip.

5. Outfit your boat safely. The ability to exit your boat quickly is an essential component of safety in rapids. It is your responsibility to see that there is absolutely nothing to cause entrapment when coming free of an upset craft, such as the following:

a. *Spray covers that won't release reliably* or that release prematurely.

b. *Boat outfitting too tight to allow a fast exit,* especially in low-volume kayaks or decked canoes. This includes low-hung thwarts in canoes lacking adequate clearance for your feet and kayak footbraces which fail or allow your feet to become wedged under them.

c. *Inadequately supported decks* that collapse on a paddler's legs when a decked boat is pinned by water pressure. Inadequate clearance with the deck because of your size or build.

d. *Loose ropes that cause entanglement.* Beware of any length of loose line attached to a whitewater boat. All items must be tied tightly and excess line eliminated; painters, throw lines, and safety-rope systems must be completely and effectively stored. Do not knot the end of a rope, as it can get caught in cracks between rocks.

6. Provide ropes that permit you to hold on to your craft so that it may be rescued. The following methods are recommended:

a. *Kayaks and covered canoes* should have grab loops of one-quarter-inch-plus rope or equivalent webbing sized to admit a normal-sized hand. Stern painters are permissible if properly secured.

b. *Open canoes* should have securely anchored bow and stern painters consisting of eight to ten feet of one-quarter-inch-plus line. These must be secured in such a way that they are readily accessible but cannot come loose accidentally. Grab loops are acceptable but are more difficult to reach after an upset.

c. *Rafts and dories* may have taut perimeter lines threaded through the loops provided. Footholds should be designed so that a paddler's feet cannot be forced through them, causing entrapment. Flip lines should be carefully and reliably stowed.

7. Know your craft's carrying capacity and how added loads affect boat handling in whitewater. Most rafts have a minimum crew size that can be added to on day trips or in easy rapids. Carrying more than two paddlers in an open canoe when running rapids is not recommended.

8. Car-top racks must be strong and attach positively to the vehicle. Lash your boat to each crossbar, then tie the ends of the boats directly to the bumpers for added security. This arrangement should survive all but the most violent vehicle accident.

III. GROUP PREPAREDNESS AND RESPONSIBILITY

1. ORGANIZATION. A river trip should be regarded as a common adventure by all participants, except on instructional or commercially guided trips as defined below. Participants share the responsibility for the conduct of the trip, and each participant is individually responsible for judging his or her own capabilities and for his or her own safety as the trip progresses. Participants are encouraged (but are not obligated) to offer advice and guidance for the independent consideration and judgment of others.

2. RIVER CONDITIONS. The group should have a reasonable knowledge of the difficulty of the run. Participants should evaluate this information and adjust their plans accordingly. Maps and guidebooks, if available, should be examined if the run is exploratory or no one is familiar with the river. The group should secure accurate flow information; the more difficult the run, the more important this will be. Be aware of possible changes in river level and how this will affect the difficulty of the run. If the trip involves tidal stretches, secure appropriate information on tides.

3. GROUP EQUIPMENT SHOULD BE SUITED TO THE DIFFICULTY OF THE RIVER. The group should always have a throw line available, and one line per boat is recommended on difficult runs. The list may include: carabiners, prussic loops, first-aid kit, flashlight, folding saw, fire starter, guidebooks, maps, food, extra clothing, and any other rescue or survival items suggested by conditions. Each item is not required on every run, and this list is not meant to be a substitute for good judgment.

4. KEEP THE GROUP COMPACT, BUT MAINTAIN SUFFICIENT SPACING TO AVOID COLLISIONS. If the group is large, consider dividing into smaller groups or using the "buddy system" as an additional safeguard. Space yourselves closely enough to permit good communication, but not so close as to interfere with one another in rapids.

  a. *A point paddler sets the pace.* When in front, do not get in over your head. Never run drops when you cannot see a clear route to the bottom or, for advanced paddlers, a sure route to the next eddy. When in doubt, stop and scout.

  b. *Keep track of all group members.* Each boat keeps the one behind it in sight, stopping if necessary. Know how many people are in your group, and take head counts regularly. No one should paddle ahead or walk out without first informing the group. Paddlers requiring additional support should stay at the center of a group and not allow themselves to lag behind in the more difficult rapids. If the group is large and contains a wide range of abilities, a "sweep boat" may be designated to bring up the rear.

  c. *Courtesy.* On heavily used rivers, do not cut in front of a boater running a drop. Always look upstream before leaving eddies to run or play. Never enter a crowded drop or eddy when no room for you exists. Passing other groups in a rapid may be hazardous: it's often safer to wait upstream until the group ahead has passed.

5. FLOAT PLAN. If the trip is into a wilderness area or for an extended period, plans should be filed with a responsible person who will contact the authorities if you are overdue. It may be wise to establish checkpoints along the way where civilization could be contacted if necessary. Knowing the location of possible help and preplanning escape routes can speed rescue.

6. DRUGS. The use of alcohol or mind-altering drugs before or during river trips is not recommended. These substances dull reflexes, reduce decision-making ability, and may interfere with important survival reflexes.

7. INSTRUCTIONAL OR COMMERCIALLY GUIDED TRIPS. In contrast to the common adventure-trip format, these trip formats involve a boating instructor or commercial guide who assumes some of the responsibilities normally exercised by the group as a whole, as appropriate under the circumstances. These formats recognize that instructional or commercially guided trips may involve participants who lack significant experience in whitewater. However, as a participant acquires experience, he or she takes on increasing responsibility for his or her own safety, in accordance with what he or she knows or should know as a result of that increased experience. Also, as in all trip formats, every participant must realize and assume the risks associated with the serious hazards of whitewater rivers. It is advisable for instructors and commercial guides or their employers to acquire trip or personal liability insurance:

a. An *"instructional trip"* is characterized by a clear teacher–pupil relationship, where the primary purpose of the trip is to teach boating skills, and which is conducted for a fee.

b. A *"commercially guided trip"* is characterized by a licensed, professional guide conducting trips for a fee.

IV. GUIDELINES FOR RIVER RESCUE

1. Recover from an upset with an Eskimo roll whenever possible. Evacuate your boat immediately if there is imminent danger of being trapped against rocks, brush, or any other kind of strainer.

2. If you swim, hold on to your boat. It has much flotation and is easy for rescuers to spot. Get to the upstream end so that you cannot be crushed between a rock and your boat by the force of the current. Persons with good balance may be able to climb on top of a swamped kayak or flipped raft and paddle to shore.

3. Release your craft if this will improve your chances, especially if the water is cold or dangerous rapids lie ahead. Actively attempt self-rescue whenever possible by swimming for safety. Be prepared to assist others who may come to your aid.

a. *When swimming in shallow or obstructed rapids, lie on your back with feet held high and pointed downstream.* Do not attempt to stand in fast-moving water; if your foot wedges on the bottom, fast water will push you under and keep you there. Get to slow or very shallow water before attempting to stand or walk. Look ahead! Avoid possible pinning situations, including undercut rocks, strainers, downed trees, holes, and other dangers, by swimming away from them.

b. *If the rapids are deep and powerful, roll over onto your stomach and swim aggressively for shore.* Watch for eddies and slackwater, and use them to get out of the current. Strong swimmers can effect a powerful upstream ferry and get to shore fast. If the shores are obstructed with strainers or undercut rocks, however, it is safer to "ride the rapid out" until a safer escape can be found.

4. If others spill and swim, go after the boaters first. Rescue boats and equipment only if this can be done safely. While participants are encouraged (but not obligated) to assist one another to the best of their ability, they should do so only if they can, in their judgment, do so safely. The first duty of a rescuer is not to compound the problem by becoming another victim.

5. The use of rescue lines requires training; uninformed use may cause injury. Never tie yourself into either end of a line without a reliable quick-release system. Have a knife handy to deal with unexpected entanglement. Learn to place set lines effectively, to throw accurately, to belay effectively, and to properly handle a rope thrown to you.

6. When reviving a drowning victim, be aware that cold water may greatly extend survival time under water. Victims of hypothermia may have depressed vital signs, causing them to look and feel dead. Don't give up; continue CPR for as long as possible without compromising safety.

V. UNIVERSAL RIVER SIGNALS

These signals may be substituted with an alternate set of signals agreed upon by the group.

STOP: *Potential hazard ahead.* Wait for "all clear" signal before proceeding, or scout ahead. Form a horizontal bar with your outstretched arms. Those seeing the signal should pass it back to others in the party.

STOP: *Potential hazard ahead.*

HELP: *Emergency.* Assist the signaler as quickly as possible. Give three long blasts on a police whistle while waving a paddle, helmet or life vest over your head. If a whistle is not available, use the visual signal alone. A whistle is best carried on a lanyard attached to your life vest.

ALL CLEAR: *Come ahead.* In the absence of other directions, proceed down the center. Form a vertical bar with your paddle or one arm held high above your head (see facing page). Paddle blade should be turned flat for maximum visibility. To signal direction or a preferred course through a rapid around obstruction, lower the previously vertical "all clear" by 45 degrees toward the side of the river with the preferred route (see right). Never point toward the obstacle you wish to avoid.

HELP: *Emergency.*

ALL CLEAR: *Come ahead.*

I'M OK: *I'm not hurt.* While holding an elbow outward toward your side, repeatedly pat the top of your head.

I'M OK: *I'm not hurt.*

VI. INTERNATIONAL SCALE OF RIVER DIFFICULTY

This is the American version of a rating system used to compare river difficulty throughout the world. This system is not exact: rivers do not always fit easily into one category, and regional or individual interpretations may cause misunderstandings. It is no substitute for a guidebook or accurate first-hand descriptions of a run.

Paddlers attempting difficult runs in unfamiliar areas should act cautiously until they get a feel for the way the scale is interpreted locally. River difficulty may change each year due to fluctuations in water level, downed trees, recent floods, geological disturbances, or bad weather. Stay alert for unexpected problems!

As river difficulty increases, the danger to swimming paddlers becomes more severe. As rapids become longer and more continuous, the challenge increases. There is a difference between running an occasional Class IV rapid and dealing with an entire river of this category. Allow an extra margin of safety between skills and river ratings when the water is cold or if the river itself is remote and inaccessible.

Examples of commonly run rapids that fit each of the classifications are presented in the document "International Scale of River Difficulty—Standard Rated Rapids." This document is available online at **www.americanwhitewater.org/content/Wiki/do-op/id/safety:internation _scale_of_river_difficulty**. Rapids of a difficulty similar to a rapids on this list are rated the same. Rivers are also rated using this scale. A river rating should take into account many factors including the difficulty of individual rapids, remoteness, hazards, etc.

APPENDIX D:
Safety Code of American Whitewater

The Six Difficulty Classes:

CLASS I: *Easy.* Fast-moving water with riffles and small waves. Few obstructions, all obvious and easily missed with little training. Risk to swimmers is slight; self-rescue is easy.

CLASS II: *Novice.* Straightforward rapids with wide, clear channels that are evident without scouting. Occasional maneuvering may be required, but rocks and medium-sized waves are easily missed by trained paddlers. Swimmers are seldom injured, and group assistance, while helpful, is seldom needed. Rapids that are at the upper end of this difficulty range are designated "Class II+."

CLASS III: *Intermediate.* Rapids with moderate, irregular waves that may be difficult to avoid and can swamp an open canoe. Complex maneuvers in fast current and good boat control in tight passages or around ledges are often required; large waves or strainers may be present but are easily avoided. Strong eddies and powerful current effects can be found, particularly on large-volume rivers. Scouting is advisable for inexperienced parties. Injuries while swimming are rare; self-rescue is usually easy, but group assistance may be required to avoid long swims. Rapids that are at the lower or upper end of this difficulty range are designated "Class III–" or "Class III+," respectively.

Class IV: *Advanced.* Intense, powerful, but predictable rapids requiring precise boat handling in turbulent water. Depending on the character of the river, it may feature large, unavoidable waves and holes or constricted passages demanding fast maneuvers under pressure. A fast, reliable eddy turn may be needed to initiate maneuvers, scout rapids, or rest. Rapids may require "must" moves above dangerous hazards. Scouting may be necessary the first time down. Risk of injury to swimmers is moderate to high, and water conditions may make self-rescue difficult. Group assistance for rescue is often essential but requires practiced skills. A strong Eskimo roll is highly recommended. Rapids that are at the upper end of this difficulty range are designated "Class IV–" or "Class IV+," respectively.

CLASS V: *Expert.* Extremely long, obstructed, or very violent rapids that expose a paddler to added risk. Drops may contain large, unavoidable waves and holes or steep, congested chutes with complex, demanding routes. Rapids may continue for long distances between pools, demanding a high level of fitness. What eddies exist may be small, turbulent, or difficult to reach. At the high end of the scale, several of these factors may be combined. Scouting is recommended but may be difficult. Swims are dangerous, and rescue is often difficult even for experts. A very reliable Eskimo roll, proper equipment, extensive experience, and practiced rescue skills are essential. Because of the large range of difficulty that exists beyond Class IV, Class 5 is an open-ended, multiple-level scale designated by 5.0, 5.1, 5.2, etc. Each of these levels is an order of magnitude more difficult than the last. Example: increasing difficulty from Class 5.0 to Class 5.1 is a similar order of magnitude as increasing from Class IV to Class 5.0.

CLASS VI: *Extreme and exploratory.* These runs have almost never been attempted and often exemplify extremes of difficulty, unpredictability, and danger. The consequences of errors are very severe, and rescue may be impossible. For teams of experts only, at favorable water levels, after close personal inspection and taking all precautions. After a Class VI rapids has been run many times, its rating may be changed to an appropriate Class 5.x rating.

INDEX

INDEX

Kevin Stiegelmaier has always been a lover of the outdoors and nature. Growing up on Long Island instilled in him a love of the ocean and led to a degree in marine biology. It also led to the purchase of his first kayak and the beginning of what has been a ten-year passion with paddling. In that time Kevin has canoed and kayaked on every type of water in every state along the East Coast, although he prefers exploring the waters of his home state, New York. Kevin currently lives on the North Shore of Long Island with his wife, Laura, and daughter, AnnaGrace, and teaches middle-school science whenever he isn't paddling. *Canoeing & Kayaking New York* is his first book.

 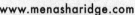

Printed in the USA
CPSIA information can be obtained
at www.ICGtesting.com
JSHW012026140824
68134JS00033B/2890